CW01217860

AMERICA'S FIRST WARTIME ELECTION

American Presidential Elections

MICHAEL NELSON

JOHN M. MCCARDELL, JR.

AMERICA'S FIRST WARTIME ELECTION

JAMES MADISON, DEWITT CLINTON, AND THE WAR OF 1812

DONALD A. ZINMAN

UNIVERSITY PRESS OF KANSAS

Published by the University Press of Kansas (Lawrence, Kansas 66045), which was organized by the Kansas Board of Regents and is operated and funded by Emporia State University, Fort Hays State University, Kansas State University, Pittsburg State University, the University of Kansas, and Wichita State University

© 2024 by the University Press of Kansas
All rights reserved

Library of Congress Cataloging-in-Publication Data

Names: Zinman, Donald A., author.
Title: America's first wartime election : James Madison, DeWitt Clinton, and the War of 1812 / Donald A. Zinman.
Other titles: James Madison, DeWitt Clinton, and the War of 1812
Description: Lawrence, Kansas : University Press of Kansas, 2024. | Series: American presidential elections | Includes bibliographical references and index.
Identifiers: LCCN 2024006739
ISBN 9780700637799 (cloth)
ISBN 9780700637805 (ebook)
Subjects: LCSH: Presidents—United States—Electionv1812. | Madison, James, 1751–1836. | Clinton, DeWitt, 1769–1828. | Political campaigns—United States—History—19th century. | United States—Politics and government—1812–1815. | United States—History—War of 1812. | BISAC: POLITICAL SCIENCE / American Government / Executive Branch | POLITICAL SCIENCE / Political Process / Political Parties
Classification: LCC E349 .Z56 2024 | DDC 971.03/4—dc23/eng/20240802
LC record available at https://lccn.loc.gov/2024006739.

British Library Cataloging-in-Publication Data is available.

10 9 8 7 6 5 4 3 2 1

The paper used in this publication is acid free and meets the minimum requirements of the American National Standard for Permanence of Paper for Printed Library Materials Z39.48-1992.

CONTENTS

Editors' Foreword vii

Preface ix

1 The Political Terrain of the Early Republic 1

2 Madison's Dilemma 37

3 Democratic-Republicans Go to War with Britain and Themselves 51

4 Federalists and Clintonians: A Wartime Alliance 89

5 The Campaign for a Wartime Presidency 120

6 In the Hands of the Legislators and Some Voters 140

7 Madison and Clinton: The War of 1812 and the Ballot Box 178

Appendix A: Elector Selection Dates and Methods in 1812 205

Appendix B: Electoral College Results in 1812 206

Appendix C: Final Roll Call Vote in the States where the Legislature Chose Presidential Electors 207

Appendix D: Available Statewide Tally where Voters Chose Presidential Electors 208

Notes 209

Bibliographic Essay 243

Index 251

A photo gallery follows page 134.

EDITORS' FOREWORD

It is more than a little surprising that historians have paid such scant attention to the presidential election of 1812. In the present volume, Donald Zinman masterfully atones for that neglect with a narrative that not only thoroughly covers the candidates and their campaigns but also demonstrates the fragility of the new republic as it faced what has often been called the "second American Revolution."

International relations—and America's proper role during international conflicts—were a constant challenge from the very beginning of nationhood. Avoiding such conflicts without compromising sovereignty constituted a recurrent theme in the presidencies of George Washington, John Adams, and Thomas Jefferson. Steering a neutral course, eschewing "entangling alliances" (as the first president noted in his Farewell Address) while asserting the right to trade freely and at the same time, managing the impact of war on an emerging and wholly unanticipated political party system (and its citizen activists) proved a persistent nuisance to America's presidents—and cost the second, in 1800, reelection.

As the "heir apparent" in 1808, James Madison brought an impressive résumé as a presidential nominee. Though having almost no executive experience, he had been a principal author of the federal Constitution, had sponsored the Bill of Rights as a member of Congress, and had served as secretary of state under his friend and mentor Thomas Jefferson. Indeed, so effective had their collaboration been that the Democratic-Republican Party they founded seemed certain to prevail over an increasingly weak and divided Federalist opposition. Madison swept to election by margins of two to one in the popular vote and three to one in the Electoral College.

Yet by the spring of 1812, events abroad seemed to be dragging the United States inexorably into war with England, this just as Madison's reelection effort was getting underway. The contest was closely fought, and Madison would barely secure a second term.

To this complex story and its far-from-inevitable outcome, Zinman brings a clarity and insight born of extensive research and intimate familiarity with his characters and sources. He reminds readers that the primitive party system remained in many ways feeble, that the processes of nomination and election continued to evolve in unexpected ways, that incumbency does not provide a smooth path to reelection, and that wartime puts political systems and ultimately presidencies to severe tests.

With this study, Donald Zinman gives the 1812 election a prominence it deserves and has for too long lacked. It is an exciting story, well told, and with implications that succeeding generations of candidates, and would-be candidates, down to our own time, have had to confront.

PREFACE

Baltimore was in tumult. All summer long, the city was plagued by violence and riots. One man observing the chaos wrote, "The Mob still remained undisbanded; and the civil authority still powerless and inert. The wounded which had been taken to the hospital, were principally carried away to the country, having been threatened with further vengeance by the barbarians." Pro-war rioters were determined to silence voices of dissent now that the United States had committed itself to a war with Great Britain. Elsewhere in the country, members of Congress were burned in effigy, or even assaulted, as partisan newspapers unleashed vitriolic rhetoric to whip up their respective readers. Opponents of the war were labeled as "Tories," "traitors," "monarchists," and treasonous citizens who had no regard for American honor. Supporters were branded as destroyers of American commerce and useful fools for French emperor Napoleon Bonaparte. Red-hot passions over the divisive War of 1812 would overlap with a presidential election that would be a referendum on the conflict itself.[1]

War creates disequilibrium in politics. Established patterns of voting behavior and public opinion are temporarily or permanently disrupted. The nascent political party system of the early republic endured a shock that it was not really ready to handle once the controversial war began. Democratic-Republicans and Federalists scrambled to position their respective parties for America's first wartime presidential election. At the same time, factional divisions and procedural squabbling on both sides complicated the campaigns of President James Madison and his challenger, New York City mayor DeWitt Clinton, who also served simultaneously as his state's lieutenant governor.

My inspiration for this project came when I was writing my first book, *The Heir Apparent Presidency*. To be elected as the heir apparent to a transformative departing predecessor is very difficult in the American political system. Madison achieved that goal in 1808 when he was elected president to succeed Thomas Jefferson, who was the leading figure behind the ideology of the Democratic-Republican Party. To win reelection to a second term is an even more arduous task for these unique heir apparent presidents, but I wanted to learn more about how they can defy the historical headwinds and earn a second term. Madison pulled it off, albeit under a set of highly unusual circumstances. The hypothesis presented here asserts that wartime presidential elections carry risks for the incumbent party, but ultimately provide the sitting president with many political advantages if the chief executive is able and willing to successfully deploy them. Incumbent presidents enjoy the advantage over their challengers of being able to maintain a greater degree of control over events and government policies. While running for reelection, presidents must continue to do the job and respond to unexpected crises. These disruptive episodes will surely alter the messaging of an incumbent's campaign. Within the context of an upcoming election, the American public and key political actors will be inclined to initially give these presidents the benefit of the doubt.

The 1812 electoral contest happened within an atmosphere of political parties struggling to communicate across state lines and exert authority, even as public passions ran very high. Federalists joined forces with anti-war Democratic-Republicans behind DeWitt Clinton's candidacy, but they found that building a fusion ticket between one party and some of the dissidents of the other party was a challenging task. To be sure, this objective was even more difficult when the parties were already institutionally weak and disorganized. Still, there were signs that the United States was slowly in transition into a more populist brand of politics. The War of 1812 has generated a voluminous record of scholarship, while the presidential election of that same year has produced comparatively little academic attention. No election for president of the United States is insignificant, especially one held in the midst of the early republic's first war.

I owe a debt of gratitude to many people who helped to make this book possible throughout the course of five years of writing and research. I give thanks to my mother, Elda Zinman, as well to as numerous friends all over this country who always kept encouraging me. The library staff at my home institution of Grand Valley State University was flexible and accommodating whenever I needed them for assistance. Similarly, I thank the university's library for providing me with easy access to the archive *America's Historical Newspapers*, which is a rich resource of archival print journalism. For seventeen years, my political science colleagues at GVSU have created a pleasant and supportive environment for me to teach and do my research. I also want to thank our student office worker, Kyla Dukes, who sometimes assisted me with finding material online. Philip Lampi's database, *A New Nation Votes*, was a valuable statistical resource for which I am very grateful. Helpful observations came from Jason Duncan in our many conversations about ancient American elections. Valuable input also came from Paul Cornish, Paul DeHart, William Adler, Jay Dow, and E. J. Fagan. I appreciate the useful comments from the staff of the University Press of Kansas, especially David Congdon and Erica Nicholson, as well as copy editor Michelle S. Asakawa and indexer Elise Hess. My own department office coordinator Ashley Savage also provided much-appreciated assistance. Behind every election there are phenomena to explain and lessons to learn. I am proud to have done my part in telling the story of America's first wartime race for the presidency.

AMERICA'S FIRST WARTIME ELECTION

1

THE POLITICAL TERRAIN OF THE EARLY REPUBLIC

Members of the Federalist Party had some grounds for cautious optimism heading into the presidential campaign of 1808, but they faced a national political landscape that was now dominated by Democratic-Republicans. Although the Federalists were feeling the political strain of multiplying factions and the economic strain of the Embargo Act these facts did not change the reality that the Democratic-Republican Party remained ascendant whereas Federalist erosion was continuing. Democratic-Republicans would have to reassemble the Jeffersonian electoral coalition under a new standard bearer, while Federalists sought to take advantage of the administration's flailing embargo policy.

As this chapter will demonstrate, by the time James Madison mounted his first presidential run he had served as a key player or passive observer of all the signature moments in the founding and first years of the American republic. In many ways, he was a stereotypical Founding Father, for his gradual and reluctant embrace of political parties was common among his colleagues. As the two parties developed, Madison's behavior revealed the tensions he experienced between public service and enlightened statesmanship on behalf of his country, verses his role as the leader of a burgeoning majority party organization.

The first challenge for Democratic-Republicans was their increasingly controversial nominating instrument. From the time of its inception through its last use in the 1824 nominating cycle, the congressional caucus winner carried the imprimatur of the national party establishment. From there the nominee could expect to receive essential backing from state party organizations and Democratic-Republican newspapers. Even so, to be tagged as the choice of the party establishment was to wear the badge of everything that was bad and unpopular about the political insiders, as well as the allegedly elitist machinations of the caucus. Supporters of candidates who did not enjoy backing from Washington, DC, insiders had every incentive to denounce anything or anybody produced by the caucus as an affront to democracy.

The 1808 presidential nomination would be the Democratic-Republicans' first truly competitive contest. In the absence of an incumbent president, the congressional caucus would be a venue for the further aggravation of intraparty divisions. Well before it commenced, the caucus for 1808 was the subject of bickering over procedures and democratic legitimacy. Supporters of each candidate sought to maximize their influence over the process at the national and state levels. Secretary of State Madison was understood to be the heir apparent to President Jefferson, given that the former had strong support in Congress, which was what counted the most in this process. Vice President George Clinton's base of support came from New York and Pennsylvania, and his boosters sought to break Virginia's domination of the early American presidency, but their candidate's support was thin outside of those two northern states. Clinton also held an inconsistent position on the Embargo Act that made him a curious choice, given that this was a signature policy of the Jefferson administration. James Monroe was thought to be the favorite within his home state of Virginia, including support from the wing associated with Representative John Randolph. They were known as Old Republicans, and in their view, Madison—and even the incumbent president himself—had strayed too far from orthodox Jeffersonianism.[1] In the end, however, Madison prevailed, as he was the candidate with the most support from the national party hierarchy. In 1808, and for more than two hundred years into the future, the establishment candidate was usually favored to win the presidential nomination as a general rule.

On January 19, 1808, Vermont senator Stephen R. Bradley, who ran the 1804 Democratic-Republican proceedings, sent out invitations for a proposed caucus just four days later.[2] This was an early date, as compared to the previous two election cycles. Madison supporters in Washington, DC, aimed to lock down the nomination early to thwart other candidates from building momentum. For his own part, Monroe had a base of support in the Virginia legislature, and backers there hastily maneuvered to hold a state caucus that would boost their candidate. The plan backfired, however, when on January 21 Madison won the overall balloting in two Virginia caucuses. Virginia's proceedings were held at two separate meetings in Richmond on that day. One caucus was held at the state capitol, where Monroe prevailed 57–10, and a second assembly was held at Bell Tavern, where Madison won 123–0.[3] Monroe's showing in the state caucuses diminished his supporters' claims that their candidate somehow represented a purer manifestation of Virginia Jeffersonianism.

Observers of today's elongated presidential nominating system sometimes say that if you are complaining about the process, then that means your candidate is losing. Similarly, supporters of Madison's rivals cried foul at the early caucus date, asserting that the national party elites were seeking to stifle debate and an open democratic process that could allow other candidates to prevail. Others denounced the existence of the congressional nominating caucus as a perversion of constitutional norms. It was "an attempt to produce an undue bias in the ensuing election . . . and virtually to transfer the appointment of those officers from the people, to a majority of the two Houses of Congress," exclaimed congressional supporters of Madison's opponents in an open letter to the *National Intelligencer*. However, Thomas Ritchie, editor of the pro-Madison *Richmond Enquirer*, argued that the caucus was a legitimate democratic exercise, asserting that "the Representatives of the people may be presumed to carry with them the wishes of the different quarters of the union." Critics also suggested that Bradley lacked the authority to call the caucus. Virginia representative Edwin Gray, a Randolph ally, expressed "abhorrence" at the invitation and called the proceedings "midnight intrigues of any set of men, who may arrogate to themselves the right, which belongs alone to the people, of selecting proper persons to fill the important offices of President and Vice President."[4]

Some men in the Monroe camp floated the idea of an alliance with Clinton, with the sitting vice president at the top of the ticket and the Virginian as vice president. John Randolph actually gave his blessing to the idea, as it would seem to be a good way to marginalize Madison for the foreseeable future. The plan got some traction, but mainline Jeffersonians continued to dominate the party within Congress, which is what counted the most in the presidential nominating process. The Clinton-Monroe proposal soon fizzled out. There were also efforts by Clintonians to place the vice president's nephew DeWitt on the ticket; the younger Clinton had already served one tour as New York City mayor and would soon begin a new tenure in that office. Strong opposition from Madison loyalists killed the DeWitt Clinton fusion proposal. Indeed, the young and ambitious flag-bearer for the Clintonian faction would have represented too much of a threat to mainline Jeffersonians in the vice presidency. From there he could spend four years positioning himself into a leading presidential candidate. George Clinton, in contrast, was a disengaged vice president who was nearing the end of his political career.[5]

The tally from the congressional nominating caucus was eighty-three votes for Madison, with only three votes each for Clinton and Monroe, and five abstentions. For the vice presidency, Clinton was overwhelmingly renominated with seventy-nine votes, while only nine votes were scattered among other candidates. Keeping Clinton on the ticket would prove to be a deft move to mollify enough of his New York and Pennsylvania supporters, who ranged from lukewarm to hostile to Madison. What was noteworthy from the caucus was its high absentee rate. Similar to the modern-day presidential nominating process, supporters of the underdog candidates can be expected to loudly denounce the process as rigged in favor of the party establishment. Congressional backers of Clinton and Monroe mostly shunned the proceedings, as approximately one-third of eligible members skipped the caucus.[6]

Outside of Washington, DC, some Monroe and Clinton enthusiasts continued to fight beyond the caucus. In Virginia, Monroe's boosters persisted with a campaign to promote their candidate. Though he would serve if elected president, Monroe neither encouraged nor disavowed the campaign on his behalf. Monroe did, however, discourage his backers from making egregious attacks on Jefferson and Madison.[7] Like Madison and Monroe, Clinton adhered to the era's norm of presidential candidates refraining from personally campaigning for the office. Some pro-Clinton newspapers and advocates, however, continued to assault the caucus process and attack Madison as too pro-French and as overly accommodating with Federalists. Clinton never accepted or declined the vice presidential nomination, and he shared his supporters' disdain with the caucus procedures. In this job, Clinton's influence in the Jefferson administration had been insignificant, and he dreaded another four years in such a constitutionally limited office.[8]

Late in the summer, Federalists convened a meeting of party elites in New York City. They renominated their 1804 ticket of General Charles Cotesworth Pinckney of South Carolina for president, and Rufus King, a former Constitutional Convention delegate, senator, and ambassador of New York, for vice president. Federalists were even more philosophically against party-building activities than their adversaries, but by 1808 they were taking greater steps toward more formal organization at the state and national levels. Although the party was so weakened that the Federalists still had little national infrastructure beyond their few members of Congress and a handful of ineffective interstate committees of correspondence, a summer gathering of party members assembled to nominate Pinckney and King.[9]

Any aspiring heir-apparent president can expect to inherit the incumbent's detractors. In the general election campaign, Federalists unsurprisingly attacked Madison as representing a third term of the Jefferson administration, with all its economic and diplomatic carnage from the embargo. A Federalist critic summed up the party's policy critique in the *Connecticut Courant*:

> They have destroyed our trade, beggared our seamen, cut off the farmer from his market, and the mechanic from his trade—our merchants are ruined because their business is broken up, credit is annihilated—and to crown the whole, we are madly rushing into a destructive war with Great Britain, because Mr. Jefferson and Mr. Madison insist upon it that they will protect deserters from British vessels.[10]

Starting in March, and throughout the campaign, Madison's dispatches as secretary of state became public. Included among these documents was correspondence pertaining to the defunct Monroe-Pinkney treaty. The dispatches portrayed Secretary Madison as an assertive, but prudent, defender of American interests abroad. Late in the campaign, Jefferson came to the aid of his heir apparent by providing Congress with further letters that demonstrated Madison's resolve toward both Britain and France.[11] These revelations likely did nothing to satisfy virulent anti-Madison partisans across the political spectrum, but they did furnish some evidence that Madison was an objective and even-handed statesman who could walk the nation through its difficulties with European powers.

Meanwhile, Democratic-Republican support continued to coalesce around the secretary of state. "The friends of the present administration will support him upon the same ground as they would have supported Mr. Jefferson—and none but those who would have opposed Mr. Jefferson, had he again become a candidate, will oppose Mr. Madison," proclaimed the *Columbian Phenix*.[12] William Duane, who edited the Philadelphia-based *Aurora*, gave his support to the official party ticket even though he preferred Clinton for the presidency. The Pennsylvania party organization followed suit with a full commitment of support for Madison.[13] Matters were more complicated in New York, but even in Clinton's home base Madison enjoyed institutional and popular support. The *Public Advertiser* in that state responded to pro-Clinton newspapers with appeals to party loyalty and a defense of the nominating caucus. Supporters of the secretary of state convened meetings to enact resolutions of support for Madison and the embargo, as well as to excoriate the Clinton campaigners as somehow not being true Democratic-Republicans.[14] In Virginia, the Monroe movement failed to gain popular traction, as voters in that state chose a full sweep of Madison electors by a vote of 14,665 for the secretary of state to 3,408 for his future presidential successor. Pinckney carried a negligible number of votes.[15]

As presidential electors were chosen throughout the autumn, Madison's momentum continued to build. The final result was a very convincing victory of 122 electoral votes for the secretary of state, with 47 for Pinckney. The Federalist candidate carried his party's strongholds in New England (save for Vermont), as well as Delaware and scattered electoral votes in North Carolina and Maryland. Clinton boosters in New York only managed to produce 6 out of the 19 electoral votes in that state, where the legislature was the final arbiter of selection. State senator DeWitt Clinton lobbied hard for the electors to be awarded to his uncle, but Governor Daniel Tompkins intervened, counseling legislators that such an act would damage party unity. Tompkins was a Madison supporter, and the rift between New York's governor and the Clintons was growing. In the end, the state's electors were allowed to make their own decisions. The Jeffersonian coalition remained resilient in Pennsylvania, the South, and the West. Madison carried over 64 percent of the popular vote among voters who were permitted to choose pledged electors in their states. Pinckney took just over 32 percent of the eligible popular vote, while Monroe and unpledged electors carried the remainder. Even if New York had fully defected to Clinton, Madison still would have easily prevailed.[16]

Congressional election results were more positive for the Federalists. Though most presidential candidates who are overwhelmingly elected can expect a coattail effect in down-ballot races, Madison was not so fortunate. In House elections held throughout 1808, Federalists posted a net gain of twenty-four seats, thereby reducing the governing party's majority. State elections did not substantially alter the dominant political equilibrium, as Democratic-Republicans maintained a commanding majority of the nation's governorships. Federalists only gained one Senate seat in the 1808 election cycle, given that Senate results were largely dependent upon state legislative elections. While the Federalists fell short of a majority, they were now well-positioned to confront the new president if they could work with the various Democratic-Republican factions in Congress that were hostile to Madison.[17]

What Federalists called the "Dambargo" failed to materialize as a game-changing policy issue in the campaign.[18] Even so, the 1808 election clearly revealed tensions within the governing party, notwithstanding the overwhelming victory for Madison. The vulnerabilities of the Jeffersonian regime had been exposed, but its basic infrastructure remained intact amid an underdeveloped party system and a still weakly organized Federalist opposition that could not create a compelling alternative. Madison had successfully reassembled a sufficient share of the Democratic-Republican electoral coalition, but he also inherited Jefferson's intraparty critics and the policy consequences of the outgoing president's embargo. Madison would carry the full baggage of an heir-apparent presidency. In addition, he would preside over a landscape that was still dominated by a post–Revolutionary War context, even though small signs of a more populist brand of politics were starting to emerge.

MADISON AND THE POLITICS OF THE EARLY REPUBLIC

James Madison fit the expectations of an early republic president: Born into a family of privilege, he was erudite, judicious, and respectful of constitutional norms. Like Thomas Jefferson before him, Madison was more skilled as a writer than an orator. He was pragmatic—but also prone to miscalculation on public policies. He had a keen understanding of human nature, but he sometimes greatly misjudged the behaviors of other political actors. He was studious and serious but also liked to partake in wisecracks and off-color jokes. Standing only five feet four inches tall, and with a small frame, Madison might not be elected president in today's political environment. Many contemporary American voters demand that their presidents appear imposing and strong, which would exclude the diminutive Madison.[19]

The future fourth president of the United States was born on March 16, 1751, at Belle Grove Plantation, located near Port Conway in colonial Virginia's King George County. The boy's father, James Madison Sr., was a prosperous planter, much of which came from inherited family wealth and his marriage to Nelly Conway. The Madison family had resided in Virginia since the middle of the seventeenth century. Madison's mother Nelly was the daughter of a well-to-do tobacco planter and merchant. The boy was the first of twelve children, although only seven survived into adulthood. As a child, young James was often in poor health, including experiencing seizures. Fast-spreading fatal diseases, such as smallpox, were common in Colonial America. So too was the persistent fear and distrust of the Native population. During his childhood, the Madison family moved to a plantation that later became known as Montpelier, in Orange County.[20]

The bookish boy was incredibly curious about everything. He was fascinated by foreign languages and literature. Private tutors provided him with a well-rounded education, and in 1769 he was ready to depart Virginia for college. The young man enrolled in what was then called the College of New Jersey, now Princeton University. He continued studying foreign languages, such as Greek and Latin, as well as religion and philosophy. Although he did not become a soaring orator in his political career, he participated in a campus debating society. Madison blitzed through his bachelor of arts program in only two years and chose to stay for another year of graduate study.[21]

In the eighteenth century, education at the graduate level was more informal than it is today. Madison's teacher was the college's president, John Witherspoon. It was under his tutelage that Madison became well-versed in the principles of the Enlightenment through a vigorous curriculum of classical political and philosophical texts. The young scholar also studied the Hebrew language. Upon coming home to Montpelier in 1772, he briefly took up the study of law, but soon gave up on any intentions of a career in that field. He always remained interested in legal studies, however, as well as the humanities.[22] Intellectual curiosity is a desirable trait in a president, even though an elite education is not a necessity for the position.

Madison's first job in government came in December 1774, when he was chosen for a spot on Orange County's Committee of Safety. This body was tasked by the First Continental Congress with enforcing the ban on trade with Great Britain, and supervising the local militia. James Sr. chaired the county committee, and James Jr. was by far the youngest man on the panel. Madison was now officially involved in revolutionary patriot activities. Many of the Committee of Safety's tactics were heavy-handed and crossed over into outright bullying. Madison, the future architect of the Bill of Rights, condoned intimidating citizens who were deemed "seditious" to the cause of defying His Majesty's authority, and confiscating and burning pamphlets and flyers that were considered soft on Britain. Although he was educated and highly intelligent, Madison was also a young man and perhaps still a bit lacking in wisdom. After war broke out, Madison was appointed as a colonel in the county militia, but this was mostly an administrative post requiring little training as a soldier. His health ailments may have constituted epilepsy, making him a poor fit for a field command, although he sometimes drilled and marched with his unit.[23]

As the son of a prominent planter, and holding a degree from a prestigious college, Madison had a clear path to a fruitful career in politics. He was a delegate to Virginia's constitutional convention in 1776, where he argued successfully for a strong plank assuring the free exercise of religion. Like most future presidents, Madison had an election loss on his résumé. In balloting for a full term to the Virginia House of Delegates, Madison was defeated in April 1777. Apparently, a major reason for this outcome was that his opponent gave away large quantities of whiskey to voters. Booze in the vicinity of American polling places was a common feature well into the nineteenth century. Madison supporters' effort to annul the election on the grounds of bribery went nowhere.[24]

This embarrassing setback was an afterthought, if not a punchline for future biographers. Madison was soon chosen for a seat on the governor's Council of State, where he served from January 1778 through the end of 1779. Virginia governors had few powers without the support of this influential body. It was here that Madison strengthened his friendship and political alliance with Thomas Jefferson, the new governor of Virginia.[25] For the rest of their careers, including during the 1812 election campaign, the two men frequently exchanged political advice, as well as counsel on public policy. They did not always agree on matters. Most notably, Madison was an enthusiastic booster of the Constitution of 1787 whereas Jefferson could be described as lukewarm about the document.

The young politician's next post was a tenure for three years in the Second Continental Congress, where Madison sharpened his skills as a legislator, refining his expertise on domestic and foreign policy issues. He also argued for a stronger bond between the states and a more robust central government, which his colleagues initially balked at supporting. For decades to come, critics charged that there was a so-called Virginia dynasty aiming to control America. Disabusing the advocates of this claim, Madison and Jefferson endorsed their state relinquishing some of its western territory to the Continental Congress.[26]

In 1784 Madison was elected to the Virginia House of Delegates, where he successfully worked to prevent official state establishment of churches as well as laws mandating a religious test for holding public office. Madison carried those principles with him into the presidency, using his veto pen to stop what he viewed as governmental favoritism of selected religious denominations. He remained an active player beyond Virginia. Serving in Congress and state government in the 1780s, he had a front-row seat to witness the multiplying problems of the Articles of Confederation, which had impotently governed the postcolonial alliance of states since 1781. The concerned legislator solicited support from colleagues for the purposes of holding a meeting in Annapolis, Maryland, to discuss reforms to the Articles, mainly pertaining to commerce and trade.[27]

Madison was part of the Virginia delegation for the Annapolis meeting, which was held in September 1786 at Mann's Tavern. Only five Middle Atlantic states sent representatives; several others simply did not have enough time to assemble teams they could send in time. The summit accomplished little, other than a consensus to call another meeting next year. The vigilant Madison arrived early in Philadelphia in May 1787 to begin preparations for a major convention to consider revisions to the Articles of Confederation. By now, he actually had little use for the Articles. Working with his cohorts Edmund Randolph and George Mason, Madison designed a model that ultimately strengthened the national government at the expense of the states. There would be a bicameral legislature, apportioned on the basis of population, and a Council of Revision, which would have enjoyed the authority to veto measures enacted by Congress. New York State had a similar body, and under the Virginians' plan the council was to include a singular chief executive, as well as some federal-level judges.[28]

Although Madison did not wish to see an overly powerful presidential office, he could also appreciate the value of independence in the executive, held accountable by the other branches of government. He advocated "a representative republic, where the executive magistracy is carefully limited; both in the extent and the duration of its power." Madison also sternly opposed any hereditary monarch, and he warned of the propensity of legislative bodies to behave in a manner resembling an angry mob: "In all very numerous assemblies, of whatever character composed, passion never fails to wrest the sceptre from reason."[29]

As a leading delegate to the Constitutional Convention of 1787, Madison and other Framers of the Constitution conceived of a democracy for grown-ups, which they interpreted as excluding many people deemed incapable of responsible participation. To be sure, a healthy republic will consist of at least some democratic institutions and processes. The worst impulses of democracy can be restrained in a republic, but limitations upon popular participation are likely to exclude the most marginalized categories of people. The restrictive democracy of this era reinforced discrimination against women, persons of color, and poorer Americans. The Constitution built a framework of diffused institutions sharing power while restraining popular participation. Senators were to be chosen by elected state legislatures. Judges would be appointed by the president and confirmed by the Senate for life terms. Executive branch officers would be appointed, subject to Senate confirmation, and serving at the pleasure of the president. The process for selecting the president was established to be highly filtered and decentralized, leaving much discretion to individual states. For several election cycles, democracy was diluted, as some states persisted in having their legislatures select presidential electors. In 1812 this was the modality in exactly half of the states; the remaining states gave this choice to voters. Slow but certain steps toward opening up democratic presidential selection were proceeding by the time Madison stood for a second term.

In addition to Madison, there were a few delegates in attendance who became major supporting actors in the 1812 presidential election, including both vice presidential nominees. Among them were Rufus King and Elbridge Gerry of Massachusetts, as well as Gouverneur Morris and Jared Ingersoll Jr. of Pennsylvania. While Madison is frequently referred to as the Father of the Constitution, this label is a little bit unfair to the other delegates who also labored very hard to arrive at a successful outcome. Madison, however, was undoubtedly a key figure in creating the document, brokering compromises and respectfully debating his colleagues. He steered the proceedings toward a replacement of the Articles of Confederation, rather than a mere revision. He took copious notes at the meetings, which didn't become public until many decades later, in accordance with the mutual agreement of secrecy between the participants. Elements of Virginia's plan were accepted, such as the two-chamber legislature and a singular executive, but the Council of Revision was dropped. Legislative apportionment by population would be balanced with equal representation by states. A national judiciary would be created, given the greater powers and authority that the federal government would be assuming. The Constitution established the necessary machinery to regulate interstate commerce and provide for national defense.[30]

During the subsequent state ratification debates, the people of New York got to see the persuasive powers of Madison's pen. Alexander Hamilton, who soon became the defining face of the federalist cause, got right to work after the Philadelphia Convention finished their task. Opposition essays were already circulating in New York newspapers and could be very influential upon elite and public opinion if not countered. Hamilton solicited his fellow New Yorker, John Jay, as a partner for the purposes of collaborating on a series of essays to defend the new Constitution. Both gentlemen then invited Madison to join the project. From October 1787 through August 1788, the three men walked readers through the provisions of the document, justifying the new powers the federal government would be undertaking. Writing under the pen name of Publius, they respectfully answered common criticisms of the Philadelphia Convention's final product. A strong republic, incorporating the principles of a filtered representative democracy, was the preferred alternative to a discombobulated confederation of states attempting to work together. The Articles of Confederation did not realistically permit the central government to exercise its already limited authority. Some powers should only be carried out by the federal government, while the states would remain free to complete those functions that are best performed at that level. "If the new Constitution be examined with accuracy and candor," Madison wrote in *Federalist*, no. 45, "it will be found that the change which it proposes consists much less in the addition of NEW POWERS to the Union, than in the invigoration of its ORIGINAL POWERS."[31]

Back at home, Madison was easily elected to serve as a delegate to Virginia's ratifying convention, which was held in June 1788. He was an active player at the proceedings, save for a short illness that sidelined him for a few days. After three weeks of extensive and detailed debate, Virginia's ratifying convention voted in the affirmative, 89–79, on June 25. Revisions were requested, however, and within much of Virginia there was concern about the Constitution's lack of protections of religious freedom. With their political momentum wobbling, Madison and other advocates of ratification conceded to support a bill of rights after the document won approval from the requisite number of states. Madison promised that the matter of religious liberty would be included among those amendments.[32]

New York was initially under the strong influence of opponents to the Constitution. Still, by the summer of 1788 the succession of other states voting in the affirmative seemed to make adoption a foregone conclusion. New Hampshire's endorsement came on June 21, which was the required ninth state needed for the Constitution to become effective. It is helpful to keep in mind that in 1788 news traveled very slowly. *The Federalist Papers* certainly served to rehabilitate the Constitution among many influential New Yorkers, although probably not until after the document was approved. Pragmatism prevailed, as joining the new government, flawed as it was, would likely be the better option than isolation from the United States. Other skeptical states had already demonstrated that asking for amendments was a legitimate way to advance their interests. A package of revisions was requested, but with New York's narrow approval on July 26, the new federal government was already planning to begin operations.[33]

Madison would surely be a significant player in crafting the amendments that so many states were asking for, but first he had to have a seat at the most relevant table. Now with the skills of a master legislator, he was well suited to either chamber of Congress. George Washington, who was unsurprisingly chosen as the first American president, encouraged Madison to run. They were personal friends and supporters of the new Constitution, and Washington assumed that Madison would be his ally in the legislative branch. Back in the state capital, however, the mischievous Patrick Henry maneuvered the Virginia legislature into snubbing Madison for selection to the US Senate. The fiery Henry was a strong opponent of the Constitution and had argued passionately against ratification at the recent Virginia convention. In a second effort at revenge, Henry and his allies worked to draft creatively shaped districts for the federal House of Representatives. The purpose was to freeze out as many federalist candidates as possible, including Madison.[34] Elbridge Gerry, Madison's future running mate in 1812, was certainly not the founding father of the practice that we all call gerrymandering today.

Madison found that Washington wasn't the only one who wanted him to run for Congress. Friends and colleagues wanted him to be a part of the new government in the legislative branch, where his experience and familiarity with the Constitution would be valuable. The district encircling his home was stacked against him, and his opponent was hardly a token candidate: James Monroe was a Revolutionary War veteran, a lawyer, and also a rising star in Virginia politics. He was a nominal opponent of the Constitution's ratification, but he was open to compromises and amendments. He and Madison had a friendship that endured through their campaign against each other.[35]

The Madison/Monroe campaign for Congress in early 1789 has attracted recent scholarly attention. The two men traveled the district together, visiting with voters, giving speeches, and engaging in policy debates. Congressional and local campaigns during the republic's early years sometimes followed this model, which was a stark contrast with how presidential races would be conducted for the next several decades. The main issue between these two candidates revolved around making amendments to the new

Constitution. Madison had already signaled his support for a bill of rights. He believed that task should be legislated in Congress, and not at another convention, which could spiral out of control. The weather was wintry, and on one occasion Madison contracted frostbite on his face, which left a permanent scar. Except for Orange County, the rest of the district was supposed to favor Monroe, but this so-called Henry-mandering failed pretty convincingly. On February 2, the voters' verdict was 1,308 for Madison and 972 for Monroe. Outperforming expectations in counties he was not supposed to win, Madison could claim vindication for his work on the Constitution and his commitment to deliver on necessary amendments.[36]

Elbridge Gerry had advocated for a bill of rights at the Philadelphia Convention. Madison and other delegates initially dismissed the need to include these amendments, which would have been aimed at securing the inherent rights of the people. Such matters were best left for the states to debate in writing their own constitutions, and arguably the current US Constitution could not be interpreted as taking away any existing rights of the people. In addition, any affirmation of specific rights might be understood as a statement that the rights of the people are restricted to just those enumerated in the document. The omission was not well-received in many states, including Virginia. In his congressional campaign, Madison worked hard to court Baptist voters by assuring them that he would fight for religious liberty as part of any bill of rights.[37]

Congressman Madison worked to keep the promise that he and other federalists made. While a constitution must empower government to perform essential functions and services, it is equally important that any social contract also limit the powers of government, lest the state become an instrument for abrogating those rights that are inherent to human beings. Bad actors will sometimes find their way into the councils of government. In *The Federalist Papers*, Madison and Hamilton also worried about the propensity of delusional popular majorities to demand measures that restrict the freedoms of an undesirable political minority. Madison was the leading figure in producing twelve new amendments that protected due process of law, freedom of speech and the press, and religious liberty. The federal government would also not be allowed to formally endorse a particular church or denomination. The states, however, would remain free to do so into the early nineteenth century.

Madison's proposals cleared the necessary two-thirds of both chambers of Congress in September 1789. By December 1791 the requisite number of states had ratified ten of the amendments. One plank, forbidding the ability of members of Congress to receive salary increases prior to elections, was not ratified until 1992. Another provision, regulating how population is to be apportioned into representation in the House of Representatives, fell short of the required approval from states. Madison had officially kept his campaign promise, and he was now on his way to being a leading member of the House. His political affiliation, however, drifted away from support for President Washington's policies.[38]

Although he was not an antisocial man, Madison remained unmarried well into adulthood. His first major courtship came when he was thirty-one years old, and his love interest was a fifteen-year-old girl named Catherine "Kitty" Floyd. She was the daughter of William Floyd, a New York signer of the Declaration of Independence. The two were briefly engaged, but the young lady broke it off in the summer of 1783, as she fell in love with another man closer to her age. The collapse of his engagement was apparently a source of shame for him, and several more years went by without any serious romance in Madison's life.[39]

Dolley Payne Todd was seventeen years younger than Madison, but that did not impede their compatibility. Charming and extroverted, she balanced Madison's occasional shyness and his more reserved personality. Dolley lost her first husband, John Todd, in Philadelphia's yellow fever epidemic of 1793, as well as her infant son. Her other son, John Payne Todd, was notoriously irresponsible and unaccomplished in life. Aaron Burr, who would someday become a politically toxic figure, helped bring Dolley together with her future husband. After a short courtship, the two were married on September 15, 1794. The couple never had children, but Madison adopted young John and looked out for him throughout his life's many peccadilloes. When Dolley joined President Madison in the executive mansion, she electrified Washington, DC, and turned her position into the capital city's most important socialite. She facilitated social events that included politicians from opposing parties, and she won the respect of citizens across demographic lines.[40]

James Madison was a slaveowner. From the cradle to the grave, he was served by enslaved Black people, and he treated the practice as a normal part of life. As a plantation owner, he held several dozen persons in bondage and had no compunction about selling them out of financial necessity. He also supported the three-fifths compromise in the Constitution, which counted slaves as 60 percent of a human being for the purposes of the census. Southern states would get to partially count slaves as persons—while granting them zero political rights—so as to enlarge their delegations in the House. Privately, Madison held some misgivings about slavery, but in his view, it could always be compromised away for the sake of something more important. Slavery, in fact, did not emerge as even a minor issue in the presidential election of 1812.

Further restrictions upon democratic participation reflected the norms of an elite-based representative democracy. In 1807 the American electorate was universally male and almost entirely white, as African American suffrage was virtually nonexistent.[41] Stringent voter qualifications, linked to property ownership or taxpaying requirements, were common across the states.[42] These policies functioned to reduce the political clout of working-class citizens and to practically eliminate African American voting rights. While the First Amendment of the Constitution permitted all Americans to partake in the political process, the suffrage laws of the era gave well-to-do white males an overall advantage. Implicit in this arrangement was the notion that working-class and poorly educated Americans should stay out of political affairs and leave the business of government to men of the gentry.

The democratic aspects of the American constitutional system were rigorously challenged during the early decades of the republic. In a case that involved Secretary Madison, the federal judiciary had to assess if Congress should be allowed to enact laws that violate the Constitution.[43] Did freedom of assembly and speech protect the right of armed citizens to forcibly resist a tax on distilled spirits? The Whiskey Rebellion of 1794 tested the proposition that any allegedly unfair tax passed by Congress somehow constituted taxation without representation, thereby warranting an armed response. As a congressman, Madison frowned upon the violent uprising in western Pennsylvania, but he also warned that the instigators could play right into the hands of actors who favored a more authoritarian form of government. "The result of the insurrection ought to be a lesson to every part of the Union against disobedience to the laws," Madison wrote. "Examples of this kind are as favorable to the enemies of Republican Government, as the experiment proves them to be dangerous to the Authors."[44]

As a leading critic of Federalist policies, Madison stepped up to defend freedom of speech from attacks by the administration of President John Adams. Could Congress and the president, under the threat of a possible war with France, create measures that stifle speech and political activism? In a package of laws known as the Alien and Sedition Acts of 1798, citizenship policies were tightened, and the president was empowered with broad rights to imprison or deport any non-American who was deemed to be a political troublemaker. The Sedition Act contained frighteningly slippery language that could have conceivably resulted in the arrest of any political activist or public critic. A person could be charged with sedition for:

> writing, printing, uttering or publishing any false, scandalous and malicious writing or writings against the government of the United States, or either house of the Congress of the United States, or the President of the United States, with intent to defame the said government, or either house of the said Congress, or the said President, or to bring them, or either of them, into contempt or disrepute; or to excite against them, or either or any of them, the hatred of the good people of the United States.[45]

Under a law like this in the political environment of the twenty-first century, any rabble-rouser on the internet or social media could find him- or herself in federal prison. Journalists sympathetic to Democratic-Republicans were especially targeted under the Sedition Act. Would the mere threat of war make it more likely that certain forms of speech could be criminalized? Amid the passion of the 1812 campaign, Madison's supporters made their position very clear that opposition to America's war against Great Britain was tantamount to treason. If the nation's leaders determined that the United States must go to war, how would that process actually play out in accordance with the Constitution? As president in 1812, Madison became the first commander-in-chief to confront that dilemma. Finally, how would the designated constitutional system for electing a president respond to the proliferation of political parties? A party system was mostly in place by 1812, but organization was spotty throughout the nation. Madison's opponents struggled to construct an anti-war electoral coalition within this environment.

Madison's views on political parties were consistent with the leading actors of his generation. In his presidential Farewell Address to the American people, George Washington warned against the ill effects of political parties:

> The spirit of party serves always to distract the public councils and enfeeble the public administration. It agitates the community with ill-rounded jealousies and false alarms; kindles the animosity of one part against another; foments occasionally riot and insurrection. It opens the door to foreign influence and corruption, which find a facilitated access to the government itself through the channels of party passion.[46]

Across the ideological spectrum, men of the Framers' generation held a general disdain for party organizations. Alexander Hamilton and Madison both dismissed parties with the pejorative label of "factions,"[47] while Jefferson asserted that "if I could not go to heaven but with a party, I would not go there at all."[48] John Adams suggested that party divisions were "to be dreaded as the greatest political evil, under our Constitution."[49] The common claims against political parties were that they were inherently divisive, and preoccupied with short-term victory at the expense of the common good. Parties were bound to attract troublemakers, demagogues, and overly ambitious characters, bringing bad influences upon the government and political life in general. Good men, who would otherwise be prone to independent thinking and acting in the nation's best interests, would succumb to the impulse to prioritize party over country. Foreign nations could even use the vehicle of a party to manipulate the outcomes of American politics and public policy.[50]

Even a revered figure such as George Washington could not escape the pull of an emerging partisan divide, however. Polarizing issues, including taxation, central banking, and relations with Britain and France, quickly drew the first president into divisive battles over the new nation's destiny. On issue after issue, the ostensibly nonpartisan Washington sided with Hamilton, his secretary of the treasury. The Hamiltonian plan called for a national bank, federal assumption of the state debts from the Revolutionary War, a national army, internal improvements, tariffs, a robust national government, and friendly relations with Britain. Manufacturing and industrialization were to be promoted over agrarianism. An advanced and modernized economy, backed by a strong national defense, would establish the credibility of the new government on the world stage. A moderate national debt would cement the confidence of bankers and investors. A healthy republic would keep democracy limited, and in the hands of gentlemen. Supporters of this policy vision were known as "Federalists," or men of the "federal interest." As Hamilton, Madison, and other supporters of the Constitution's ratification also called themselves federalists, they viewed themselves as the lineal descendants of the architects of that document.[51]

Critics of administration policies formed a coalition in Congress that became known as "Republicans," or "Democratic-Republicans," or men of the "Republican interest." This organized opposition gained momentum during the Washington presidency and intensified further under President John Adams. Democratic-Republicans opposed the Hamilton economic program, regarding it as a blueprint for government centralization and favoritism of bankers and speculators. They favored low tariffs, sufficient to fund governmental expenses, as protectionism was prone to political mischief in support of powerful industries. Short of a national emergency, defense of the country was best left to state militias, with a small federal army and navy. The Democratic-Republican view held that an overly large and centralized military could be dangerous to liberty. Relations with Britain were to be kept at arm's length. As a general rule, the locus of governmental powers should be left to the states, the federal judiciary should be limited, and the legislative branch should function as the main driver of public policy. Internal improvements to the nation's infrastructure should generally be relegated to the states, where actors at that level would best know how to address their needs. The president was to act as a dutiful steward, charged with carrying out the will of Congress, backed by a limited executive branch. The United States, in the Democratic-Republican vision, was to be a predominantly agrarian nation. Democracy, at least among the free white male population, was to be celebrated as consistent with the principles of the American Revolution. There was some lineage with the old anti-federalists who had opposed the Constitution's ratification on the grounds that the document infringed upon the proper powers of the states. However, the historical linkage between anti-federalists and Democratic-Republicans is far from perfect.[52]

Outside of the national capital, Federalist/Democratic-Republican divisions also emerged, though with varying levels of intensity as well as quite a bit of variation in each state's political balances of power. Politicians in state legislatures and local offices lined up behind party labels. Overtly partisan newspapers surfaced to spread the gospel to loyal supporters in city after city. During the war and election campaign of 1812, inflammatory newspaper rhetoric spread throughout the nation. The cleavage that developed was real, and polarizing at times, but less sophisticated than subsequent party systems.[53] The same men who had once denounced parties as troublesome pests now helped to build two major parties. Madison was a reluctant participant, as much as he tried to remain above the fray as president. Still, the ethos of this era was that parties were a necessary evil that must be tolerated. Federalists and Democratic-Republicans justified their existence for the purposes of stopping their opponents' allegedly sinister designs upon American constitutional government. The notion that one's party affiliation is predominantly rooted in dislike, fear, and even hatred for the opposition is what political scientists today call *negative partisanship*.[54] Surely this phenomenon existed in the days long before survey research and public opinion polls. Hopefully, these party architects believed, there would someday be a time when such organizations would no longer be necessary, and the affairs of government would be handled by enlightened statesmen.[55]

Both parties relied upon constituencies of supporters, though there could be variation from state to state, as a truly nationalized party system had not yet materialized. The support base for both parties did not sharply divide along rural and urban lines in many states. Federalists positioned themselves as the party of industrialization, mercantilism, and economic modernization. They also evolved into an Anglo-American party. As tensions with France escalated in the 1790s, Federalists began to support restrictive immigration policies that were especially aimed at people of non-British heritage.[56] They had the support of citizens who favored a robust central government that could act as an agent of economic development and a defender of national security. Prosperous merchants, bankers, and speculators were more likely to support the Federalist cause.[57] The party's regional base was in New England, though even here, cracks in its dominance began to appear in the decade of the 1800s. Federalist support in the South and the Middle Atlantic states also began weakening after 1800. The party's erosion resumed after a limited northern comeback in the years leading up to and during the War of 1812. The states of Connecticut and Delaware, however, remained stubborn Federalist strongholds well into the 1810s.

Democratic-Republicans positioned themselves as guardians of limited government, which was also a central principle of the American Revolution. While some of them had previously been anti-federalist opponents of the Constitution, they now held that the document could work best if it was a device for restraining government, rather than expanding it. While they championed the virtue of the small yeoman farmer—and agrarianism in general—Democratic-Republicans did not enjoy universal support from rural citizens. There was far from a national consensus on economic policies, and voters of this era were just as prone to being mobilized on the basis of social and cultural issues as they are today. The party won the support of citizens who shared their skepticism of the federal government's undue meddling in economic affairs. For voters who favored a politics of egalitarianism, as it was understood around the year 1800, the Democratic-Republican Party was a natural fit. Upwardly mobile Americans could be attracted to the party's anti-elitist message. Settlers of new lands out west would find the Democratic-Republican emphasis on agrarian policies to be appealing. In addition, people who settled in new western states, far away from the national capital, would be more likely to view the central government with suspicion or hostility. Newcomers of French and Irish heritage preferred Democratic-Republicans, and the party accordingly favored liberalized immigration policies. The South served as the sectional base for Democratic-Republicans, though the party became at least competitive in all regions, even in Federalist-dominated states. Newly established states in the West, such as Ohio, Tennessee, and Louisiana, favored Democratic-Republicans. By the standards of the early 1800s, the party was well-positioned to be a big tent that was ready to embrace a diversifying nation. In 1812 the party's demographic and geographical advantages proved to be valuable for Madison's reelection, even as Democratic-Republicans were divided over the war.

Religion sometimes divided Federalists and Democratic-Republicans. As a party that embraced separation of church and state, Democratic-Republicans would be attractive to religious minorities. Catholics generally supported Democratic-Republicans, as did Jews. Federalists were particularly strong among New England Congregationalists, where some states officially established that church.[58] In their opposition to established state churches, Episcopalians in New England preferred Democratic-Republicans, while favoring Federalists in other states.[59] Baptists, given their strong opposition to governmental establishment of churches, strongly supported Democratic-Republicans.[60] Methodists, with their egalitarian ethos, favored Democratic-Republicans, though a pocket of Federalist support could be found among that denomination in the Delmarva Peninsula.[61] Presbyterians were divided between their Old and New Light wings, with the former favoring Federalists, and the latter evangelical group in the Democratic-Republican camp. Among Quakers, Federalists were generally the preferred party.[62]

As Federalists initially rallied around the economic plans and constitutional philosophy of Hamilton, he became their intellectual leader. Even after he left the Washington administration Cabinet, Hamilton continued to wield some influence in Federalist circles. In an extensive essay that became public ahead of the 1800 presidential election, Hamilton denounced President Adams's judgment, temperament, and fitness for office, though the former treasury secretary gave his reluctant support. Hamilton and his allies made a failed attempt to replace their party's president with Charles Cotesworth Pinckney, a Revolutionary War officer and former Constitutional Convention delegate. The document helped to weaken Adams's support from Federalists and further divide the party, as Democratic-Republicans were happy to disseminate it through the newspapers.[63] Adamant supporters of Hamilton and his policies were known as High Federalists, and they held a particular disdain for the idea that Democratic-Republicans should be treated as a legitimate and loyal opposition.

Federalists in 1812 awkwardly positioned themselves as the peace party against Madison, though this was a reversal of their historical stance. More than a decade earlier, High Federalists had pushed for a full military solution to American grievances with France. The two countries had been engaged in two years of periodic skirmishes on the seas, disrupting the shipping operations of both nations. Adams was just as determined to prevent a war that the United States was scarcely ready fight, though he appreciated the importance of preparation. As he worked to broker a peace agreement, Adams agreed to the formation of a national army and a buildup of the navy. Upon peace being achieved, Adams and Congress had the army disbanded.[64] Meanwhile, in the Cabinet, the president became frustrated as three of his secretaries looked to Hamilton for leadership, rather than to the elected head of government. In May 1800, exasperated by their loyalty to the former treasury secretary, as well as their hawkish stance vis-à-vis France, Adams forced the resignation of Secretary of War James McHenry and fired Secretary of State Timothy Pickering. Secretary of the Treasury Oliver Wolcott Jr. was forced to resign later in the year. The intra-Federalist feuding over relations with France further diminished Adams's prospects for a second term. In addition, as news in this era traveled at a glacial pace across the ocean, word of the peace agreement only reached American ears after the election.

Thomas Jefferson was the leading critic of Hamilton's policies within George Washington's Cabinet, and he emerged as the political and intellectual embodiment of the Democratic-Republican Party. During his tenure as secretary of state, Jefferson asserted what would become his party's vision for the young republic, and Congressman Madison was increasingly his ally. In an administration that purported to be nonpartisan, however, Washington's policy choices repeatedly favored the Federalist approach, leaving Jefferson politically isolated. In the House, Madison led the opposition to kill Hamilton's economic plans, which were stalled by the summer of 1790. Then at Hamilton and Jefferson's urging, a sort of dinner summit was held between themselves and Madison. Jefferson found Hamilton's banking and economic plans to be an alarming consolidation of the central government. Madison resented federal assumption of all state debts because he considered such a policy unfair to the states that had retired the bulk of their post-war debt after much sacrifice, while other states remained indebted. Jefferson and Madison acquiesced in Hamilton's proposal for federal assumption of state debts, along with a pledge to revise Virginia's debt downward. The permanent national capital would be situated along the Potomac River, which would place it on southern soil. The government would be temporarily relocated from New York City to Philadelphia. Madison did not agree to vote in favor of Hamilton's plans, but he made it clear that he would not mount a full-throated legislative effort to defeat the treasury secretary's agenda.[65]

In spite of this deal, the rift between Jefferson and the Cabinet continued. Though he shared President Washington's aversion to foreign entanglements, Jefferson held a sympathetic view of the French Revolution, believing that it represented the advancement of democracy in opposition to monarchy.[66] When Washington asserted a formal policy of American neutrality in the ongoing war between France and Britain, Jefferson objected to the president's unilateral action. Jefferson opposed American military intervention, but he encouraged Madison to publicly challenge Hamilton's claim that Washington enjoyed executive authority to proclaim official neutrality.[67] Having lost the most important policy debates within the administration, Jefferson resigned in December 1793, but he remained as the closest thing Democratic-Republicans had to a national face.

By that time, Madison had formed an alliance with Jefferson and Democratic-Republicans. Formerly aligned with the federalist architects of the Constitution, Washington's broad use of executive power to proclaim American neutrality was disturbing to the congressman, for he was a fierce guardian of the strict boundaries of responsibility between the three branches of government. Madison was also especially concerned about Hamilton's nationalistic economic plans. A governmental establishment so closely tied to banking and commercial interests was dangerous to Madison—and it was inconsistent with the constitutional vision he laid out in *The Federalist Papers* just a few years prior. Given that Virginia had mostly paid its debts from the war, Madison saw the Hamiltonian program as skewed to the advantage of speculators. The treasury secretary's plans mostly favored northern states and functioned to the disadvantage of southern states and agricultural interests. As for the national bank, Madison regarded that idea as unauthorized by the Constitution, although he would evolve on this matter in the years to come. To be sure, when war broke out in 1812, the absence of a national bank created uncertainty for President Madison's ability to finance the nation's new military commitments.[68]

The now former Hamilton ally also denounced the 1795 Jay Treaty with Britain, which was aimed at rectifying post-war differences between the two countries. One issue that would bedevil the Washington administration and three subsequent presidents was the impressment of American sailors into the British Royal Navy. Under this policy, British vessels were authorized to intercept American ships and seize Americans on the grounds that they were allegedly deserters from the Royal Navy. Although some of these impressed seamen certainly were British deserters or nationals, many others were in fact American citizens. Thousands of American seamen were wrongfully impressed by British naval authorities, detained, and forced to prove their citizenship status before being released.[69] Not only were these practices flagrant violations of due process of law, but American shipping was greatly disrupted by impressment. For their own part, Britain needed a steady stream of seamen for its navy, given the many threats and conflicts the country regularly experienced, namely the Napoleonic Wars. In addition to the impressment issue, American grievances included lost slaves from the Revolutionary War. There were also the matters of merchant ships that had recently been seized, British occupation of forts around the Great Lakes, British arming of Native Americans in the Northwest Territory, trade in the West Indies, and border disputes between the United States and British Canada. The pact, negotiated by Supreme Court chief justice and special envoy John Jay, made several concessions to the British that Madison and Democratic-Republicans found unacceptable.

Arbitration would resolve several disputes, the British would withdraw from American forts, and trade restrictions were mostly liberalized on terms favorable to Britain. The impressment issue remained unresolved, slaveholders would not be compensated for their lost slaves, and the border dispute would be negotiated by way of commissioners. Madison vehemently denounced the treaty as a sellout to Britain. The Senate ratified the treaty with the bare constitutional minimum two-thirds vote. In the House, Madison mounted a campaign to force the Washington administration to hand over documents concerning the negotiation process, under the threat of withholding congressional appropriations to implement the treaty. Washington rejected Madison's demands as an unconstitutional encroachment on the president's executive authority (though the documents were submitted to the Senate), and the House voted to fund the treaty's implementation anyway.[70] Public antagonism toward the agreement helped to galvanize the new opposition party, as it rallied around Jefferson for the first truly competitive presidential election in 1796.[71]

First as a force of opposition, and then as a governing party after 1800, Democratic-Republicans became a disparate coalition. From the beginning, the party found itself managing a fragile collection of factions, rivalries, and personality conflicts. With little national cohesion in the entire party system, any one salient issue had the potential to tear Democratic-Republicans apart. As the party grew larger, these challenges only multiplied, even as the Federalists continued to weaken. Under Madison's tenure as president, the national party was a bloated and fragile apparatus with a very open rupture as the 1812 election campaign got underway. As Democratic-Republicans increasingly dominated the national landscape, the governing party began to absorb its old Federalist opponents. Future president John Quincy Adams, for example, switched his allegiance from nominal Federalist toward a gradual affiliation with Democratic-Republicans late in the Jefferson administration, though he retained a strong nationalist outlook for the duration of his career.[72] Holding to the Founding-era disdain of partisanship, Democratic-Republicans now aimed to dilute any sharp differences between the parties. James Monroe, presidential predecessor to the junior Adams, spoke of a great "amalgamation" of the two parties—under the Jeffersonian tent, of course—that would once and for all bring the country toward the Founders' ideal of a nation without partisan combat.[73]

Both parties were loose confederations of state organizations, with varying levels of depth and sophistication across the nation. There was nothing resembling the centralizing agents that would only begin to emerge in the 1830s. National party conventions, committees, and platforms were still decades away. Parties communicated through state and local organs, as there was no national news media. Nor did presidents embrace the role of party leader. Rather, presidents held to the Founding-generation view of parties as unfortunate assemblies of citizens, politicians, and activists that must be tolerated in a representative democracy. At the national level, the closest thing to any kind of nationalized organization was the quadrennial congressional nominating caucus.

The Constitution was silent on the process of presidential nominations, leaving the task to the organized supporters of individual candidates. After George Washington's departure from the office, partisan tensions were bound to further escalate in the absence of the nation's most unifying figure. Aspiring politicians jockeyed for position within their respective parties, building cadres of followers and sharpening internal divisions. Similar to conventions and presidential primaries in later decades, the congressional nominating caucus would serve as a venue to chart the party's future national direction and leadership. Also analogous to conventions and primaries in the modern era, the nominating caucus soon became a controversial method, riddled with accusations of elitism and inherent bias in favor of insider candidates. Critics resorted to calling the procedure unconstitutional, on the grounds that members of Congress were not authorized with a formal role in the selection of candidates.[74]

In the first American party system, decisions were often made in small meetings of elites and other politically well-connected citizens. The caucus served as the most notable example of exclusivity. Presidential candidates were chosen by other politicians. Grassroots participation by ordinary citizens was not part of the process. In each presidential election year from 1796 to 1824, party members in both houses of Congress would deliberate and select presidential and vice presidential nominees. Meetings were initially rather informal, and attendance was far from universal. As the Democratic-Republican Party was ascendant after 1800, its assembly took on a greater importance than that of the Federalist Party, which discontinued its caucus in 1804. Losing or underdog candidates often brushed the caucus aside as illegitimate and received unofficial nominations from supporters in state legislatures. Because the nomination rested in the hands of the legislative branch, presidents and aspiring presidents had a vested interest in placating the congressional wings of their respective party.[75] As the years went by, the Jeffersonian coalition became larger, and included more populist factions, making this procedure increasingly controversial. Accordingly, Democratic-Republican opponents of Madison repeated these criticisms of the nominating process during the 1812 campaign.

A JEFFERSONIAN MAJORITY

The America that Madison presided over in 1812 was politically dominated by a fractious Democratic-Republican majority, with divisions that had been intensifying for years. The pivotal moment in establishing a growing Democratic-Republican supremacy was the presidential election of 1800. Jefferson himself likened the election's outcome to the significance of the American Revolution.[76] In a rematch of the 1796 contest, the much better organized and energized Democratic-Republican Party engineered the defeat of the incumbent President Adams. The campaign was vitriolic, with hyperbolic accusations, rumors, and smears that a contemporary observer of American politics would easily recognize. Adams was denounced as a quasi-monarchist who was plotting to once again subordinate the United States to Great Britain by marrying off one of his sons to a daughter of King George III. Jefferson was accused of being an atheist, a pro-French Jacobin, and a dishonest hypocrite who had committed financial improprieties.[77]

Over-the-top accusations of both candidates were shouted from party publications that resembled the emotionally charged and partisan tone of twenty-first-century cable news and social media memes.

The Electoral College outcome left no doubt that Adams was defeated, but the original constitutional design for presidential elections generated a deadlocked result due to the parties' nominating running mates for president and vice president. The Constitution called for members of the Electoral College to vote for two candidates, with no distinction between president and vice president. The winner would be president, and the runner-up would be vice president. Democratic-Republican electors voted for Jefferson and his running mate, Aaron Burr of New York. One Jefferson elector was supposed to discard his second vote to ensure that Burr finished as runner-up, but miscommunications and misunderstandings produced a tie vote between the two candidates.[78]

Though Democratic-Republicans had also captured control of Congress in the election, the Constitution called for the presidential contest to be resolved by the outgoing House of Representatives, which was controlled by Federalists. Burr commanded a following in his state and elsewhere; he was an equally, if not more, controversial figure than Jefferson. He was also a man of considerable deficiencies of character. The prospect of elevating him to the presidency was rather alarming to many Democratic-Republicans. Had Burr simply stood down and stressed that he was intended to be Jefferson's vice president, a long standoff might have been avoided. This, however, the ambitious Burr refused to do, and some Federalists were eager to create mischief by installing the unpredictable New Yorker into the presidency. A prolonged deadlock in the House occurred, dragging well into the winter of 1801.

At this point Alexander Hamilton got involved. Though now just a private citizen, he still exerted influence in Federalist circles. Warning congressmen of his party that Burr would be dangerous to the very survival of the republic, Hamilton urged them to let Jefferson prevail. Burr was "unfit" and an "embryo Caesar," and while Jefferson had his own issues of character, he would at least respect the American system of constitutional government.[79] "If we must have an *enemy* at the head of the Government," Hamilton wrote to House Speaker Theodore Sedgwick during the 1800 campaign, "let it be one whom we can oppose & for whom we are not responsible, who will not involve our party in the disgrace of his foolish and bad measures."[80] Enough Federalist congressmen were convinced by Hamilton to abstain, and on the thirty-sixth round of voting Jefferson was selected as chief executive. Burr's clumsy attempt at a collusion with the Federalists was spoiled, thereby making it seem disingenuous and dishonest to cross party lines in pursuit of the presidency.

The enmity between Hamilton and Burr continued, as the former treasury secretary successfully used his influence to thwart Burr's 1804 campaign for governor of New York. Hamilton reluctantly agreed to resolve his differences with Burr in an ill-fated duel at Weehawken, New Jersey, on July 11, 1804. After Burr killed Hamilton in this misguided altercation, his reputation continued to decline. The vice president had already been dumped from the 1804 Democratic-Republican ticket earlier in the year, and he then allegedly engaged in a bizarre conspiracy to establish a new nation in North America. Burr was tried for treason and acquitted, for the hard evidence was flimsy, but his political career was over.[81]

The Electoral College deadlock, as well as Burr's intransigence, created considerable unnecessary political tension. As presidential elections were now fully partisan affairs, the constitutional model would have to be revised. Now in the US Senate for a brief tenure, DeWitt Clinton and most of his fellow congressional Democratic-Republicans advocated for passage of the Twelfth Amendment to the Constitution. Ratification from the necessary states was completed by June 1804. The new rules would be in effect for the 1804 race, so as to preclude the confusing debacle of 1800 from occurring again. The new amendment called for presidential electors to cast separate ballots for president and vice president. Revisions were also made to the congressional selection process that governed how winners would be chosen if no candidate should win a majority of electoral votes. Federalists opposed the amendment, perhaps cognizant of their weakening national status, and calculating that the old, discombobulated selection system still gave them a fighting chance to install a president or vice president.[82]

Madison was handling personal matters and recurring health ailments when Jefferson tapped him to be secretary of state. Although his father had recently died, Madison was able to arrive in the new national capital a few weeks after the inauguration to be at the president's side as Jefferson's top lieutenant. The closeness of the 1800 presidential election belied the coming era of Democratic-Republican dominance. Federalists were still well-positioned within the national government, including the civil service, the judiciary, and the military's officer corps. Secretary Madison not only would be involved in foreign policy but would also be a major player in the Jefferson administration's efforts to steer the nation away from Federalist practices at home.[83]

When the country was on the brink of a possible war with France, Federalists stood in a formidable position in Congress and in the states. As subsequent election results demonstrated, the late 1790s proved to be the Federalist apex. Democratic-Republican gains in Congress steadily grew throughout the Jefferson presidency, as did their state governorships.[84] Jefferson's 1804 reelection was overwhelming, as the party even carried some old Federalist strongholds in New England. Accordingly, as the dominant party grew ever larger and inclusive of some former Federalists, more and more factions began to emerge. Alliances were formed and reformed, and coalitions could be fluid depending on the issues at stake. There was the purist and generally southern Old Republican faction that fiercely celebrated limited government and states' rights, as well as the concept of a restrained executive, who is held accountable by Congress.[85] There were the Quid factions, predominantly based in New York and Pennsylvania, who were known for their cooperation with Federalists.[86] Burr commanded a loyal following, as did supporters of New York governor and future vice president George Clinton. Finally, there were the mainline party supporters of the Jefferson administration, who could be expected to regularly back the president's initiatives. When they dissented, it would be done quietly and respectfully, often for local political reasons. They kept an arm's-length relationship with the other factions until the onset of war with Britain, when these party regulars essentially merged with the most aggressive supporters of military action, who were known as War Hawks. Mainline Jeffersonians were guided by their ideologies, pragmatism, and the task of managing an overly large governing party coalition. Save for the Old Republicans, every faction supported some degree of greater responsibility for the federal government. Nationalistic voices steadily gained influence within the party during the Jefferson and Madison presidencies. Under Madison's tenure, the intraparty divisions intensified, and seemed to peak during his reelection contest.

As presidents are party leaders, they must carefully manage competing factions in tandem with the political circumstances and policy demands of their governing environment. Even Jefferson himself was subject to criticism for ideological apostasy. During his administration, Virginia representative John Randolph of Roanoke became the defining face of the Old Republican wing of the party. As early as the spring of 1804, Randolph and other Old Republicans began attacking the administration. Old Republicans denounced the administration's efforts to rectify the Yazoo land fraud that had wreaked havoc in Georgia. The bribe-riddled land sale was the subject of a major scandal in that state, and while Old Republicans were appalled, they rejected federal intervention as an affront to the rights of states. Old Republicans also criticized the administration's plans to acquire the Spanish territory of West Florida. Jefferson and Madison claimed that the land was part of the Louisiana Purchase, though Spain disagreed. Randolph's Old Republicans disapproved of the administration's negotiating tactics, which they viewed as akin to bribery, and claimed that Congress was disrespected throughout the process. Old Republicans further staked out their independence when they unsuccessfully opposed the protectionist Non-Importation Act of 1806, which was backed by the administration to retaliate against Great Britain's polices on trade and impressment. Randolph was an eccentric man whose ideology and hyperbole could get the best of him, but his faction reflected grievances with the Jefferson administration's pragmatism and the president's slow steps toward a more robust role for the national government. Still, as vocal as the Old Republicans were, their influence was limited, and they began declining in the latter years of the Jefferson administration. Indeed, Randolph was replaced as chair of the House Ways and Means Committee in the 1807 session of Congress.[87]

The Old Republicans of the Randolph faction were sometimes referred to as Tertium Quids, as if to suggest that they represented a third party, or a coherent alliance of dissidents from the Federalist and Democratic-Republican camps. Third-party splinters in this era were sometimes casually called "Quid" in various states. The Quid label, however, was more accurately applied to organized Democratic-Republican factions in Pennsylvania and New York. Randolph's Old Republicans and the latter Quid factions had little in common. While the Old Republicans were stern critics of the Jefferson administration, the New York and Pennsylvania Quids generally supported the president's policies. Pennsylvania Quids called themselves "Constitutional Republicans" and were organized around Governor Thomas McKean; they also enjoyed some support from Federalists in that state. New York Quids were led by one-term governor Morgan Lewis, rivaled by the Clinton political family, as they both jockeyed for power in that state's party. As Democratic-Republicans of this era were far more decentralized than today's party organizations, these Pennsylvania and New York alliances were rooted in personal rivalries and state and local politics.[88]

The Clinton faction of New York presented another challenge for Jefferson, Madison, and other party regulars. George Clinton was an imposing figure over the state's politics, which also gave him a major national platform. Clinton had a distinguished career as an army officer going back to the French and Indian War. His career then turned to the law and politics. After a stint as New York City district attorney, Clinton served as the state's governor for a total of nearly twenty-one years, stepping down for the first time in 1795. As the American Revolution overlapped Clinton's long governorship, he nonetheless was commissioned as a brigadier general in the Continental Army. Initially, Clinton agreed with Hamilton's assertion that the federal government had to be enhanced, favoring a convention to revise the Articles of Confederation, but the governor objected to the extent of national consolidation embodied in the new constitution. Hamilton, Clinton, and their respective allies quarreled with each other through New York newspapers. Now in full opposition to the new constitution, Clinton was a leading anti-federalist voice, and he was the likely author of anonymous essays (under the pen name of "Cato") that were published to critique the new form of government.[89]

In July 1801 Clinton returned to the governorship for one final tour in office. In this capacity, he remained the leading figure in a coalition of supporters that remained generally loyal to the Jefferson administration in its first six years, all while they jockeyed for position within the fractious New York party. The troublesome Burr was replaced on the national ticket, as the party's congressional nominating caucus overwhelmingly chose Clinton for the vice presidency on February 25, 1804. Although he lacked enthusiasm for the job, Clinton maintained a duty to serve, and he accepted the nomination.[90] This move helped to secure the state's electoral votes for Jefferson and isolate a potential rival to Madison into a job that carried little influence in this era. However, the Clintonian faction became increasingly hostile to the Jefferson administration in the latter two years. Most notably, its members objected to the government's moves toward retaliatory trade restrictions, as their faction spoke for the commercial, manufacturing, and shipping sectors that stood to be harmed. The Clintonians proceeded to contest Madison's nomination in 1808 and were in full opposition to the new president by the time war with Britain came.

The existence of a strong agent of outside opposition will force the governing party to sharply define a central ideology, organizing principles, and clear stances on vital public policy issues. The governing party will have to arrive at its best possible consensus on these matters. However, now freed from serious national political competition from Federalists, Democratic-Republicans had the ability to modify, rather than repeal, the policy legacy of their adversaries. The overarching political cleavage in the nation centered on moderation verses cancelation of the Hamiltonian program. In the absence of a viable Federalist opposition to enforce accountability, Democratic-Republicans were liberated to do some of both, all while navigating an increasingly incoherent national party.

The old Federalist program was accommodated, but it was gradually redirected toward Jeffersonian principles. Steadily, the Jefferson administration adapted much of the Hamiltonian economic system to the Democratic-Republican ideology. The Bank of the United States was retained, and three new branches were established. Jefferson, however, continued to promote state-chartered banks.[91] Numerous federal taxes were eliminated, including the long-hated whiskey tax.[92] Spending on wasteful administrative costs was phased out. Jefferson did not engage in a full-throated campaign to remove Washington and Adams appointees from the government; rather, he limited firings to only the most partisan Federalists. Through attrition, eventually the government's workforce would be made up of Democratic-Republican civil servants.[93] Though Jefferson opposed an overly large military establishment, he could appreciate the value of professionalization. In March 1802 he signed a law creating a national military academy. The Jefferson administration downsized and reorganized the army and navy in ways that reduced the influence of the Federalist-dominated officer corps, but the cutbacks may have left the nation ill-prepared for the conflicts to come.[94] A naval altercation with the Barbary States of northern Africa disrupted the administration's fiscal plans, especially with regard to trimming the navy's budget.[95] A national road was chartered by a Democratic-Republican Congress and president in 1806,[96] even though their party took a dim view to federal sponsorship of internal improvements. Although Jefferson professed to deplore independent executive leadership and loose interpretations of government's constitutional authority, nonetheless he authorized the bargain purchase of the massive Louisiana Territory from France. Over Federalist objections, Congress approved the deal. The new land would reinforce the Jeffersonian ideal of a predominantly agrarian nation for several more decades.

During John Adams's final days in office, he installed John Marshall as chief justice of the Supreme Court. A strong Virginia Federalist, Marshall would preside over the high court for the next thirty-four years, fiercely protecting national supremacy and the integrity of a federal system of government. Some of his party cohorts even mentioned his name as a possible candidate for the presidential ticket in 1812. Marshall ensured that long after the Federalists were vanquished in the political arena, their constitutional philosophy would retain a strong influence over public policy at both the state and national levels of government. However, after a period of many years in power, Democratic-Republicans were able to shape the judicial branch to their liking.

TOWARD A WAR FOOTING

Foreign trade presented another dilemma for the Jefferson administration. Jeffersonian orthodoxy held that international commerce should be as free from political meddling as possible. Even so, trade restrictions and tariffs were then—and remain today—available to any administration as potential weapons of foreign policy. At the same time, hastily concocted or vengeful trade policies can produce unanticipated consequences and anger elements of a president's domestic political base. As the Democratic-Republican national coalition broadened to include manufacturing interests, and foreign aggressions at sea mounted, the Jefferson administration opened the door to greater politicization of trade. The results were disastrous for the economy, and the nation began its slow movement toward a war footing. In addition, Democratic-Republican miscues could have been successfully exploited by a well-organized and disciplined Federalist opposition.

The Non-Importation Act was enacted in April 1806. The law represented a clumsy effort to combat belligerent British actions at sea, for the measure placed an embargo on various selected items from that country. This ineffective law was repeatedly suspended before it was fully implemented in December 1807.[97] Madison seemed to view the policy with skepticism, and he argued for a more robust response. His views ultimately prevailed, as the law failed to achieve its objectives and the British did not take American grievances seriously.[98] Nor did Jefferson and Madison find diplomatic efforts to be useful. James Monroe, then the American minister to Great Britain, along with Maryland politician and diplomat William Pinkney, negotiated a treaty that achieved very little and notably made no progress toward ending impressments of American seamen. Madison had insisted on settlement of the impressment issue in his instructions to the diplomats. Accordingly, after receiving the treaty in early March 1807, Jefferson, Madison, and the Cabinet chose not to send the document to the Senate for consideration.[99] As a result, Monroe's relationship with Madison and the president became strained.[100]

The United States had been drawn into Britain's rivalry with Napoleonic France by way of diplomatic miscalculations, misunderstandings, and bad luck. French emperor Napoleon Bonaparte issued the Berlin Decree in November 1806. This measure deemed "the British islands . . . in a state of blockade" and barred "all commerce and correspondence with the British islands." France would now be authorized to seize ships that were allegedly in violation of the policy.[101] The British responded in January and November 1807 with Orders in Council that further complicated the ability for American vessels to engage in commerce. Now the British asserted a right to bar any trade that did not include their country's products, unless those vessels docked in England and paid a transit duty beforehand. Napoleon retaliated with the Milan Decree, which stipulated that any ships complying with these British policies would be fair game for being seized by the French.[102] Given their maritime commercial activity in the region, the likelihood of American vessels becoming submerged in these two warring nations' escalating measures was almost assured. The weak presence of American naval ships at sea made any kind of forceful response to these policies very unrealistic.

A new level of aggression emerged with the USS *Chesapeake* incident on June 22, 1807. Near Hampton Roads, Virginia, the British vessel HMS *Leopard* attacked the American ship, resulting in twenty-one casualties. In a search for deserters from the Royal Navy, the *Leopard* fired upon the *Chesapeake* until crew from the former was able to board the American ship. The British apprehended four alleged deserters, but three of these men were actually Americans who had escaped impressment into the Royal Navy before joining the *Chesapeake* crew. The Jefferson administration took a restrained response, given the absence of a strong American naval position vis-à-vis Britain. Madison was among those in the Cabinet who called for a more assertive public stance, but the president chose a measured course of action. The Jefferson administration demanded a British withdrawal from American harbors and instructed US ambassadors in Europe to pursue reparations and an end to impressments. Hastily, the administration prepared the armed forces for possible future conflicts.[103]

The norms of this era dictated that chief executives should not interfere too deeply into the legislative process. Presidential lobbying of Congress to enact a specific agenda, which is what we expect to see today, was considered an inappropriate intrusion into a separate branch of government. Respectful presidential suggestions to Congress, however, were still considered acceptable. Madison urged Jefferson to support a comprehensive embargo.[104] To supplement the Non-Importation Act, Congress acted promptly upon Jefferson's request to enact the Embargo Act. The statute was signed into law on December 22, 1807. Federalists were almost unanimously opposed, and Democratic-Republicans from the Randolph wing were adamant in their disagreement as well, but the legislation passed both houses of Congress overwhelmingly.[105] The policy closed all American ports from trading with the world, though the target countries were Britain and France.

American ships were effectively grounded, and the economic damage began to appear rather quickly. In the election year of 1808, when Madison would stand for the presidency, there was a plunge of approximately 80 percent in American exports and an almost 60 percent drop in imports. Job losses mounted in cities and towns that were dependent on shipping and related industries.[106] The law proved extraordinarily difficult to enforce, given the lean apparatus of the federal government. The embargo was routinely flouted, and various loopholes were quickly found and exploited. Less than a month after the enactment of the Embargo Act, Congress passed another bill to restrict foreign commerce by coasting vessels, as well as from fishing and whaling ships. Penalties for violators were significantly enhanced. Then, in March 1808 Congress followed up with additional enforcement legislation containing specific exemption provisions that would be at the discretion of the president, as well as new penalties. The repeated requests from shippers for exemptions became a political headache for Jefferson. The following month saw the enactment of another enforcement act that tightened the exemption provisions. The overarching policy became ever more heavy-handed and confusing. The various enforcement acts gave significant arbitrary powers to port collectors and navy commanders.[107]

Congress also provided Jefferson with authority to lift the embargo on France and/or Britain if he determined that those two nations had ceased their aggressive behaviors at sea. Resources were contributed to an army and naval buildup, both to enforce the embargo and in preparation for a possible war with France or Britain. Congress authorized $4 million to expand and modernize the military and further fortify American ports. Still, the planned upgrades to the armed forces were not yet complete by the time Jefferson left office.[108] As Britain and France continued to shrug off American trading restrictions, Jefferson's policy was creating political baggage for Madison going into the presidential campaign.

A presidential candidate of the same party as the outgoing administration must make a political calculus as to how much he or she wishes to embrace the policy trajectory of the current chief executive. The candidate can choose a full embrace of the outgoing president, with only very minor differences in the execution of public policies, and some differences in political style. This approach is preferable if the outgoing president is popular and enjoys strong support from elsewhere in the political system. Unsurprisingly, the candidate will also inherit the outgoing president's supporters and adversaries. Even as the embargo was creating major political liabilities for Democratic-Republicans, Madison was positioned to take this approach in 1808.

Publicly and privately, Madison was a big booster of the embargo policy, and he was slow to acknowledge its political and economic shortcomings. The secretary of state penned three anonymous letters of support in the *National Intelligencer*, a Jeffersonian newspaper.[109] "It is singularly fortunate that an embargo, whilst it guards our essential resources," Madison argued, "will have the collateral effect of making it the interest of all nations to change the system which has driven our commerce from the ocean."[110] The letters also dismissed concerns about the economic impact on the United States, and suggested that the embargo would only extract a small sacrifice from the American people for the greater good of upholding national honor and boosting domestic industries in the long-run.[111] In private correspondence, Madison further argued that the legislation was a "precaution only," with no hostile intentions toward Britain or any other nation.[112] He already had a history of supporting trade restrictions with that country as a means of countering its commercial and naval behaviors.

Secretary of the Treasury Albert Gallatin lamented the difficulties of enforcing the embargo, warning that increasingly heavy-handed approaches and augmentations of federal power would be necessary to make the policy effective. "Congress must either invest the Executive with the most arbitrary powers and sufficient force to carry the embargo into effect, or give it up altogether," Gallatin wrote. Madison had hitched himself to the administration's most unpopular policy as he positioned himself as Jefferson's heir apparent; he insisted in the first half of 1808 that the policy was working and enjoyed public support. "The public mind everywhere is rallying," Madison wrote in a private letter to Pinkney in the spring of 1808, as the secretary of state further claimed that the embargo was increasingly effective. By the summer months, however, Madison had begun to acknowledge the ferocious opposition to the embargo, and the economic anxiety it was causing in shipping-dependent communities. However, he blamed these phenomena on Federalist public agitation and foreign meddling in American politics.[113] Nevertheless, as the secretary of state succeeded Jefferson as president, Madison was compelled to deal with the economic damage from the embargo. He was also obligated to devise a replacement policy that could mollify most of his party, all while still asserting American interests abroad.

2

MADISON'S DILEMMA

On Saturday, March 4, 1809, James Madison stood before his inauguration ceremony in the chamber of the House of Representatives. The new president's tone was optimistic and conciliatory, while still acknowledging the diplomatic challenges the republic faced. In his remarks, Madison dismissed the hardship from the embargo and celebrated the country's continued economic growth and innovation. Although he was not a man of soaring rhetoric, the fourth president revealed his distaste for undue involvement in foreign wars:

> Under the benign influence of our republican institutions, and the maintenance of peace with all nations whilst so many of them were engaged in bloody and wasteful wars, the fruits of a just policy were enjoyed in an unrivaled growth of our faculties and resources. Proofs of this were seen in the improvements of agriculture, in the successful enterprises of commerce, in the progress of manufacturers and useful arts, in the increase of the public revenue and the use made of it in reducing the public debt, and in the valuable works and establishments everywhere multiplying over the face of our land.
>
> It is a precious reflection that the transition from this prosperous condition of our country to the scene which has for some time been distressing us is not chargeable on any unwarrantable views, nor, as I trust, on any involuntary errors in the public councils. Indulging no pas-

sions which trespass on the rights or the repose of other nations, it has been the true glory of the United States to cultivate peace by observing justice, and to entitle themselves to the respect of the nations at war by fulfilling their neutral obligations with the most scrupulous impartiality.[1]

As this chapter reveals, the new president found himself at the head of a squabbling governing party, as well as an underperforming and bickering Cabinet that became the source of much criticism of the Madison administration. If Jefferson's election in 1800 was deemed a "revolution" in government and politics, Madison's job was to preserve, protect, and defend the policy achievements and principles of the Democratic-Republican governing regime. In this capacity, the new president's role was not to be a revolutionary who was tasked with tearing down an old Federalist order but a custodian who was charged with maintaining Jeffersonian commitments in government and politics. Madison would have to manage the large Democratic-Republican coalition, placating the various camps under the Jeffersonian banner, even as some of these multiplying factions viewed the new president with suspicion or contempt. The Federalist minority, meanwhile, would see opportunities for a rebound under Jefferson's more politically constrained successor. Not only would Madison be expected to protect his predecessor's achievements, but he would also be expected to follow through on unfinished policies and agendas. In addition, Jefferson's successor would be responsible for correcting and modifying the previous administration's policies where circumstances made such a course of action necessary.

Madison was the heir apparent to a president who himself departed from his own orthodoxy. By the end of Jefferson's tenure, there were restive and hostile camps under the Democratic-Republican banner, all of whom were prepared to direct their ire toward Madison. When Jefferson's heir apparent embarked on new adaptations of Democratic-Republican ideology, some coalition partners would predictably regard such actions as fraudulent and a further unfaithfulness to the Jeffersonian creed. Madison faced a changing domestic political environment as well as an unstable international arena. Some degree of modification, fixing, or even outright repeal of Jefferson administration initiatives would be necessary.

Support for Madison in 1808, as affirmed by his boosters, was understood as an endorsement of the general thrust of Jefferson's embargo policy. For example, at a Democratic-Republican Party meeting in New Castle

County, Delaware, a resolution was adopted asserting that the embargo "promoted the real benefit of this great community" and that "the selection of James Madison to fill the office of President of the United States, after the expiration of the present term of Presidency, was dictated by a wise policy."[2] At the same time, the new president inherited the economic and political baggage from the Jefferson administration's trade policies and diplomatic woes vis-à-vis Britain and France. Many alternatives were available, but these options only created even more confusion while doing nothing to reverse the nation's inexorable march to war.

To be sure, the political party system remained in an undeveloped and nebulous state during Madison's tenure. His party remained in firm control of the Washington, DC, governmental establishment, as well as the vast majority of statehouses. Madison's Federalist adversaries were hardly irrelevant, and signs of some revitalization in the Northeast were already apparent. Their party did adopt some new organizational and messaging techniques, but their comeback was temporary and regional.[3] Madison instead encountered far more difficulties from his own party. Within the Jeffersonian coalition there were the Clintonians, the Old Republicans, the nationalistic War Hawks, and the Invisibles. All these Democratic-Republican factions demonstrated varying levels of strength during Madison's first term, but one or more of these groups could create significant headaches for the president and mainline supporters of the administration. Madison opened himself up to accusations that his governance lacked ideological and programmatic coherence.

PRESIDENT MADISON'S TANGLED DAMBARGO

The controversial and ever-changing embargo policy would be the main course on the new president's plate, as it was closely intertwined with economic output and the tenuous diplomatic situation with European powers. Any modification of the policy in the late months of the Jefferson administration would become Madison's political responsibility, given the new president's close ties to his predecessor. An additional enforcement act, approved by Congress and Jefferson in January 1809, further tightened the screws. Now the army, navy, and customs agents would be empowered with new tools to intercept illegal commerce. Civil liberties, once a trademark of Jeffersonian ideology, were subordinated to the greater importance of doing economic damage to Britain and France.[4]

Notwithstanding the generally favorable outcome in the recent election, Democratic-Republicans all over the country continued to express their displeasure with the Embargo Act and its mounting economic damage. Acts of civil disobedience were growing, which angered the outgoing president and strengthened his commitment to enforce the law.[5] As president-elect, Madison was now well aware of the public restiveness, while hinting that war was becoming increasingly likely. As he wrote to William Pinkney, "the impatience under the Embargo, more particularly in Massachusetts, is becoming extremely acute under the artificial excitements given to it; and a preference of war within a very limited period is everywhere gaining ground."[6]

Just three days before leaving office, Jefferson agreed to replace the Embargo Act by signing the Non-Intercourse Act, which was adopted by Congress on a generally party-line vote: most Democratic-Republicans approved, while most Federalists and Democratic-Republicans from the Randolph wing were in opposition. The new policy called for the resumption of international trade but left a conditional embargo on Britain and France. If, however, one of those two nations were to respect American neutrality at sea, and remove trading restrictions, then the United States would resume commerce with that respective country. The president would be empowered to certify that one of those countries was in compliance with American demands, and then trade could resume. Few believed the new policy could be rigorously enforced, or that the two European powers would yield to the demands of the United States. A proposal to allow the president to grant letters of marque and reprisal as an enforcement tool was defeated.[7] Senators and representatives agreed that the new Congress would assemble at the end of May (early by the standards of that era) and deliberate on further actions as events dictated.[8]

Madison himself was bewildered by the embargo policy's erratic changes, which he attributed to political agitators. "You will see with regret," the president-elect wrote Pinkney in February, "the difficulty experienced in collecting the mind of Congress into some proper focus. On no occasion were the ideas so unstable and so scattered." The new president believed he would be inheriting a policy that would not fundamentally rectify American trading and maritime grievances, while still producing negative economic consequences at home. Though cognizant of its unpopularity in some precincts, Madison wanted the core policy objectives of the Embargo Act to be retained.[9]

Unfortunately, the nonintercourse policy proved to be as ineffectual as most observers expected, thus accelerating the movement to a war footing with Britain and creating early political turmoil for Madison's presidency.

American ships could not be realistically stopped from docking in the forbidden foreign ports, and trade with Britain could very easily be conducted in neutral locations.[10] Although Jefferson acquiesced in the correction of his own flawed policy, the repair job became even more complicated for his successor. Madison's corrective task was hampered by equally ineffective policy alternatives, diplomatic miscues, and constant political bickering within his own party.

The British government now had to contend with a new American president and a new policy. There was an opportunity for a possible fresh start, and maybe even a chance to gain an advantage vis-à-vis France. David Erskine, the British minister to the United States, got right to work on negotiating terms with Madison. The deal that was hammered out called for the British to rescind their Orders in Council by June 10, after which Anglo-American free trade would resume. Madison announced the pact in a triumphant proclamation on April 19, pursuant to his powers under the Non-Intercourse Act.[11] Perhaps Jefferson and Madison's embargo policies were finally producing the desired results. Indeed, there was considerable public praise for Madison, even from Federalist newspapers, for this seemingly peaceful resolution of American trading and maritime grievances with the British.[12] The *Northern Whig*, a Federalist publication out of Hudson, New York, commended Madison for departing from "the mad scheme of his immediate predecessor" and saluted his good judgment: "While he continues to pursue the track which he has taken, we will follow and applaud him."[13] Another Federalist newspaper, the *American*, in Providence, Rhode Island, was magnanimous: "So the peace of the country is preserved, and its Commercial Prosperity restored, the Federalists are perfectly indifferent at who claims or receives the credit."[14]

Or so everybody thought. Madison's apparent first diplomatic victory as president was scotched when word of the agreement reached London. Erskine had in fact disobeyed his government's instructions by failing to insist on British naval enforcement of American nonintercourse with France. This was a provision that Madison would never agree to, for it would be politically unpopular at home and contrary to American sovereignty. Erskine then abandoned this demand, and he and Madison made their deal. Upon London's rejection of the pact, Erskine was recalled; after Madison's Cabinet deliberated on the situation, Anglo-American nonintercourse was resumed in a bland August 9 presidential proclamation.[15]

Now matters were about to become even more unstable and confusing. Treasury Secretary Gallatin, who Madison had retained in his position, warned that the nonintercourse policy was straining the federal budget.[16] Gallatin worked on a revised policy with Democratic-Republican representative Nathaniel Macon of North Carolina, who was a former House Speaker and an ally of the Old Republican faction. Their first effort, however, was a bust. What was called Macon's Bill #1 failed to clear both houses of Congress. That measure called for maintaining an embargo on French and British ships until such time as one or both countries certified that it would respect American neutrality and trading rights; importation of goods from Britain and France would be restricted to US vessels. Various members critiqued the bill for being too harsh, whereas some found it too lenient. The legislation was defeated by an alliance of Federalists and hawkish Democratic-Republicans following much bickering between the House and Senate.[17]

The next alternative did pass Congress, though few were happy with the outcome, including Madison. Macon's Bill #2 was enacted and signed by the president on May 1, 1810. The new law restored free trade, but with the proviso that once either Britain or France could be certified as officially respecting American neutrality and trading rights, the president would be authorized to order a policy of nonintercourse with the other respective country. Macon personally opposed the measure that was named after him (and he did not write), and Madison called Macon's Bill #2 "a botch of a bill." The president did, however, sign the legislation as the least bad alternative available for the moment, hoping that it just might force Britain's hand because surely then France would halt its aggressive actions at sea if doing so would put its European enemy at a disadvantage. Then, Madison hoped, the British would repeal their Orders in Council.[18] The norms of this era also dictated that presidents should only use the veto if they held constitutional objections to a bill. Disagreement with the substance of public policies enacted by Congress was not considered an appropriate basis on which to exercise the veto.[19] The existence of an unwritten taboo against using the veto as a bargaining chip in the legislative process, as modern presidents would do, greatly constrained the ability of early chief executives to achieve their goals with Congress.

Then the United States got played by Napoleon Bonaparte. The emperor took advantage of the new policy to deceive Madison into weakening Britain's position vis-à-vis France. In a letter dated August 5, 1810, the French foreign minister Jean-Baptiste de Nompère de Champagny (the Duc de Cadore) informed US officials that his country would respect American trading rights and neutrality by November 1, contingent upon a reinstitution of American nonintercourse with the British.[20] After learning of France's promises, Madison delivered on his end of the bargain by lifting trade restrictions on the French in a November 2 proclamation.[21] The British would now have ninety days to repeal their Orders in Council or face a restoration of American nonintercourse, though this did not occur because the government in London was skeptical that France would honor its commitment to halt its belligerent behavior against the United States.[22]

The other problem was that Napoleon hoodwinked the Madison administration, as his country persisted with hostile actions against Americans at sea. France simply wanted its European enemy to be pushed into a war with the United States. Nor was the Cadore letter fully compliant with the Macon law, which called for Britain and/or France to attach no strings. The letter, however, suggested that American nonintercourse would have to be levied on Britain for France to stand down against the United States. Left unspoken was the status of American ships and cargo the French had seized beforehand, and various other loopholes France could employ to ultimately continue bullying the United States at sea. Members of both political parties had warned that Cadore's letter was deceptive and not to be trusted. Secretary of State Robert Smith had opposed agreeing to the French terms. John Randolph denounced the "imbecility" of accepting the deal. Federalists accused the president of being a Francophile. Madison, however, was anxious to find a feasible exit from this crisis, especially given the comparative weakness of the United States vis-à-vis Britain and France. Madison and Congress formally reinstated the nonintercourse policy on Britain in early March 1811.[23]

Now matters were worse. Britain and France were still violating Americans at sea, and the French even implemented new tariffs and trading constraints.[24] Napoleon had successfully manipulated the United States into standing down against his country, which set forces in motion that would distract his British adversary with a possible war overseas. Hostilities between the United States and Britain were now careening toward a war the young country was not prepared to fight. Critics across the political spectrum who questioned Madison's competence, judgment, and resolve were now armed with more evidence. If there was to be a war, the president could be fairly scolded for poor decisions that brought the United States to this predicament. The 1812 presidential election campaign would be a venue for these grievances to be aired and debated.

TEARING AT THE JEFFERSONIAN FABRIC

Madison's on-again, off-again trading policies created uncertainty in the economy, outraged his adversaries, and confused his supporters. Meanwhile, other political crises during the president's first term functioned to both disrupt the fragile Democratic-Republican coalition he would need for reelection and provide opportunities for Federalists to make a comeback. The delicate state of political equilibrium that brought Madison to the presidency was disturbed not only by the march toward war but also by territorial expansion, national banking, bickering in the Cabinet, and a more assertive Congress than his predecessor faced. As he navigated an unmanageable party coalition, Madison's actions on multiple fronts revealed a president who was trying to govern along Jeffersonian principles while otherwise pragmatically departing from orthodoxy when necessary.

Like his predecessor, President Madison transitioned from a virulent opponent of the National Bank of the United States to a position of tolerance and accommodation toward the powerful institution. In early 1811 the Bank's twenty-year charter was about to expire, and Madison nominally favored renewal. Despite Jefferson and Madison making their peace with the Bank, the institution still had its enemies who never gave up their arguments that this brainchild of Alexander Hamilton was an instrument of economic favoritism for foreigners, speculators, and the politically well-connected. Nor were they persuaded that the Bank simply became constitutional due to the passage of twenty years and broader political acceptance from former skeptics. "If, in 1791, it was unconstitutional, it must be so now. The constitution does not change with the times," asserted Kentucky Democratic-Republican representative William T. Barry.[25]

In keeping with the norm of this era, Madison personally maintained a respectful distance from congressional deliberations over a possible renewal of the Bank's charter. Treasury Secretary Gallatin, however, was more aggressive in his advocacy for a renewal, stressing that the National Bank was a linchpin for economic stability. Though the Bank was controversial, it had proven to be a reliable institution for the government to conduct financial transactions and raise capital. Fiscal uncertainty created by the on-again, off-again trade embargoes only made recharter even more necessary for the Bank's proponents. Many years in office under Madison and Jefferson meant that Gallatin had inherited both presidents' political enemies, including within the Democratic-Republican camp. Consistent with their long record of support for central banking, the Federalist minority in both chambers of Congress voted to recharter. Gallatin and pro-administration

Democratic-Republicans, however, could not overcome the anti-bank and anti-Madison factions within their own party. In January 1811 the recharter bill went down to a one-vote defeat in the House. The following month in the Senate, the measure again fell one vote short due to the tiebreaking roll call of Vice President George Clinton, who continued to voice constitutional objections to the Bank.[26]

In contrast to the present era, when vice presidents serve as strong loyalists for their respective administration's legislative agenda, the men who held this office in the early republic often did not share some of the chief executive's policy commitments. Given the naked political calculations and electoral coalition-building among disparate factions that came with vice presidential selections, we should not find this fact surprising. As he cast his vote in the Senate, Clinton told the chamber that the power to charter governmental corporations was not authorized in the Constitution, and that doing so "has an inevitable tendency to consolidation, and affords just and serious cause of alarm."[27]

The debate in Congress and the newspapers was a venue for various anti-Madison factions (and even some supporters of the administration) to air their grievances. Depicting a political adversary as a flip-flopper was apparently a good strategy in the era of the early republic. The president was accused of abandoning his once strict constitutional scruples. Other Bank critics gleefully disseminated Madison's previous statements in opposition to national banking. Representative Joseph Desha, a Democratic-Republican of Kentucky, noted that Madison had once argued as a congressman that incorporation of a national bank was not authorized by the Constitution. Desha pointed to an old House speech by Madison where the future president revealed that the power to charter a bank was "expunged" from the Constitution "as a power dangerous and improper to be vested in the General Government."[28] Even the normally pro-Madison *Richmond Enquirer* came out in opposition to recharter, as editor Thomas Ritchie had a vested financial interest in the state-chartered Bank of Virginia. Such institutions would conceivably benefit from the National Bank's demise. In lieu of central banking, opponents promoted banks chartered by individual states, as they had become more numerous in the past decade. At the same time, these state-based institutions could be just as prone to political manipulation as the Bank of the United States.[29] Nor was their financial stability guaranteed. Now with the National Bank losing its congressional charter, any future war with a European power would have to be financed by various state banks.[30]

This embarrassing legislative defeat for Madison fully exposed the vulnerabilities of an unusually large and increasingly incoherent Democratic-Republican coalition. The president had his supporters in Congress, but every action and reaction of the Madison administration served to further antagonize festering tensions within his party, and created opportunities for a Federalist resurgence. In the era of the early republic, Congress and the Cabinet functioned as institutions with as much or even more political and governmental influence than the president. Madison's critics were well represented within both these centers of power, and this president was not normally inclined to enhance executive power arrangements in the American system of constitutional government. He did, however, use the veto more frequently than his three predecessors combined.

Although other variables certainly come into play, the volume of a president's vetoes is one factor that can indicate how harmonious his relationship is with Congress. Consistent with George Washington's rare use of the veto, Madison only vetoed legislation on constitutional grounds, as revealed by his written messages. The veto was one tool that Madison could use to maintain strict adherence to Jeffersonian orthodoxy, even as he departed from those principles in other arenas. While Adams and Jefferson issued no vetoes during their presidencies, Madison used his pen to veto three bills in his first term.

The first two vetoes were cast on the grounds of the First Amendment's establishment clause that prohibited state endorsement of religion. Jeffersonian orthodoxy held that the affairs of government should be divorced from the machinery of religious institutions. Pursuant to that principle, the president should uphold his constitutional oath by preventing an entanglement of religious functions and governmental activities, even though there was no feasible way to detach faith-based values from the rough-and-tumble world of politics. On February 21, 1811, Madison vetoed a bill that would have incorporated the Episcopal Church in Washington, DC. Though the church would provide social services for the poor, Madison asserted in his veto message that the measure set "a precedent for giving to religious societies as such a legal agency in carrying into effect a public and civil duty."[31] One week later, Madison vetoed a bill that would have provided a parcel of land for the Baptist Church in the Mississippi Territory. In a terse message, Madison denounced the measure as "contrary to the article of the Constitution which declares that 'Congress shall make no law respecting a religious establishment.'"[32] Many Baptist leaders applauded Madison's veto as appropriately maintaining the distance between church and state.[33]

Madison's third veto was consistent with the Jeffersonian view of a limited role for the federal judiciary. On April 3, 1812, Madison rejected legislation that would have expanded the powers of Supreme Court justices as circuit-riding judges. The early republic practice of Supreme Court justices riding circuit to preside over cases throughout the country was a system that in Madison's view was unconstitutional, and should be phased out.[34] In his message, Madison denounced the bill as "a precedent for modifications and extensions of judicial services encroaching on the constitutional tenure of judicial offices."[35]

The problem for Madison, however, was not the courts but his unhinged Cabinet. In the early republic, the Cabinet played a significant role in the president's administration. To achieve a careful sectional and political balance, presidents were expected to fill their Cabinet with men from all regions of the country, as well as all politically relevant factions within the governing party.[36] In contrast to the twentieth and twenty-first centuries, when presidents were surrounded by a large corps of White House staffers, policy advisers, and independent agency heads, the Cabinet served as an institutional base for an early chief executive to receive advice and deliberate upon the administration's actions. Some nineteenth-century presidents consulted with or even preferred an informal "Kitchen Cabinet" of trusted confidants who may have been private citizens, political operatives, or other government officials.[37] In addition, it was considered perfectly appropriate for an early president to consult individual members of Congress about the administration's ongoing actions or possible forthcoming initiatives.

Madison's Cabinet was carefully constructed around the imperatives of his overly large and diverse political coalition. There was some individual talent in these men, but collectively Madison's first-term Cabinet was beset by bickering and by secretaries who did not meet the expectations of their jobs in a nation stumbling into war. The Cabinet's star was the Genevan-born Gallatin of Pennsylvania, the Jefferson administration holdover at Treasury. Madison trusted Gallatin's advice on political and policy matters, and the latter was commonly used as a liaison with members of Congress. Still, Gallatin's close ties to Jefferson and Madison meant that the treasury secretary also inherited all the Democratic-Republican critics who were becoming exasperated with the current administration's policies. Madison had wanted Gallatin as secretary of state, but Senator Samuel Smith of Maryland and his allies would not permit that to happen, for this was the most prestigious Cabinet post in the early republic, and a possible stepping stone to the presidency for any occupant. Senator Smith was the leader of an adamant anti-Madison Democratic-Republican faction known as the Invisibles. To avoid a political fight, Madison yielded to the Invisibles and installed Senator Smith's brother Robert at State, while retaining Gallatin as treasury secretary, which would prevent an ugly Senate confirmation process.[38] Titles notwithstanding, Gallatin became the most influential Cabinet secretary in practice.

To give due representation to New England, the most tenuous of the Democratic-Republican regions, Madison selected William Eustis of Massachusetts as secretary of war. Eustis was a former congressman and army surgeon during the war for independence, who appeared to be suited for the job, but he resigned six months into the War of 1812 as American forces were generally slumping on the battlefield. Attorney General Caesar Rodney of Delaware held limited influence in the administration, for the job was not considered a major Cabinet position during the first few American presidencies. William Pinkney of Maryland, who succeeded Rodney in December 1811, was not a regular contributor to the Cabinet, though he did draft the first version of the House bill declaring war on Britain. The secretary of the Department of the Navy, which was then a Cabinet position, was Paul Hamilton of South Carolina. The drunkard secretary was not especially qualified for the job and had poor relations with the president and Congress. He too resigned at the end of 1812, in spite of some naval victories early in the war.[39]

In the president's first term, his biggest Cabinet problem was the ego of Secretary of State Robert Smith of Maryland. After serving nearly the entirety of Jefferson's presidency as secretary of the navy, as well as a brief stint as attorney general, Smith had become the source of political headaches that spilled over into the press, the Senate, and possibly the state of Maryland in next year's election. Their permanent rupture came when the president agreed to the French terms in the Cadore letter, which Smith was disinclined to take seriously. Secretary Smith was so stringent and public in his opposition to the deal that he was willing to undercut the Madison administration by openly voicing his personal skepticism of the new policy in conversations with British diplomats.[40] These actions arguably constituted insubordination in the midst of a fragile and fluid international situation at sea. Smith was openly mocking the president's policies in discussions with government officials from rival countries, which can conceivably influence the behaviors of foreign actors.

Meanwhile, exasperated by the failure of the National Bank recharter, as well as by the political attacks from the secretary of state and his congressional allies, Gallatin tendered his resignation on March 5, 1811. Madison, however, did not accept it, and the secretary of the treasury was persuaded to stay. Instead, the president committed to pushing Smith out.[41] No longer holding confidence in his secretary of state, Madison encouraged Smith to resign, even offering to ease him out with an appointment as American minister to Russia. After some hemming and hawing, Smith declined the appointment and resigned effective April 1, 1811. In a confidential presidential memorandum, Madison laid out multiple grievances with the performance of the recently departed secretary of state. "The business of the Dept. had not been conducted in the systematic and punctual manner," the president said, "which was necessary, particularly in the foreign correspondence, and that I had become daily more dissatisfied with it." Among other criticisms, there was Smith's careless disregard for confidentiality, disloyalty to administration objectives, and his generally poor diplomatic skills.[42]

The fired Cabinet secretary subsequently wrote a lengthy and angry public defense of himself that did little to restore his reputation while revealing his hostility to the Madison administration. "To ensure the duration of the republican party," Smith said in a closing swipe at Madison's character, "as well as to preserve the honour and the best interests of the United States, it has become indispensibly necessary, that our President be a man of energetic mind, of enlarged and liberal views, of temperate and dignified deportment, of honourable and manly feelings, and as efficient in maintaining, as sagacious in discerning the rights of our much-injured and insulted country."[43] As part of a common historical pattern that persists to the present day, Smith would hardly be the last disgruntled Cabinet secretary or marginalized administration official to write an adversarial kiss-and-tell manuscript after leaving the president's team. The consequence of Smith's departure from the Cabinet was to create even greater political conflict between Madison and the Invisibles, who had not been inclined to trust the president in the first place.

With Gallatin retained and the troublemaking Smith jettisoned, Madison installed James Monroe as secretary of state. The two Virginians had a rivalry that went back more than a decade, but the rift was healing. Monroe was well respected by the Old Republican faction, and though he had some critics from the Invisible faction and William Duane's *Aurora* in Philadelphia, the new secretary of state was confirmed by the Senate unanimously in November 1811.[44] The appointment was an important move toward ameliorating any lingering divisions within the Democratic-Republican Party in Virginia, an essential state for Madison's reelection.

Finally, the Clintonian faction was represented by Vice President George Clinton. Consistent with vice presidents of the early republic, his influence within the administration was almost nonexistent. The vice president's tie-breaking negative vote on the National Bank recharter was only one part of his overarching opposition to the administration. Like many past and recent vice presidents, Clinton was not personally close with the chief executive, having been placed on the 1808 ticket out of political necessity. Clinton did not even attend Madison's presidential inauguration, apparently taking his own constitutional oath elsewhere.[45] The seventy-two-year-old Clinton died of natural causes on April 20, 1812, leaving the office vacant for the remainder of Madison's term. Mayor DeWitt Clinton was now effectively the leading figure of this faction. Going into the 1812 election, pro-Madison Democratic-Republicans would have to either defeat the Clintonians outright or accommodate them as had been done in 1808. The congressional nominating caucus, however, would be the final arbiter in the selection of a new presidential running mate.

Madison's Cabinet mirrored the factions in his own party, as Democratic-Republicans' internal divisions burst into the open. Within Congress and the states, rivalries, policy disagreements, and personal animosities continued to play out, setting the stage for a possible Federalist comeback, a full-on Democratic-Republican implosion, or both. Democratic-Republican discord occurred alongside, and partially because of, the nation's slow but certain march into hostilities with the British. Meanwhile, Madison increasingly acceded to the demands of the pro-war elements of his party. In the months to follow, wartime politics proved to be a source both for unity within the governing party and a major rift within the bloated Democratic-Republican coalition.

3

DEMOCRATIC-REPUBLICANS GO TO WAR WITH BRITAIN AND THEMSELVES

The *Columbian* was in an awkward situation. The New York City newspaper was strongly affiliated with the Clintonian faction, but the outbreak of war compelled the publication to rally its readers behind the same president who they had mocked and denounced for months. As word of the declaration of war spread, the *Columbian* called upon citizens to give their support "with all the vigor and unanimity the great occasion can inspire." At this point, any American who would "doubt or waver between his choice and duty in the case, must be lost to all sense of moral obligation and social ties." However, the newspaper pivoted to remind readers that the administration left the nation unprepared through a pattern of feckless and aloof leadership. Madison's government brought America to this position by way of "weakness or irresolution which has protracted the past ruinous condition of the republic," as well as an "incapacity which is to manage the national concerns through the struggle." Then the *Columbian* pivoted back to pledging its full support for the upcoming war effort.[1]

As this chapter will show, momentum for war with Great Britain steadily grew during Madison's first term. The president might have enjoyed a moment of national patriotic fervor once the shooting started, but his political vulnerabilities remained palpable with an election just a few months away. Unlike so many future American wars, there was no single military attack that would galvanize a clear consensus of politicians and ordinary citizens behind a second war with Britain. Nothing took place that was comparable to a Confederate bombardment of Fort Sumter, a Japanese raid on Pearl Harbor, or Al Qaeda terrorist attacks on 9/11. The Madison administration gradually steered the governing party and the nation into war after years of legitimate grievances were subsumed by bungled diplomacy, misunderstandings, and outright distortions. Most congressional Democratic-Republicans voted to authorize war, and Madison's caucus renomination was technically unanimous. Outside of New York, Democratic-Republicans fell into line behind their president, but the party remained in a state of unrest. Criticisms of Madison's competence, judgment, and motives persisted as the nation entered into its first constitutionally declared war. DeWitt Clinton, a rising star in national politics, emerged as the possible beneficiary of these shortcomings.

THE MISCHIEFS OF JEFFERSONIAN FACTIONS

The same president who once warned of the "mischiefs of faction" in *Federalist*, no. 10 seemed to have his concerns vindicated, for he was tormented by various wings of his own party during his tenure. Going into the 1812 presidential campaign, the multiplicity of Democratic-Republican factions presented a significant challenge for Madison and created quite a bit of uncertainty for his reelection prospects. During his first term, Madison made his peace with some factions, while driving a deeper rupture with other groups in the party. Throughout this term, the factions made temporary alliances with each other and Federalists to support or oppose the Madison administration. Coalitions would shift depending on the issue at hand and the existing political environment. Given the magnitude of the Democratic-Republican congressional majorities during Madison's first term, the most important political bargaining and maneuvering was within the governing party's ranks.

First, there were the mainline Jeffersonians who counted themselves as consistent allies of the Madison administration. Within their ranks, they appreciated the necessity of accommodating the Hamiltonian financial system and took a dim view to the states' rights militancy of some of the Old Republicans and other Jeffersonian purists. They also recognized the need for greater military professionalization and credibility at a time when the United States was still not taken very seriously by many European powers. The War Hawk wing generally spun off from this faction. Mainline Jeffersonians would maintain a respectful stance if they held any disagreements with Madison administration initiatives. Well-represented in all regions of the country, plenty of these men were prone to disagreeing with the president on an individual issue, perhaps due to the interests of state and local affairs, or differences over political tactics. Secretary Gallatin was the most prominent of the regular Jeffersonians in the Cabinet, while Senator William H. Crawford of Georgia, and Representative and then Senator John Taylor of South Carolina were examples of pro-administration members of Congress. Pro-Madison printings could be found in every state, but the *National Intelligencer* was arguably the closet thing America had to a truly national newspaper in the early nineteenth century. It also served as the Madison administration's communications organ in the capital, as this periodical was read by the movers and shakers in Washington, DC.[2] Published thrice per week, dispatches from the *National Intelligencer* were also frequently carried by newspapers all over the country.

The political strength of the Old Republicans was on the decline during Madison's first term, but these party dissidents were hardly an irrelevancy. Battling their own party that was becoming increasingly complicit in—or even advocating—a stronger federal government, Old Republicans remained on the political scene to ensure that doctrinaire Jeffersonian arguments still had a place at the table. They were a presence in the southern US House delegations, particularly from Virginia and North Carolina, and held only small influence in the Senate. Representative John Randolph remained their vociferous leader, though he presided over a marginalized faction, and his own influence over national political outcomes had dwindled since the Jefferson years. As purist Jeffersonians, who were not necessarily averse to compromise, their voting behavior in Congress was not always easy to predict. Nor were the Old Republicans always even unified among themselves. A greater level of unity might have enhanced their political clout as a faction. Even on the National Bank recharter, their House votes were split, perhaps owing to divided feelings about Secretary Gallatin. Some Old Republicans could at least respect that the pro-Bank treasury secretary was committed to frugality in government spending, and they gave him the benefit of the doubt on the recharter bill. Other Old Republicans continued to voice constitutional objections to the institution's existence.[3]

The men of this faction lacked the communications machinery of a state party organization, making their presence in the newspapers rather limited. In Richmond, Monroe supporters did establish the *Spirit of '76* late in the 1808 campaign, which then became a favored organ for Old Republicans. Monroe, of course, was never really a part of the Old Republican faction, but he commanded their respect given his past record as an advocate of states' rights and his critique of Madison. The new secretary of state's reconciliation with the Madison administration only further marginalized Old Republican hardliners as extremists, though some men in this faction accepted the rapprochement.[4] For its part, the *Spirit of '76* was defunct by early 1814.[5]

When the time came to make a decision about declaring war in June 1812, many Old Republicans struggled with their distrust of Britain, alongside their dislike of military solutions to international disputes. They also tended to oppose building up the armed forces in the months prior to the war, lest they condone the enlargement of the federal bureaucracy and legitimize standing armies and navies. Still, a flailing policy of on-and-off-again trade embargoes, disruption to the economy, and injured national pride seemed to push many Old Republicans into a reluctant acquiescence into war. When the roll calls were held on declaring war in June 1812, a majority of congressional Old Republicans voted in the affirmative. Randolph gave a passionate speech in opposition, but in the end his House partners scattered in varying directions. Randolph ally Richard Stanford of North Carolina voted no, while Virginia's Edwin Gray and Matthew Clay skipped the final roll call on the declaration. Persuadable Old Republicans, like Nathaniel Macon, voted yes. The war and the peace that followed only drove the Old Republicans further into obscurity.[6]

Madison's effectiveness as a chief administrator was targeted by all the dissident wings of his party, but the factions' internal distrust of each other precluded them from unifying around an alternative candidate or policy agenda. Old Republicans frequently critiqued Madison's motives and competence, which sometimes overlapped with the same arguments of the Invisibles, but these Jeffersonian purists still vitriolically opposed the latter party wing and their scheming. Nathaniel Macon, who was hardly the firebreather that Randolph was, compared the Invisibles to Federalists—a vile slur within the Jeffersonian party. For his own part, Randolph called his rival faction "the worst men in our country."[7]

All presidents attract inexplicable critics: adversaries who reflexively oppose the chief executive's actions, deplore his personal behaviors, and distrust his character and motives. Even in contradiction of their own policy positions and ideologies, these are the fastidious critics who will exploit every presidential shortcoming for their own political gain. The cantankerous Invisibles—sometimes referred to as "malcontents"—were a thorn in Madison's side within the Senate. As a general rule, they favored a stronger federal government, but their dislike of the president was paramount. With allies in the press and key members of Congress, they were anything but invisible. Maryland senator Samuel Smith was their leader, along with lieutenants William Branch Giles of Virginia and Michael Leib of Pennsylvania. Their sometime allies in Congress included Senators Obadiah German of New York, Tennessee's Joseph Anderson, and Pennsylvania's Andrew Gregg, as well as Representatives Robert Wright of Maryland and Samuel Mitchill of New York.[8]

William Duane's *Aurora*, which had only reluctantly backed Madison in 1808, turned against the president after the fiasco surrounding Secretary Smith's dismissal. On top of the Clintonian sympathies of the *Aurora*, the newspaper now aligned with the Invisibles and Gallatin's Pennsylvania critics. Duane now began to publish slashing anti-Madison articles, denouncing Gallatin as an evil mastermind who was somehow controlling the executive branch. Smith's firing meant that Gallatin would "rule all things, so long as the people will submit thereto," and Duane called the treasury secretary "the next president." Duane was surely also upset that his endorsement of Madison in 1808 did not result in the publisher receiving printing contracts from the federal government.[9] Indeed, partisan newspapers could sometimes expect government patronage in the nineteenth century.

Invisibles had an intense dislike and distrust of Gallatin, who they regarded as disloyal, given his foreign birth and accent. After blocking Madison from appointing him as secretary of state, the Invisibles continued to make the treasury secretary their chief enemy in the administration. Accordingly, opposition to the National Bank recharter was a rallying cry for this faction.[10] Madison's fragile working relationship with the Invisibles deteriorated after Robert Smith was pushed out of the State Department. The men of this faction critiqued Madison for inept diplomacy and a weak stance toward Britain. The Invisible trio in the Senate, along with their allies, Andrew Gregg and Joseph Anderson, all voted to declare unconditional war. However, their votes on amendments were mixed prior to the final war declaration roll call, thereby revealing the Invisibles' ideological incoherence. In the House, Wright voted yes, while Mitchill voted no, as the latter was also part of the Clintonian faction.[11]

The label "War Hawk" or just "hawk" is still a commonly used nomenclature to refer to supporters of muscular foreign policy, as well as of military solutions to American grievances and international disputes. The hawk is known to be an aggressive bird, while doves are not. War Hawks were Democratic-Republican politicians, mostly from the South and the West, that vigorously pushed for the United States to resolve its quarrels with Britain through a military remedy. John Randolph applied the label pejoratively to the advocates of military preparation and aggressive foreign policy.[12] Never one who was inclined toward an aggressive foreign policy, and cognizant of American military limitations, Madison initially resisted, then accommodated and advanced the War Hawks' arguments. By June 1812 the president was legitimizing the War Hawk position (though less belligerently) after claiming that all peaceful alternatives had been exhausted.

The House War Hawks were led by the young new Speaker of the House, Henry Clay of Kentucky. Their ranks included South Carolina representatives John C. Calhoun, Langdon Cheves, and William Lowndes, as well as Felix Grundy of Tennessee, George Troup of Georgia, and Richard Johnson of Kentucky. In the Senate, there was William H. Crawford and Charles Tait, both of Georgia. Some War Hawks were rising stars who had yet to reach the prime of their political careers. Generally, War Hawks came from the ranks of mainline Jeffersonians, but they did not share Madison's reluctance to steer the United States toward a war footing. In their view, protecting American honor through military solutions would safeguard national commerce and earn the long-term respect of European powers.[13]

As diplomacy floundered, the War Hawks' arguments gained credibility and increasingly earned the respect of other Democratic-Republican factions, as well as Madison himself. Even Federalists were willing to consider measures that promoted military preparation for hostilities. Madison's Annual Message to Congress on November 5, 1811, maintained a firm resolve, stressing the need for preparation while avoiding some of the belligerent rhetoric of the War Hawks. "With this evidence of hostile inflexibility," Madison asserted, "in trampling on rights which no independent nation can relinquish, Congress will feel the duty of putting the United States into an armor and an attitude demanded by the crisis, and corresponding with the national spirit and expectations."[14] Congress then began debates upon how (and not so much if) to prepare militarily. Between December 1811 and April 1812, Congress overwhelmingly enacted measures to boost the size of the army, raise military pay, and grant the president authority to activate the state militias. An appropriation of $1.9 million was passed for weapons and materials. Other legislation was approved to authorize borrowing money and levy higher duties, contingent upon war being declared. However, Congress balked at expanding the navy, as many Democratic-Republicans regarded it as an expensive and losing proposition to attempt out-arming the Royal Navy. What Congress did opt to do was to improve the existing naval infrastructure, and increase coastal fortifications. The Madison administration got the core of what it sought for war preparations, though it preferred use of state militias and volunteers rather than boosting the permanent army. In addition, Madison issued an amnesty to all existing army deserters if they returned to duty.[15]

Though many Americans and politicians were still not yet convinced that hostilities were inevitable, the political choices from Washington, DC, as well as events on the ground, gradually brought the United States—and Madison—into an irreversible war stance. Long-simmering friction between American citizens of the Northwest Territory and Native American peoples inexorably became subsumed into the United States' rationale for war. The War Hawks were certainly all too happy to exploit the tensions to achieve their goals. That included publicizing claims that Native Americans were being egged on to violent action by the British, as well as inaccurate assertions of Federalist collusion with the enemy.

DEWITT CLINTON AND THE CLINTONIANS

Throughout Madison's first term, one or more of the aforementioned factions was displeased with the president. Conversely, there were issues and moments when one or more factions were on board with Madison's policies and initiatives. Even some mainline Jeffersonians challenged the administration by increasingly accepting arguments from War Hawk members of Congress. Only the Clintonians, however, would turn their opposition into a frontal attack upon Madison's continuation in office. When war with Britain commenced, no faction was more stridently opposed than the Clintonians, and their criticisms—however clumsily—formed the basis for the first anti-war presidential campaign in American history. Much of the Clintonian critique revolved around the economic consequences a war with this European power—and American trading partner—could produce. Their arguments were consistent with the case that would be made by a skeptic who disapproved of the war on pragmatic grounds, rather than an ideological basis for opposition. From the beginning, however, their stance was nuanced, and arguably inconsistent and confusing.

The flagship Clintonian newspapers were centered in New York. In 1812 this included the *Columbian*, published by Connecticut native Charles Holt and based in New York City, and the *Albany Register*, disseminated out of the state capital and published by Solomon Southwick. In 1797 Holt created the *Bee* in New London, Connecticut, at just twenty-five years of age. The Jeffersonian newspaper was in the wilderness in a state where Federalists dominated. In 1800 Holt was fined and briefly imprisoned for violating the Sedition Act, although Jefferson helped the editor with the payment of his fine. In 1802 Holt founded another newspaper called the *Bee* in Hudson, New York. Then in 1809 he was recruited to come to New York City to edit the newspaper that would become the messenger for the state's Clintonian wing, although the *Columbian* was initially supportive of the Madison administration.[16]

Similar to Holt, Solomon Southwick was very well plugged into party affairs. Southwick was a native of Rhode Island, where his father was also a newspaper publisher. The young man had training not only in the printing business but also as a cook and a sailor. Upon moving to New York, he joined the *Albany Register* and worked his way up to being the newspaper's editor and publisher. He became an official printer for the state of New York in 1809. Southwick also worked his way up the ladder of the Democratic-Republican organization, with clerkships in the legislature, followed by a two-year tenure as the sheriff of Albany County.[17]

Just like with the Invisibles, the Clintonians' early support for Madison was fragile and unlikely to last long. Representing commercial locales, centrally in New York, but also with support in New Hampshire, New Jersey, and Pennsylvania, the Clintonians opposed overly restrictive and arbitrary trade embargoes that would surely harm American industry and shipping. Tariffs, in comparison, were considered appropriate to protect domestic industries. They opposed the agrarianism of Old Republicans and some mainline Jeffersonians, and supported federal sponsorship of internal improvements to build up the nation's infrastructure. Their failure to end the Virginia dynasty of the presidency in 1808 only contributed to the Clintonians' suspicion of Madison, and now the men of this faction were aggrieved that they did not receive the patronage they felt was due.[18] The Clintonians' lukewarm support for the party ticket in 1808—which was by no means universal—served to marginalize this faction from the beginning of the new president's tenure. The April 1812 death of Vice President Clinton removed even a nominal figure from the senior ranks of the Madison administration.

Most ordinary Americans are no longer familiar with the old Clinton family of New York that was prominent well into the nineteenth century. The New York Clintons we all know today (that is, Bill and Hilary) began their political activities in the 1970s in Arkansas and migrated up to New York in 2000. They are not related to the Clinton political family of the early republic. In that era, just like today, any gentleman with a famous family name would enjoy some advantages in his pursuit of elected office. By the time DeWitt Clinton ran for president, his family was nationally well-established in military and political life. George Clinton, DeWitt's uncle, was a Revolutionary War officer, a long-tenured governor of New York, and a former vice president of the United States. James Clinton, George's older brother, ultimately achieved the rank of brevet major general, distinguishing himself as a veteran of the French and Indian War, as well as the American Revolution. After ending his career in the army, James served a few terms in both houses of the New York legislature. James Clinton's wife Mary DeWitt descended from a Dutch family, and the couple had seven children.

Their third son was DeWitt Clinton, who was born on March 2, 1769, in Little Britain in Orange County, New York. The boy liked books and science while growing up in the context of the Revolutionary War. Colonel James Clinton was wounded during the siege of Quebec, and young DeWitt worried for years about his father's welfare in the field. His older brother Alexander also served. After a few years of private tutoring, thirteen-year-old DeWitt was sent to the Kingston Academy to complete his childhood education. He was a member of the school's debating society and met other boys from New York's most elite families.[19]

DeWitt Clinton intended to begin his higher education pursuits in 1784 at the College of New Jersey. His stay there did not last long, however, as King's College in New York City was set to reopen. The notion of the governor's nephew attending college out of state was politically embarrassing. City and state leaders resolved to get King's College up and running again after falling into disrepair during the war, including a period of British occupation. Clinton soon enrolled at the institution, which was renamed Columbia College and is now known as Columbia University. In 1786 he graduated at the top of his class.[20]

Soon thereafter, Clinton began studying law in the office of the highly regarded attorney Samuel Jones. In 1790 he passed the bar exam and became a practicing lawyer in New York City. Meanwhile, as New York and other states were deliberating upon the new Constitution, the young Clinton provided support for his uncle George, who opposed ratification. Beginning in late 1787, and into early 1788, DeWitt Clinton's essays were published under the pen name of Countryman. DeWitt Clinton assailed the new Constitution as an undue interference with the proper powers of the states. In contrast with the rhetorical eloquence of *The Federalist Papers* (which do carry a tinge of pomposity), the Countryman letters were deliberately written to sound like the honest concerns of a common citizen. Clinton made efforts not to sound like the son of a politician and a graduate of an elite college:

I have seen enough to convince me very fully, that the new constitution is a very bad one, and a hundred-fold worse than our present government; and I do not perceive, that any of the writers in favour of it (although some of them use a vast many fine words, and shew a great deal of learning) are able to remove any of the objections which are made against it.[21]

As an aspiring young politician, DeWitt Clinton was building relationships and earning the trust of key citizens. One of the benefits of his family connections was his receipt of a commission in the state militia; by 1794 he had worked his way up to the rank of captain. Like many elite gentlemen in politics, he was a Freemason. He also joined the St. Tammany Society (later to be known as Tammany Hall) just before the group became highly politicized. In fact, by 1802 Clinton and the Tammany Society were bitter opponents. Another relationship concerned Clinton's new wife. In February 1796 he married Maria Franklin. The young woman was the beneficiary of a large inheritance upon the death of her father Walter Franklin, who was a successful merchant. The couple had ten children, including George W. Clinton, who would serve for a year as the mayor of Buffalo, and then as a US Attorney.[22]

A man of great intellectual curiosity, DeWitt was a strong supporter of government promoting culture, the arts, public education, and infrastructure. He cofounded the New-York Historical Society, the American Academy of the Arts, and the Literary and Philosophical Society. A calculating politician, who was more than willing to engage in the horse-trading necessary to get things done, Clinton believed that state and local governments existed to provide necessary services to improve human welfare. As New York City's mayor, he devoted himself to the proactive use of government as an agent for economic modernization. A more advanced economy and activist government would lift the happiness of the people and make life better for the underprivileged. Clinton also stepped up in defense of his state's Irish American immigrants and favored liberalizing the nation's laws concerning naturalized citizenship. While DeWitt Clinton never aggressively defended slavery, he came from a family of slaveholders. He owned at least two persons in his adult lifetime, although one was freed in 1810.[23] Given the absence of slavery from the issue agenda in the 1812 campaign, Clinton's potential liabilities on this matter were never exploited.

The Clintons followed most anti-federalists into the Democratic-Republican Party, although in the 1790s New York was very hospitable for Federalists. When George Clinton departed the governorship, he was replaced by Federalist John Jay. Dewitt Clinton's own political career began in the state Assembly, although he lost his first bid in a multi-candidate race in 1795. He tried again the following year and lost, but in April 1797 Clinton was elected to the lower house of the state legislature. He took office in January 1798, but later in the year he was elected to the New York Senate from the Southern District.[24]

By 1800, New York was a political battleground state. Clinton supported Jefferson for the presidency, even taking up his pen to defend the vice president from baseless charges of being an atheist. With his influence in the legislature growing quickly, Clinton was chosen for the state's powerful Council of Appointment late in 1800. The body was made up of four senators, who were selected by the Assembly; each councilman had a one-year term, and the governor served as an ex officio member. The Council of Appointment—which was created in 1777—existed to provide some level of accountability over appointments to statewide and local offices, as well as the selection of judgeships. Over the years, however, it took growing control of all appointments, even down to very minor local posts. It also functioned as an engine of patronage. Clinton and Governor Jay clashed over appointments, and the state constitution was soon changed to clarify the power arrangement between the chief executive and the council. Later in his political career, the council became a source of much frustration for Clinton.[25]

After voters sent George Clinton back to the governorship in 1801, the Federalists began declining in the state, albeit with sporadic signs of a comeback. Now more than ever, New York's Democratic-Republican Party was a hotbed of rivalries and factions. Vice President Aaron Burr and his supporters, including the Tammany Society, increasingly butted heads with the Clintons and their allies. The rhetorical warfare in the newspapers and pamphlets degenerated into character attacks, unfounded accusations, and conspiracy theories. Such attacks can be treated as part of the normal sparring of politics, but matters took a more serious turn in the summer of 1802.

Burr's supporters remained embittered over their man losing out on the presidency in 1800, even though Jefferson was always the intended Democratic-Republican nominee for the top job. Clinton was not involved in the machinations to keep Burr out of the presidency when the House was deliberating, but by now there were other scores to settle. The Clinton family had recently maneuvered to remove Burr as one of the directors of the Manhattan Company, which he founded in 1799. The Manhattan

Company was established to deliver clean water to residents, but actually the organization was created to challenge the Federalist domination over banking in New York City. To this day, the Manhattan Company is one of the ancestors of JPMorgan Chase & Co. Not only was Burr displaced, but so too was his top ally, John Swartwout. The back-and-forth verbal attacks continued, and Clinton apparently crossed a line, denouncing Swartwout as "a liar, a scoundrel, and a villain." In early nineteenth-century America, slurs to this degree would prompt code duello.[26]

In Colonial America, and for several decades beyond, dueling was the accepted manner in which two gentlemen would resolve a conflict involving a perceived insult to a man's honor. Some citizens regarded the practice as primitive, but in 1802 it was considered the civilized alternative to brawling and family feuds. Efforts to achieve a peaceful reconciliation failed. The two quarreling men convened on July 31, 1802, at a field in Weehawken, New Jersey—the same site where the famous duel took place between Burr and Alexander Hamilton two years later. The encounter followed the recognized rules of dueling at the time, and after several exchanges, Swartwout had two wounds in the leg. Clinton was unharmed and content to walk away, even though Swartwout wanted to continue.[27] The whole episode put Clinton's career and his life at risk. Over two decades later, a history of dueling was not prohibitive to the presidential candidacy of Andrew Jackson, and Clinton met the expectations that a man of his social standing was expected to follow.

Prior to the duel, Clinton had moved from the statehouse to the US Senate. The legislature appointed him to fill a midterm vacancy, and in February 1802 he took his seat. His tenure in the national capital was brief but not without some accomplishments. Coming from an immigrant-rich city, Clinton successfully advocated for more lenient naturalization policies. He also played a leading role in the adoption of the Twelfth Amendment to the Constitution, which reformed the Electoral College. Clinton introduced the measure in October 1803, which was enacted by Congress with very few changes, and subsequently ratified by the states ahead of the next presidential race. During the Senate debate over the amendment, Clinton almost ended up in another duel. New Jersey senator Jonathan Dayton, who was a Burr ally, opposed the amendment and proposed major alterations. Bickering ensued, and Dayton accused Clinton of insulting his honor and attacking his motives. He demanded from Clinton either an apology or a challenge to a duel. Clinton opted to be the adult in the dispute and issued a limited apology. His work in the Senate was done now anyway, for he was preparing to return home for a new position: mayor of New York City.[28]

The Council of Appointment chose Clinton for the mayorship, and he assumed office in late 1803. In many ways, he behaved like a conventional politician, as he engaged in patronage politics to build support, but he also took a keen interest in public policy. His approach to the job was very hands-on and visionary, as Clinton personally supervised the city's police operations and intervened to stop violent mobs on more than one occasion. He appeared in the streets to help suppress an anti-Catholic riot, and offered a monetary reward to bring the perpetrators to justice. As the mayor of a crowded city, he took public health and sanitation seriously, for he was always attentive to measures that could be taken to reduce the impact of periodic waves of yellow fever and other contagious diseases. A major port city like New York also received numerous foreign ships, which sometimes required the mayor's intervention to stave off international incidents. There was little the federal government was able to do to prevent European powers from harassing American vessels, and the neutrality of New York City's harbor was often not taken seriously by the British and French when their ships were in the vicinity.[29]

By 1805 the Clinton family was rising in American politics, as George was now Jefferson's vice president, and DeWitt's younger brother George Jr. was a congressman. Aaron Burr was losing influence in New York following his disgrace on the Weehawken dueling grounds and his defeat in the 1804 gubernatorial race. Mayor Clinton, however, found himself in more political fights that likely could have been avoided. The new governor was Morgan Lewis, who was initially allied with the Clintonians, but he and Clinton soon had a falling out. The two disagreed over a state charter for a Federalist-controlled bank. That institution would have been a competitor of Clinton's Manhattan Company, which he basically controlled. Not only did Clinton oppose the bank charter, but he recruited candidates to run for the legislature who shared that stance. Clinton was also elected to return to the New York Senate in April 1805, an office he was allowed to hold while still serving as mayor. In the Senate, Clinton consolidated his control over the Council of Appointment and used his position to remove the supporters of Governor Lewis from their state jobs.[30]

DeWitt Clinton demonstrated his capacity to behave with vindictiveness, and he showed no compunction about bringing the full weight of his growing political machine upon a former ally. The recent episode also did little to convince skeptics that Clinton was not an ambitious politician. Efforts to achieve a reconciliation between Clintonians and supporters of Aaron Burr also seemed to backfire and only created the appearance of political opportunism. Clintonians lost their legislative majority in 1806, and, not surprisingly, in February 1807 a new Council of Appointment fired Clinton from the mayorship of New York City.[31]

He was still a state senator, however, and the Clintonian influence remained robust in New York. Daniel Tompkins, a state supreme court justice and a Clinton ally, defeated Lewis in the April 1807 gubernatorial election, reversing any signs of a political decline for DeWitt Clinton. The Council of Appointment reinstalled him into the mayorship in February 1808. At this point, Clinton's flip-flopping on issues would start causing problems for his future presidential campaign. Initially opposing the federal Embargo Act, Clinton then walked back his criticisms and supported his president's policy. Subsequently, he continued to defend the embargo, pledged his support to Jefferson's successor, and denounced the Federalists as unpatriotic.[32]

As mayor, Clinton obviously had a front-row seat to witness the rapid economic devastation this foolish policy produced for his city that was so dependent on shipping. Signs of a Federalist comeback were percolating in New York, and especially in New York City. In April 1809 Federalists gained control of the Assembly. Clinton knew what this meant: the new assemblymen got to choose their own Council of Appointment, and sure enough, Mayor Clinton was removed from his office in early 1810. The setback was temporary, however, in the volatile environment of his state's politics. In spite of intraparty tensions, he continued to support Tompkins and endorsed him for reelection that year. The governor won a second term, and Clinton remained in the good graces of his party. When Democratic-Republicans regained the Assembly in the April 1810 elections, he was well-positioned to be sent back to the mayorship by a new Council of Appointment.[33]

In February 1811, Clinton was mayor again. That same year, however, the Tammany Society maneuvered to successfully deny him renomination for his Senate seat. As he was aiming to improve his relations with Federalists, he took advantage of the New York law that permitted politicians to hold more than one office at a time. Clinton made himself available to run for the lieutenant governorship. The incumbent had recently died, and the state constitution called for a special election to be held. In April, he won his first statewide election by a margin of about 6 percent over Federalist Nicholas Fish. The mayor was clearly losing popularity at home, however, as Fish carried New York City, and a candidate nominated by the Tammany Society came in second. Clinton won just 18 percent in his own city.[34]

Vice President Clinton's death elevated DeWitt's fast-rising stock in state and national politics, and considerable attention shifted in his direction as the new leader of a powerful Democratic-Republican faction. Having served his uncle as a personal secretary, the forty-three-year-old Clinton could capitalize off the many connections the family name provided. The Clintonians' anti-war stance, however, was nuanced and complicated. While they are categorized as opponents of the War of 1812, the Clintonians were not pacifists. Their plan was to respond to British and French outrages on the seas not through embargoes, but by building up the military and muscular diplomacy. Hopefully then the two European bullies would get serious about a peaceful resolution.

Clintonians advocated for a delay in the congressional declaration of war, ostensibly to create more time for diplomacy and military preparation. Clintonians in the House, largely in the New York and New Jersey delegations, voted against the final war declaration on Britain. New York's Obadiah German, New Hampshire's Nicholas Gilman, and New Jersey's John Lambert were the Clintonians in the Senate, while Kentucky's John Pope was hard to neatly categorize into any particular faction; they all voted against the final declaration for unrestricted war on Britain. However, prior to the final roll call, the Clintonian senators did vote with Federalists for some alternative versions of a war declaration, as well as a failed effort to delay the final war resolution. The Clintonian senators backed unsuccessful roll-call votes that called for a maritime-only war declaration, as well as a triangular war declaration that would include France *and* Britain as targets of the United States.[35] The inconsistency of the Clintonian senators in their 1812 votes on war was a harbinger of the problems DeWitt Clinton would have on this issue in his presidential campaign.

The growing likelihood of war also appeared to delay the most important public works project of Clinton's career—and maybe in American history up to that point. The Erie Canal project was completed more than a decade after the 1812 presidential election, although plans were already in the works even before he sought the presidency. The idea, which did not originate with Clinton, was to link the Hudson River around Albany with Lake Erie to the west. Under the plan, access to all of the Great Lakes would be eased, not only for New Yorkers but for commerce more generally. In 1810 Clinton accepted an invitation to serve on the state's Erie Canal Commission, which would conduct research and field trips before construction would begin. It would take a long time for the project to build political support and obtain the necessary funding. Many Federalists supported the proposal, but bipartisan buy-in was necessary for an undertaking of this magnitude. Clinton emerged as a major booster and eventually became the public face of the project. The legislature sent him to Washington, DC, to try to procure federal funding from Congress and President Madison.[36]

Clinton and his fellow commissioner, Gouverneur Morris, were in the national capital in December 1811 and January 1812. The president agreed to meet with the two men. Consistent with a mainstream Jeffersonian Democratic-Republican at the time, Madison took the position that federal aid for internal improvements was generally unconstitutional. To be sure, he was not opposed to the Erie Canal project. In a message to Congress, the president praised New York's plans, but he was deferential to the judgment of the legislative branch about what, if any, action the federal government should take. "The utility of canal navigation is universally admitted," Madison wrote on December 23, 1811, as he then kicked the ball to Congress to "suggest to their consideration, whatever steps may be proper on their part, towards its introduction and accomplishment." With the House and Senate making war preparations, a major appropriation of federal dollars for an ambitious public works project was not in the cards. A House committee shelved the funding request in February 1812.[37]

For the time being, the Erie Canal venture would have to do without money from Washington, DC. Other observers were more cynical, seeing the sticky fingers of politics on Clinton and Morris. Federalists normally advocated for internal improvements, but Senator James A. Bayard of Delaware was dismissive, asserting that "the characters of the two men are pretty well known, and it is rather supposed that they mean to open a road to the presidency than a Canal from the lakes." The canal proposal didn't emerge as an issue in the 1812 campaign, but it was well known in New York that Clinton had presidential ambitions—if not in 1812, then in the future.[38]

PRE-WAR EPISODES

The British, who controlled Canada, maintained an arm's-length alliance with the tribes in the Northwest Territory, but American settlers were suspicious, and not without some justification. Britain traded and forged economic relations with the Native peoples in this region, for it was in was in the interest of their country to keep good relations, given the persistent post–Revolutionary War Anglo-American tensions. Fairly or not, any outbreak of violence between Americans and Native peoples would therefore be easy to scapegoat upon Britain. For settlers in the American West, the prospect of alleged mischief perpetuated by Indian peoples with British assistance was very easy to believe. In addition, demagogues who cared little for facts and nuance could easily exploit any outbreak of violence as a justification for a broader war on Britain.[39]

One trigger was a small Anglo-American naval skirmish off the coast of North Carolina. Misunderstandings, miscommunications, and mutual distrust produced the battle on May 16, 1811. The USS *President*, patrolling the Carolina coast, engaged the small British sloop HMS *Little Belt*. Commodore John Rodgers's much larger *President* defeated the *Little Belt* in a clash that killed eleven Britons and injured one American. Bickering ensued between London and Washington, DC, over who was to blame over the pointless battle. The United States prevailed in this encounter, but the politically costly victory further unleashed the domestic momentum for war.[40]

As expected, anti-British sentiment bubbled up in the newspapers. The *National Intelligencer* applauded Rodgers "in repelling and chastising the attack so causelessly and rashly made on the United States frigate President." The *Boston Patriot* celebrated the victory, reporting that citizens toasted the naval triumph on Independence Day: "May the *President* dissever every *Little Belt* that tends to harm in American commerce." Meanwhile, an American court of inquiry faulted the British and vindicated Rodgers. Navy Secretary Paul Hamilton told Madison that the proceedings "all combine in forming a Mass of Evidence not to be resisted, and which places the Commodore above the reach of censure or even of suspicion."[41]

The greater trigger would come in the form of the Battle of Tippecanoe on November 7, 1811, just two days after Madison's Annual Message. The battle was the culmination of years of tensions that had little or nothing to do with the British. In the previous decade, a spiritual revival led by Tenskwatawa, a Shawnee, who was referred to as the Prophet, attracted much Native American support from various tribes. The movement rejected white American culture and assimilation while increasingly promoting self-defense and noncooperation with the federal government. Existing treaties, the Prophet's followers believed, were coercive, unfair, and contrary to the preservation of Indian peoples. The Prophet's brother Tecumseh helped to militarize their movement and promote good relations with the British. In the vicinity of the Wabash and Tippecanoe Rivers, near what is now Lafayette, Indiana, a camp called Prophetstown was established for followers of the cause.[42]

Indiana's territorial governor William Henry Harrison, an army officer with experience fighting Native Americans in the Northwest Territory, was resolved to bring the defiant Indian peoples into submission. Harrison warned Madison throughout 1810 that the Prophet's followers were becoming more militant, as more and more violent incidents occurred. Diplomacy with Tecumseh failed, and Harrison was now even more convinced that the British were pulling the strings of the restive tribes in his territory. After some hesitation, Madison sent Harrison more troops, even though the president's hands were full and the armed forces stretched thin, given matters in Florida and the tense situations with Britain and France at sea.[43]

In the fall of 1811, Harrison took his army to Prophetstown to confront the Prophet and apprehend those whom the governor claimed were responsible for violent and criminal acts. Arguably, this move was in violation of Madison's orders to seek peace with the Native peoples, but Secretary of War Eustis gave Harrison contradictory directives urging more aggressive action.[44] On November 7 the battle commenced. The Prophet rallied his men, as Tecumseh was in the South recruiting other Native American tribes when the battle took place. The Native peoples attacked Harrison's men and inflicted many casualties, but the governor's forces counterattacked and burned Prophetstown to the ground. On paper, it was a military victory for the United States, but the sentiments that popularized the Prophet's movement persisted in the Northwest Territory.[45] In a written message to Congress on December 18, Madison declared victory, saluted the bravery of American troops, and denounced the "combination of savages" that he held responsible for the battle. Though he did not make any explicit accusation of British meddling, Madison expressed his hope that the clash would result in "a cessation of the murders and depredations committed on our frontier" and "the prevention of any hostile incursions."[46]

Newspapers had a field day, using the battle as evidence for Anglo-Indian collusion, which could only be rectified by war. The Lexington, Kentucky, *Reporter* charged that *"the war on the Wabash is purely* BRITISH.*"*[47] The *Republican* in Savannah, Georgia, shrieked, "Indian War!!" In a racist rant, the *Republican Star* in Easton, Maryland, argued, "We are then persuaded that the Indian war will be found to be really *British*. The Savages [are] only the allies of GREATER *Savages*." Even the *Supporter* in Chillicothe, Ohio, which was a Federalist publication, screeched, "War! War! War!"[48] Any careful nuance or thoughtful consideration of the facts and context surrounding these events was lost amid anti-Indian prejudices and predispositions to distrust the British. The Madison team was all too willing to stoke those fears.

John Henry was an Irish immigrant to the United States, an army veteran, and a one-time fur trader in Montreal. Since the first Embargo Act, Henry had been paid by the British governor of Lower Canada to monitor the political situation in New England, particularly Massachusetts. Opposition to a possible Anglo-American war was strong in this region, and ripe for British utilization, perhaps even culminating in a secession crisis. Henry eventually demanded significant rewards that British officials would not pay. Following the advice of Paul Emile Soubrian, a French con artist, Henry contacted the State Department with the assistance of Democratic-Republican governor Elbridge Gerry of Massachusetts. Eager for evidence that would boost the case for war, Monroe's State Department in February 1812 paid $50,000 (about $883,000 in 2022 dollars) for Henry's documents. The secretary of state then arranged to keep the papers private until after Henry had quietly left the United States.[49]

Madison made his move on March 9, when he sent Henry's papers to Congress. The presidential communication with Congress asserted that the documents "prove that at a recent period," the British hired "a secret agent," who was charged with "fomenting disaffection to the constituted authorities of the nation, and in intrigues with the disaffected, for the purpose of bringing about resistance to the laws, and eventually, in concert with a British force, of destroying the Union and forming the eastern part thereof into a political connection with Great Britain."[50] The Madison administration was doing more than accusing the British of violating American sovereignty at sea. Now the president was indicting Britain as an official sponsor in an alleged secession scheme to break up the United States in collusion with New England Federalists.

Given the shamelessness with which the Madison administration exploited the Henry affair, it could be said that there was now little separating mainline Jeffersonians from the belligerent anti-British elements in American politics. Accordingly, the *National Intelligencer* responded with arguments that placed it squarely in the War Hawk camp, denouncing the British for "perfidiously stirring up rebellion and ... feeling for the vitals of the Republic, to which she might in the dead of night direct her poisoned dagger." Any sympathizer of Britain should be "marked as the foe to freedom, as the parricidal enemy of his country!" To gin up the Madison administration's case for war, the newspaper subsequently published a series of articles on the pain and suffering of American seamen who had been impressed by the British.[51]

Federalists found themselves on the defensive, though their newspapers denounced the release of the documents as a political stunt, and impugned Henry's character. "ANOTHER DEMOCRATIC LIE DETECTED," bellowed the *Boston Gazette*. "Henry the Counterfeiter," claimed Baltimore's *Federal Republican*. The payoff to Henry was cited as evidence of his suspect motives and low credibility, and Madison was attacked for partaking in the manipulative scheme. "We feel mortified," the *Concord Gazette* said, "to see the Chief Magistrate of our country descending from the dignity of his office, to retail the slanders of a traitor, and add to their virulence."[52]

To be sure, the Federalist critics had a point, for the evidence of a British concoction to separate the United States was flimsy at best. That New England was opposed to trade embargoes and war with the British was no secret, but Henry's papers never identified any specific Americans involved in a cabal to dissolve the federal union. In addition, Henry's credibility was problematic given his disappearance, as well as his insistence on being paid by the government of the United States for information about what would clearly constitute a treasonous scheme. If anybody was disloyal to the United States, it was him, for Henry was the one who received payment from a hostile foreign power to spy on his own adopted country, only to then demand more. The fact that the president and Monroe acquiesced in paying him revealed not an anti-American Federalist/British plot but rather that the Madison administration had made a political decision and these documents could burnish the public case for declaring war.[53]

Partisans on the issue of war heard what they wanted to hear. For antiwar Americans, the Henry affair was evidence of dishonesty and political intrigue to further a march to war. For War Hawks, the episode was proof of a long train of British insults to the honor of the United States, and the disloyalty of Federalist citizens.[54] Although this was hardly the last time an American president would sanction the use of questionable evidence to take the country to war, there was little political price for Madison during his tenure. In a contemporary presidential administration, the Henry affair—bribery, espionage, con men, poor intelligence reports, politicians eager to start a war—would have all the makings of a major scandal, possible impeachment proceedings, or even criminal charges. In 1812, however, momentum for war continued to build, even on other fronts.

Matters concerning the Spanish-controlled Florida Territory produced a mixed bag of results for Madison, but quite a few political headaches, and distractions from the inevitable war with Britain that the administration prioritized. Florida was poorly defended by Spain and was replete with escaped slaves, smugglers, Indigenous peoples, and American citizens yearning for annexation. The possibility also existed that the British or French could take advantage of this unstable state of affairs and step up their meddling in the territory. Jefferson believed that the Louisiana Purchase made West Florida American territory. As president, Madison sought to fulfill his predecessor's unfinished task by pursuing annexation when the right opportunity presented itself.[55] Events, however, did not transpire completely according to plans, and Madison's political standing within his party was put at further risk going into his reelection campaign.

Madison decided to move on West Florida first, so as to head off any British or French advantage in the region. Additional access to the waterways would also be an obvious economic benefit to the United States. William Wycoff, a representative who was dispatched to act on behalf of the Madison administration, mounted a public pro-American movement within West Florida in the summer of 1810. The campaign took place, but like so many political separatist movements, it mushroomed out of control and into violence. After first calling a convention, the revolutionaries subsequently attacked Baton Rouge, captured the Spanish governor, declared West Florida to be an independent nation, and asserted that annexation by the United States *might* be negotiable.[56]

At a time when American relations with Britain and France were precarious at best, a conflict with a third European power was the last thing Madison needed. Dispatch was necessary, given the unstable situation, and the possibility of a power vacuum or a conflagration in West Florida. On October 27, with Congress out of session, the president issued a secret proclamation annexing the territory; American troops were sent to West Florida accordingly, so as to enforce the presidential decree.[57] No legitimacy would be given to any notion of West Florida being an independent nation, for Madison's position was that the Louisiana Purchase deemed this American territory all along. Not until his written Annual Message to Congress on December 5 did Madison make the proclamation public.[58]

The pursuit of East Florida, in contrast, was a bust, and it created preelection troubles for the president at a time when the release of the Henry papers was also causing political embarrassment. In early 1811 Madison drafted a covert plan to acquire the territory, and in a confidential message to Congress, he requested and received authorization and funding for the project.[59] Through the use of heavy-handed tactics, however, the plan fizzled. The two agents, General George Mathews and John McKee, began the process of facilitating a full-scale armed uprising that would hopefully culminate in American annexation of East Florida. With assistance from

US Navy gunboats, Mathews and his followers captured Amelia Island at the town of Fernandina in northeastern Florida on March 17, 1812. The land was promptly transferred over to the United States, presumably for annexation, but this insurgency in Florida also went awry. Mathews and his "Florida Patriots," as they were called, then proceeded south toward St. Augustine along with US Army forces. The troops met little resistance, but when word reached Washington, DC, the Madison administration was aghast at the unneeded diplomatic conundrum that now existed. Mathews's campaign could antagonize Spain's British allies at a time when Madison and Monroe were making last-ditch attempts to avoid an Anglo-American war. In April 1812 the administration disavowed and dismissed Mathews on the grounds that he disobeyed his official instructions. In a letter to Jefferson, Madison lamented Mathews's campaign as "a tragi-comedy, in the face of common sense," and asserted that the general's "extravagances place us in the most distressing dilemma."[60]

Whereas the bungled East Florida mission was at least authorized by Congress, Madison's West Florida proclamation was a unilateral act, which was bound to alarm this president's usual critics. Federalist publications denounced the West Florida decree as a warmongering abuse of executive power, while Democratic-Republican newspapers praised Madison's resolve.[61] Mathews was displeased by his sudden abandonment by the Madison administration in East Florida but died on August 30 before he could travel to Washington, DC, and personally defend himself before the president. From Mathews's point of view, his actions were consistent with the Madison administration's arguably vague orders. The defiant general also apparently considered revealing the details of his aborted secret mission and making public all of his official correspondence with the Madison administration. Doing so could have added further humiliation to the president just as a controversial war with Britain was commencing. Still, Mathews declined to go public, lest he politically damage Madison at a moment when war with Britain was imminent and the president's reelection was far from a guarantee. "I think it highly improper at the present crisis to do any act that would lessen or injure the President in the opinion of his fellow citizens, or in the approaching Election," Mathews wrote to Secretary Monroe. "The good of our country may require all his influence aided by the best of our citizens," the dismissed general said.[62]

Breaking publicly with a wartime president would be a risky move and possibly further damage Mathews's credibility. Hence, this embarrassing evidence never hit the newspapers during the presidential campaign, which could have otherwise given Madison's opponents even more grounds to attack him as a reckless warmonger. As word of the siege became public, Federalist periodicals wasted no time in denouncing the East Florida mission and the Madison administration's use of ad hoc militias to achieve territorial conquest. The *Charleston Courier* compared Madison's actions to the bullying behaviors of European powers. The newspaper also dismissed the notion that Florida was in danger of falling into British hands, and it mocked the administration-backed project as irresponsible: "The farce of receiving the Province from a handful of insurgents, assuming to themselves the glorious name of the Spanish *patriots* in the mother country, is disgraceful in the extreme. If Florida must be ours, let the arms of the U. States take it, and not receive it at second hand."[63]

Nor did the East Florida mission exactly command universal support from Democratic-Republican factions who generally endorsed expansionist policies. Some in their ranks also frowned upon outsourcing the project to the unpredictable Patriot revolutionaries, as opposed to a standard military operation or diplomatic channels. Other southern party members expressed sympathy for the mission and acknowledged that Mathews's disavowal was a product of unfortunate political circumstances. Senator William H. Crawford of Georgia wrote from his state to Secretary Monroe claiming that Mathews "believes that the disavowal of his arrangement was entirely the result of Henry's discovery and he is not very singular in that opinion in this country, so far as I have been able to collect public opinion." Crawford wrote approvingly of the Florida revolutionaries and lamented the "embarrassing" situation the Madison administration had created for itself.[64]

Meanwhile, Monroe replaced Mathews with Georgia governor David Mitchell. The new commander had a similar mandate to continue the East Florida mission, which descended into chaos throughout 1812 as the nation's attention turned to the war with Britain.[65] American war fervor, however, did not extend to a full-throated congressional endorsement for a military seizure of East Florida. On June 19, the day Madison issued the Anglo-American war proclamation, War Hawk representative George Troup of Georgia proposed a measure that would authorize the president to militarily seize the whole Florida Territory. In the House, where the War Hawks and administration loyalists held the balance of power, the bill passed easily. In the Senate, however, Federalists, Clintonians, and the Invisible trio joined forces to defeat the measure by a vote of 14–16 on July 3.[66]

Presidents are well-advised to bring the country together on the eve of a war with a major foreign power. At a time when the Henry documents were circulating in the newspapers and inflaming partisan divisions, the conflagration in East Florida only poured more fuel on a volatile political situation. Far from uniting a nation about to go to war with Britain, both of these episodes only served to do the opposite. The Henry affair demonstrated that the Madison administration held a clear preference for an Anglo-American war, while engaging in a militarily risky side project in Florida that delivered no political benefits. When the misadventure in East Florida took an embarrassing turn, the Madison team deprioritized the mission, and the Senate rebuked the administration. The War of 1812 would be America's first politically divisive war, with a national election about to occur in just a few months.

WAR ARRIVES

Madison's actions now placed him in the position of assuming full ownership of the inevitable hostilities with Britain. Opponents would label the clash "Mr. Madison's War," as if to suggest that the conflict was a presidential concoction for some sinister purpose, rather than a necessity for national security.[67] Events escalated as the War Hawks demanded and received presidential support for a new and total embargo upon Britain. Madison and Monroe, on the advice of Speaker Clay, originally proposed a thirty-day embargo as a prelude to war. Americans also awaited news from the USS *Hornet* from overseas, which was rumored to be bringing news of British responses to the unfolding situation. Monroe then amended his request to increase the length of the embargo to sixty days, perhaps to await the ship's arrival and boost military preparations in the meantime. "Considering it as expedient," Madison told Congress on April 1, 1812, "under existing circumstances and prospects, that a general embargo be laid on all vessels now in port, or hereafter arriving, for the period of sixty days, I recommend the immediate passage of a law to that effect."[68] Not only did Congress quickly oblige, but the embargo that was enacted was extended to ninety days. Shippers scurried to move their goods to market on the seas before the new policy took effect.[69] The House majority was now under the firm control of the War Hawks.

If anything, the Federalist comeback that showed signs of manifesting in the 1808 presidential race seemed to stall out in the 1810 congressional elections. Democratic-Republicans netted thirteen House seats, while Senate elections produced virtually no change in the governing party's overwhelming majority.[70] What was noteworthy about this round of elections was that War Hawk candidates strengthened their position relative to other party factions. In the context of ever-changing, confusing, and ineffective trade policies, as well as a continuation of disrespect on the seas from the European powers, House campaign appeals featured aggressive anti-British rhetoric and pro-war cadences. Partisan newspapers ginned up the belligerent language as well, denouncing Madison's flailing stance against American adversaries. The *Aurora* called for the election of pro-war congressmen, and the *Baltimore Whig* attacked the president's "pusillanimous" leadership. "Arise! Arise! Columbia's sons arise! And shake of [sic] the torper of sloth and inactivity," exclaimed the *Carthage Gazette*.[71]

This War Hawk cohort that came to Congress consisted of a large freshman class committed to war, or at least to a more muscular stance against America's European adversaries. In fact, about half of the incoming Twelfth Congress would be composed of new members. Henry Clay of Kentucky was among this group of War Hawks, as he was elected to the House from a district based around Fayette County. The young politician was not only a War Hawk but also something of a nationalist, committed to a federal program of internal improvements, trade restrictions, and building up the nation's defenses. He opposed the National Bank, a position that he would reverse in subsequent years as he refined what was called his American System of economic development.[72]

The freshman congressman was selected as Speaker of the House of Representatives with support from his fellow War Hawks. In the first two decades following ratification of the Constitution, the position of Speaker was not an especially strong office. The document established that the Speaker shall be third in line for the presidency and that he (or she) is to preside over the proceedings of the House. In the early years of the republic, the Speaker held no institutional or political authority beyond what was explicated in the Constitution. Save for his task as a presiding officer, the Speaker then did not wield significant control over the House's legislative process. Nor was the Speakership a senior position of party leadership.

Clay enhanced the Speaker's role in the House, and in government more generally. Just shy of thirty-four years old, Clay was an ambitious and experienced politician as well as a shrewd operator. Before becoming Speaker, Clay had already served two separate stints in the Kentucky legislature and two nonconsecutive partial terms in the US Senate. As a state representative, Clay engineered the gerrymander (before that word was used) of Kentucky's districts for the purposes of securing a unanimous electoral vote for Jefferson's 1804 reelection.[73] After being chosen as Speaker of the

US House of Representatives in March 1811, Clay got right to work on the task of using his office to maximize the influence of his policy agenda. The new Speaker used the large War Hawk contingent in the House to form a national political base of power. Key Clay allies were installed on influential committees and chosen as chairs. The Rules Committee was brought under control of the Speaker of the House, effectively giving him control over the flow of legislation in the chamber. Clay was also a stern parliamentarian from the rostrum of the Speaker's chair, as he rigidly enforced rules and reined in loquacious members like John Randolph, among others.[74]

As a strict believer in the Constitution, James Madison also took seriously the notion that the document was written to prevent the United States from marching into war on presidential fiat and without careful deliberation. For the first time, Congress would be using the constitutional provision concerning a declaration of war in 1812. Nothing in the Constitution explicitly grants the president any powers over this process. The chief executive is the commander-in-chief of the armed forces, charged with prosecuting a war if one is declared—not deciding whether or not the nation is to go into a protracted armed engagement. Madison's behavior here would establish precedents for future presidential behavior, as well as for the wartime relationship between the legislative and executive branches. Does the president have a duty to formally ask Congress to declare war? Or should the president not use the influence of his office in this way, and allow the people's representatives in the legislative branch to debate the matter? If the president is the commander-in-chief, shouldn't he have some say in the congressional deliberative process? If and when Congress declares war, must that body provide reasons for taking the nation down this path? Should debates on declaring war be public, as if it was just another bill in Congress on tariffs and banks? However implausible, what if Congress declared war and the president opposed the measure?

The *Hornet* arrived in New York on May 19, the day after Madison's renomination at the congressional caucus. The vessel revealed no new news to indicate changes in behavior by either of the European belligerents. Correspondence from British foreign secretary Lord Castlereagh also confirmed in April that British policy would not change, given the continued French aggressions. The Madison administration and the War Hawks continued to direct their ire at Britain, however, as that nation had a greater record than France of recent hostile acts toward American ships and personnel. In a message disseminated to the *National Intelligencer*, possibly written by an administration insider, the focus was kept on British outrages. "Let it not be said that the misconduct of France neutralizes in the least that of Great Britain," the editorial lectured. While military action against France should remain on the table, the nation should prioritize the "unremitted infractions of our rights by Great Britain."[75]

Last-ditch diplomatic maneuvers failed, or fell victim to the slow communications of the era. Rumors of British concessions percolated but were hard to verify. Britain did agree to resolve long-standing grievances from the *Chesapeake* incident and pay reparations. The Royal Navy stood down in the early months of 1812 by avoiding the American coast and deescalating any contacts with American vessels and citizens. An offer was made to suspend the Orders in Council if the United States would agree to British trade licensing requirements, but the Madison administration rebuffed this proposal, surely aware that Americans would regard this measure as an insulting attack on national sovereignty. Further disruption shook British politics when the hardline prime minister, Spencer Perceval, was assassinated by an insane man on May 11, for reasons having nothing to do with the Orders in Council. That said, British industrialists and shippers were also applying pressure to lift the policy, as it was causing them harm. The power vacuum created an opportunity for a new stance vis-à-vis the United States, but it was too late. As fate would have it, none of these occurrences made much of a difference, even as Britain suspended the Orders in Council on June 17, the very day the Senate approved a declaration of war. Word did not reach American shores for weeks, and by that time the diplomatic rupture had reached a point of no return. The arguably more serious matter of impressments remained.[76]

The instantaneous communications and rapid transportation that we all take for granted today might have very well stopped the War of 1812 from occurring. Nor did anything like professionalized objective journalism then exist, which could have fairly assessed facts on the ground. In the spring of 1812, all indications in the United States pointed toward the British as remaining generally hostile at sea. Distrust of the British and their motives so permeated American politics for decades that resolution of old matters like the *Chesapeake* did little to slow the onward march to war. Speculating about counterfactual scenarios is a fruitless exercise, as politicians of Madison's era were guided by the whims of public opinion, imperfect information, and their own biases, just as they are today.

Amid little evidence of substantial changes to the situation, Madison had already begun drafting a carefully worded war message to Congress. The statement never made an explicit request for a war declaration, but instead focused upon grievances against the United States perpetuated by the British. In a message sent to Congress on June 1, Madison's lengthy statement articulated American arguments in firm language that stopped short of bellicosity. Impressment, arguably the most outrageous of the British infringements, formed a major part of the message. "British cruisers have been in the continued practice of violating the American flag on the great highway of nations, and of seizing and carrying off persons sailing under it," Madison noted. American citizens "have been dragged on board ships of war of a foreign nation and exposed, under the severities of their discipline, to be exiled to the most distant and deadly climes, to risk their lives in the battles of their oppressors, and to be the melancholy instruments of taking away those of their own brethren." The United States, the president noted, has worked for years "in vain" and "exhausted remonstrances and expostulations" to peacefully resolve these injustices.

Madison also addressed other hostile behaviors at sea, taking care to note that the United States was not the aggressor, and had in fact shown great restraint in the face of flagrant violations of "the law of nations" and diplomatic deceptions. "British cruisers," he said, "hover over and harass our entering and departing commerce." Captured personnel on American vessels, he asserted, are subjected to "lawless proceedings." Illegal blockades had "plundered" American commerce "in every sea." Despite the patient and peaceful efforts of the United States, it was evident that Great Britain sought a "monopoly" over commerce on the seas by way of "forgeries and perjuries."

With a clear reference to the recent battle at Tippecanoe, Madison launched a racist accusation of British-Indian collusion to make war on the United States. "Our attention is necessarily drawn to the warfare just renewed by the savages on one of our extensive frontiers," the president charged. "It is difficult to account for the activity and combinations which have for some time been developing," Madison explained, "among tribes in constant intercourse with British traders and garrisons without connecting their hostility with that influence and without recollecting the authenticated examples of such interpositions heretofore furnished by the officers and agents of that Government."

Though he showed respect for congressional prerogatives, Madison left no doubt where he stood. The decision to declare war was a "solemn question which the Constitution wisely confides to the legislative department of the Government. In recommending it to their early deliberations I am happy in the assurance that the decision will be worthy the enlightened and patriotic councils of a virtuous, a free, and a powerful nation."[77] Although

Madison gave due attention to French transgressions, he urged Congress to await further information from diplomats before taking additional actions. At Madison's request, the House debate that followed was in secret,[78] which clearly contradicted the spirit of the Constitution's mandate that legislative debates be transparent, especially on matters as serious as war. The House vote to declare war on June 4 was 79–49, with all Federalists in opposition, along with Clintonian Democratic-Republicans and a small number of Old Republicans.

The Senate moved slower, as that body usually does, but the outcome was never in doubt. After debate on alternatives was exhausted, the Senate approved a declaration of war on Britain by a vote of 19–13 on June 17. After the House approved slight amendments from the Senate, Madison signed the congressional war resolution on June 18. The following day, in a proclamation tinged with jingoism, the president instructed

> the good people of the United States, as they love their country, as they value the precious heritage derived from the virtue and valor of their fathers, as they feel the wrongs which have forced on them the last resort of injured nations, and as they consult the best means under the blessing of Divine Providence of abridging its calamities, that they exert themselves in preserving order, in promoting concord, in maintaining the authority and efficacy of the laws, and in supporting and invigorating all the measures which may be adopted by the constituted authorities for obtaining a speedy, a just, and an honorable peace.[79]

The cadences here dropped a hint of the themes that would color Madison's upcoming reelection campaign, insinuating that the time for debate was over, and good citizens had no choice but to support the war effort. War opponents across the political spectrum did not share that view. Clintonians and Federalists aimed to bring doves into their coalition, as well as those who were sympathetic to the need to take military action but also had no confidence in Madison's abilities as a commander-in-chief. Meanwhile, Samuel Harrison, a Madison ally from Vermont, advised the president that the nation was unprepared for war, and that offensive military action would not command public support. "You may lay aside all expectations of a new election to the Presidency, if you do *declare War*," Harrison warned.[80]

RENOMINATION

As early as 1812, rumors and speculation circulated that Madison was pressured by the War Hawks to push for a declaration of war. These claims suggest that Clay and his allies went so far as to threaten the president with denial of renomination at the congressional caucus if he did not proactively call for war with the British. Opponents had an incentive to make these accusations. Such an indictment would delegitimize the president's case for war as being not the solemn arguments of a commander-in-chief taking his country into battle as a last resort, but rather, as a desperate and feckless politician giving in to the powerful War Hawk faction so as to be renominated. Anti-war Old Republicans made these accusations, insinuating that the caucus's delay was part of a strategy to goad Madison into asking for a war declaration. "These president-makers, who are all for war, I presume may expect by delaying it to cause certain gentlemen to commit themselves for battle," former Virginia congressman James Garnett told Randolph. The British minister in Washington, DC, Augustus Foster, claimed that he was told by an American politician that the caucus was delayed due to Madison's hesitation on the war issue. Anti-Madison newspapers and congressmen continued with these lines of attack during the war and beyond.[81]

Madison biographers like Irving Brant and other historians have found no proof to support these assertions of nefarious political dealmaking. There was little to no evidence of an internal party groundswell to depose Madison, save for the Clinton candidacy, and the New Yorker lacked much support beyond his own faction. In addition, the president's behavior in the Henry affair does not seem to place him in the role of reluctant warrior. Madison was affirmatively building a case for war on the basis of unsubstantiated and vague evidence that was provided by a paid agent with questionable motives. False rumors also circulated in the spring of 1812 that Madison had launched a last-minute peace mission to Britain.[82] Time and again, going back to at least the first half of 1811, we see Madison accommodating the demands of the War Hawks and treating their positions as legitimate, rather than pushing back against them.

Before the congressional nominating caucus convened, Madison's support as party standard bearer was already very secure. Any effort to oust Madison would require some degree of support from key Democratic-Republican power brokers in large states like New York, Pennsylvania, and Virginia. Instead, the opposite occurred, as Madison critics within the party were defeated and marginalized. First, Virginia state legislators demonstrated full loyalty to their favorite son by nominating a slate of twenty-five presidential electors in a February caucus. As the *Richmond Enquirer* reported, "It is proper to say, that but one sentiment reigned through the Meeting—and that the only test laid down, whether *they* should or should not vote for such and such a Elector, was, whether *he* would or would not vote for James Madison as President of the U.S."[83]

In Pennsylvania, Democratic-Republican divisions fizzled when it came time to choose a presidential nominee, although the state had seen considerable signs of dissention within the party during Madison's first term. Pennsylvania certainly contained pockets of support for the Clintonian faction and the Invisibles. Additionally, in Madison's rookie year as president, he was brought into an internal party conflict with Governor Simon Snyder. The matter concerned a long-brewing feud over an old British sloop, the *Active*, that was captured during the Revolutionary War. The controversy upended Pennsylvania politics, causing riots and a near armed clash between the state militia and federal marshals, as well as rumblings of a possible civil war. Cooler heads, however, eventually prevailed.

American prisoners mutinied on board the *Active* in the summer of 1778, but they apparently didn't have full control of the vessel when it was brought into the port of Philadelphia by privateers operating under the auspices of the state of Pennsylvania. Decades of litigation followed, wending through state and federal courts, wrangling over who had a rightful claim to the money generated from the sale of the ship. Pennsylvania's late state treasurer, David Rittenhouse, had held the cash in a private account while the messy case inched through the court system. Upon his death, the money was part of his estate, which was controlled by his two daughters. The estate was then successfully sued in federal court by Captain Gideon Olmsted, the organizer of the original mutiny on the *Active*. The US Supreme Court upheld the ruling with instructions that Olmsted be paid. Believing the ruling to be an affront to state sovereignty, the Pennsylvania legislature went so far as to enact a law blocking payment to Olmsted. Governor Snyder appealed to Madison to respect his state's autonomy, asserting that surely one of the leading Framers of the Constitution would be "no less disposed to protect the sovreignty [sic] and independence of the several states, as guaranteed to them, than to defend the rights and legitimate powers of the General government."[84] But now as president, charged with taking care that the laws and court orders be faithfully executed, Madison showed his old federalist leanings when he told Snyder that "the Executive of the U. States, is not only unauthorized to prevent the execution of a Decree sanctioned by the Supreme Court of the U. States, but is expressly enjoined by Statute, to carry into effect any such decree, where opposition may be made to it."[85]

A full-scale fiasco followed that nearly brought Pennsylvania into a state of civil war with the United States in 1809. The governor called out the state militia to prevent federal marshals from arresting the elderly Rittenhouse daughters, and a minor physical clash ensued. Some Pennsylvanians, including newspaperman William Duane in his *Aurora*, chastised Snyder for potentially starting a civil war over what was ultimately just a fight over a dead man's estate. As Pennsylvania Federalists humorously watched their opposition party clash over state verses federal powers, the governor's critics poured into the streets of Philadelphia. Riots followed, and even some of the state militiamen abstained from duty over what they believed to be an overblown conflict. Eventually a federal marshal was forced to elude the state militia guarding the Rittenhouse home so he could present a writ of arrest to the women. Snyder then retreated and called back his militia, and the state supreme court refused to intervene in the dispute.

Meanwhile, the Madison administration brought criminal charges on the state militiamen and their commanding officer for their physical resistance and defiance toward a federal marshal. The men were convicted and sentenced to short prison terms and fines. Having prevailed in this fight, Madison heeded the demands of the *Aurora* and acted with grace and political skill by pardoning the rebellious citizen soldiers of Pennsylvania, and even refunded their fines. The crisis was over, and the state party began reconciling.[86] The whole episode was an unneeded source of division among Pennsylvania Democratic-Republicans, given the volatile politics over the embargo and the many personal rivalries that complicated party unity. By early 1812, however, Madison and Snyder had patched up their differences. The governor actually publicly toasted in support of Madison's reelection. Likewise, on March 7, Democratic-Republican state legislators assembled and unanimously chose pro-Madison presidential electors who would stand for the president if he carried the state in the autumn's popular vote. The ailing George Clinton was also renominated for the vice presidency, as a possible gesture toward party unity.[87]

Such party divisions had not been smoothed out in the state of New York. Nor would they be. Clintonians did not fully control the apparatus of the state Democratic-Republican organization, but they had a strong base in the state legislature and could therefore cause considerable headaches for pro-Madison forces. Whether the Clintonians would collaborate with the Federalists in a fusion ticket remained an open question, offering advantages and disadvantages. First, however, New York would have to lead the way in promoting Clinton, and with as much national appeal as possible. Standing in the way was Governor Daniel Tompkins, a full supporter of Madison. On March 27 Tompkins maneuvered to delay the convening of the legislature until May 21, thereby forestalling the inevitable nomination of DeWitt Clinton, which would take place on May 29.[88]

In his official message announcing the executive action (called "prorogation"), the governor claimed that the state was now subsumed by a scandal concerning bribery and the proposed Bank of America, which was to be chartered in New York. The institution was meant to assume many of the responsibilities of the old national bank, but some legislators were allegedly offered bribes to vote for the charter. Solomon Southwick, a bank supporter, was himself caught up in this mischief, as he was indicted and tried for efforts to bribe the Speaker of the Assembly. He was acquitted, but one of his associates was convicted. Federalists and Clintonians were big boosters of the Bank of America, although DeWitt Clinton was a nominal opponent. Saying nothing about the presidential election, Tompkins declared the delay was necessary "in order that time may be afforded for reflection, and for the complete ascertainment of public sentiment upon a measure fraught with such important consequences."[89] Of course, Clintonians saw the matter differently, as Southwick's *Albany Register* denounced Tompkins's move as a transparent action on behalf of Madison, and an affront to New Yorkers' right to have their first American president. "Virginia has nominated, and so has Pennsylvania. Why, then, should New York remain silent?," Southwick asked his readers. "SILENT! NO!," he continued. "This great State, this proud pillar of the American confederacy will no longer sleep in inglorious indifference to the destinies that naturally await her."[90]

As Vice President George Clinton was in poor health, the possibility of a Madison–DeWitt Clinton ticket was raised by some pro-administration members of Congress.[91] Such an alliance might mollify enough Clintonians, and save some of New York's electoral votes for Madison, while satisfying mainline Jeffersonians by placing the younger Clinton in the insignificant office of the vice presidency. Federalist cooperation with the Clintonians could also be choked off. However, such a partnership was no longer realistic, and it never materialized. Unlike the context of the Madison-Clinton ticket in 1808, now the nation stood on the precipice of an Anglo-American war that sharply divided these wings of the Jeffersonian party. Clintonians determined that the only rational way forward was independent of the Democratic-Republican establishment, and Federalists concluded that a wartime alliance with dissident Jeffersonians was necessary to mount a national comeback.

While political news and developments moved at a slower pace in the era, as compared to today, momentum still mattered. By the time of the congressional nominating caucus, any prospect for an intraparty revolt against the president was dead. The anticlimactic event took place on May 18 in the Senate chamber, four months later than in 1808. The presidential tally on that day was eighty-two for Madison, none for other candidates, and only one abstention from the Clintonian representative Thomas Sammons of New York. As in 1808, the caucus continued to be a controversial instrument, with the usual accusations of favoritism toward political insiders and the party establishment. Outnumbered at the national level, the vast majority of Clintonian members of Congress, as well as some men from other factions, boycotted the proceedings. Among the Senate Invisible trio, only Leib attended. The Old Republicans' leading voice, John Randolph, was not present.[92] Other Madison supporters were not at the caucus that day for personal reasons. The pro-Madison *Weekly Register* crowed that "the unanimity in favor of Mr. Madison speaks loudly in his behalf, to his political friends."[93]

The vice presidential nomination was a source of minor disruption. The first round of balloting was won by John Langdon of New Hampshire, a venerable former president pro tempore of the Senate, governor of his state, and delegate to the Constitutional Convention. The vote was sixty-four for Langdon to sixteen for the outgoing governor of Massachusetts, Elbridge Gerry, and two for other candidates. In a letter to Langdon, the caucus appealed to his sense of duty and the need for wartime unity. "In this awful period of arms and calamities," the caucus said, "the republic has a right to the service of its citizens," for "there is a peculiar fitness in your presiding over the deliberations of the senate of the United States." Langdon, however, replied with a respectful decline of the party's nomination. After thanking the caucus, the old statesman expressed his desire to retire from public life, given his "advanced age" of seventy-one years. "To launch again into the ocean of politics, at my time of life, appears to me highly improper." The letter makes no mention of the current political climate, nor is there any expression of dissatisfaction with the Madison administration. Langdon did indeed retire from public life in 1812.[94]

A second congressional nominating caucus was held in the Senate chamber on the evening of June 8 to select a running mate. Elbridge Gerry, now the former governor of his state, was the choice of seventy-four senators and representatives, with only three scattered votes for other candidates. Speaker Clay then gave members who had not attended the previous caucus the chance to add their names to the tally of Madison supporters. The incumbent president collected an additional ten votes from mainline

Jeffersonians and War Hawks, with no dissenters. After both caucuses, Madison held the support of 69 percent, or 92 out of 133 Democratic-Republicans in Congress—a respectable showing, given the many different factions in the party.[95]

Gerry was a full player in the important chapters in the founding of the American republic. Not only was he a signer of the Declaration of Independence, but he was also a delegate to the Constitutional Convention a decade later. Making standard anti-federalist arguments, Gerry was one of just three sitting delegates who declined to sign the document. He was also one of three American peace commissioners sent to France in 1797 by President Adams. When the French made efforts to procure bribes from the three gentlemen as a condition for continuing diplomacy, Americans were outraged. The episode became known as the XYZ Affair. While Adams stood behind his Massachusetts commissioner, Federalists smeared Gerry for allegedly being soft on France and supposedly ruining the negotiations. The previously nonpartisan Gerry became a Democratic-Republican in 1800.[96]

Now the vice presidential nomination would provide him with a dignified way to manage his declining political career. On April 6, 1812, Gerry narrowly lost his bid for reelection as Massachusetts governor to Federalist Caleb Strong. As a Madison ally in the midst of an inevitable war that was unpopular in his state, Gerry carried this baggage into his defeat. In addition, Governor Gerry suffered the consequences for using his office to conduct a partisan vendetta against the Federalists, as he now considered them to be dangerous monarchists. The formerly moderate Gerry endorsed various measures to weaken his political adversaries, including targeting Federalist newspapers with prosecutions for libel, and efforts to purge the opposition party from other powerful institutions in his state.[97]

Most famously, Gerry became the namesake of a scheme that still creates controversy to this day. The Democratic-Republican majority in the state legislature altered congressional and legislative districts so as to further marginalize the Federalists. Some districts were oddly shaped, including one that looked like a salamander. Gerry privately disapproved of this hardball tactic, but he signed the redistricting bill anyway. The practice of engineering creative political districts to achieve a disproportionate advantage had existed elsewhere in the country prior to Gerry's governorship, but the salamander was called the "Gerry-mander" by the *Boston Gazette*, and the pejorative name became permanent. Energized Federalists mocked the gerrymandering and capitalized on the governor's bitter partisanship and association with Madison's ramp-up to war.[98]

Now unemployed, and holding several debts, Gerry asked Madison for a patronage job. The defeated governor inquired about being appointed collector for the port of Boston, or any other position that could keep him financially solvent. "I will frankly declare to you, Sir, that if any office of the kind mentioned should be offered, it will at this time be of great service to me; as well by furnishing me, with a pecuniary supply, requisite for the subsistence & education of a large & lovely circle of eight fine children," the humbled Gerry wrote.[99] The job of a federal port collector was an influential and lucrative patronage post in the early republic, arguably more prestigious than the vice presidency.[100]

Madison and his party, however, needed Gerry on the presidential ballot to deliver the necessary political benefits. As a New Englander, Gerry could make the Democratic-Republican ticket competitive in the party's weakest region, and his hawkish stance on war would play well in the South and the West. Some mainline party members, however, expressed concern that Gerry had now become a polarizing figure. Treasury Secretary Gallatin wrote to Joseph Nicholson, a Maryland lawyer and Democratic-Republican politician, in the hopes that Langdon could be talked out of declining the vice presidential nomination. Gerry was a divisive figure, Gallatin said, in contrast to the more statesmanlike reputation of Langdon. Demonstrating his concern about electability, the treasury secretary said, "We want as much popularity as is attainable; and Mr. Langdon's name is by far the most popular we can get. How beloved his person by all who know him I need not tell you. Gerry is, in both respects, the reverse." In addition, elevating Gerry could saddle Madison with another disloyal and unreliable lieutenant, like George Clinton. "I much fear that, if elected," Gallatin warned, "he would give us as much trouble as our late Vice-President."[101]

The anti-Gerry ruminations, however, never got off the ground. The congressional party caucus appealed to Gerry's duty to serve and the necessity of Democratic-Republican unity as the nation stood on the precipice of an imminent war. "Nothing short of unanimity," they wrote to Gerry, "at least in the Republican ranks, can insure success to those measures which the national councils have judged to be imperiously necessary for the vindication of the injured rights and insulted honor of the nation." In a June 18 letter to the congressional party caucus, Gerry gave his thanks and accepted the nomination.[102]

Although the controversial caucus in Washington, DC, was technically a win for Madison, it was his strength within the state nominating contests that bolstered his legitimacy as the national choice for Democratic-Republicans. The incumbent president carried nominations across a diverse assortment of states, which belied the intraparty critiques of Madison. The strength of mainline Jeffersonians within the party was reflected by the additional caucus or convention nominations of Madison in Kentucky, Maryland, Massachusetts, New Hampshire, New Jersey, Ohio, Vermont, and Rhode Island.[103] The state nominations continued after the congressional caucus verdict. After renominating the president in Boston on June 10, Massachusetts Democratic-Republican legislators released a statement that was effusive with praise: "The undeviating adherence to the principles of the Constitution by JAMES MADISON, his inflexible integrity, and the able and impartial manner in which he has administered the Executive Government of the U. States, have increased the confidence of this meeting in this enlightened and virtuous Statesman."[104] The Democratic-Republican governor and legislators of Maryland convened in Annapolis on June 18 to unanimously nominate the Madison-Gerry ticket, expressing their "highest opinion of the integrity, patriotism and ability" of the two men.[105]

A Democratic-Republican state convention in Trenton, New Jersey, met on July 10 and "*Resolved*, unanimously, That this Convention approve heartily of the nomination" of the Madison-Gerry ticket. The convention sent Madison a letter framing their choice as a show of support for a wartime president and cheering him on to a "vigorous prosecution of the war until our wrongs are redressed and our rights respected" and praising the president for his "conduct, as well in your endeavors to preserve peace, as in your final recommendation of a resort to arms, meets with our most decided approbation."[106] In a reply to his New Jersey supporters, Madison praised their convention message for affirming "the character of Citizens, who know the value of the National rights at stake in the present contest; and who are willing to do justice to the sincere & persevering efforts which have been employed to obtain respect to them without a resort to arms." Then Madison laid out a standard defense of his administration's war policy.[107]

In Newport, Rhode Island, Democratic-Republican legislators and delegates convened on July 8 to unanimously nominate and "highly approve" of the Madison-Gerry ticket and "cordially recommend to the Citizens of this State, that they exert their influence, and make use of all honorable means, to effect the election of the above named gentlemen."[108] Late in the campaign cycle, Democratic-Republican legislators in Vermont met on October 9 in Montpelier to unanimously renominate the incumbent president. Framing their choice in the language of patriotism and wartime solidarity, the declaration affirmed that "in times of danger from abroad, it is our most important duty, to strengthen the government of our country with the confidence of the people." The Madison administration had earned another term because it "labored with unwearied fidelity to preserve us from the entangling alliances and destructive broils of Europe—who, by the most patient forbearance have evinced their love of peace, while consistent with safety and honor, and when peace had become dishonorable and dangerous, have with promptitude relied upon the patriotism of the people in an appeal to arms."[109]

On the one hand, Madison's domination of the state and congressional nominating caucuses revealed an impressive show of support from Democratic-Republican Party officeholders within the mainline ranks and the War Hawk faction. Alternatively, other factions remained restive, and with the nation about to carelessly embark on a second war with Britain, the real possibility of unknown disruptions to political equilibrium made Madison's reelection very uncertain. The imminent defection of the Clintonian faction serves as the best example of how normal domestic political alliances can be scrambled when a country goes to war. Now the Federalists had to make a difficult decision about forging a coalition with some of their old adversaries.

4
FEDERALISTS AND CLINTONIANS
A WARTIME ALLIANCE

Rumors were circulating. Influential Federalists from all over America descended upon New York City for a secret meeting in September. Word of the gathering soon got out, and speculation mounted as to what had been discussed. Opponents jumped at the chance to assert that something sinister was taking place. Federalist elites, they charged, were plotting an alliance with Clintonians. Perhaps they were cutting a deal to nominate Mayor Clinton, whereby he would promise to end the war within twenty-four hours. Other fear-mongering claims suggested that Federalists would be guaranteed seats in the Cabinet, move the national capital to Philadelphia or New York, and establish a hereditary senate in the national government. The "Grand Caucus," as the *Public Advertiser* called it, was somewhat of a new thing for Federalists, although they had held a similar and smaller nominating event four years earlier.[1]

The election cycle of 1812 was the best opportunity for Federalists to reverse a decade of national decline. As this chapter demonstrates, Federalists adapted their organizing tactics in response to the openings presented by the outbreak of a controversial war. The process they followed was often clumsy and lacking in coherence, but it revealed that Federalists had to depart from their traditional views about the role of political parties. As for the Clintonians, they lacked a strong national base, and in order for their anti-war message to gain credibility, they needed to form an alliance with their opponents across the partisan aisle.

The Federalists were born for the purpose of being a

governing coalition, not a political party. They frowned upon organizing outside of the context of administering state and federal institutions, but reluctantly embraced political and electoral activism when it became a necessity to survive. To campaign openly for an elected position also ran contrary to the Federalist notion that statesmen should not seek office, but rather, should serve only after being asked by citizens or elites. Federalists maintained an identity as the party of gentlemen, wisdom, good temperament, and responsible stewards of government. Claiming the Constitution as the product of their own work, Federalists believed they had the inherent right to govern during the document's tenuous early years of existence. Fisher Ames, a prominent party figure in Massachusetts, asserted that "the only chance of safety lies in the revival of the energy of the federalists, who alone will or can preserve liberty, property or Constitution," lest the United States descend into a "monarchical mobocracy" like revolutionary France.[2]

Federalists justified their collective existence on the basis of stopping what they believed to be the dangerous plans of the opposition party. In their view, Democratic-Republicans were a motley collection of the most untrustworthy elements of society, who would hazardously pervert the carefully designed model in the Constitution. Federalists sneered at their adversaries as rabble rousers who held an unrealistic expectation of democracy and failed to appreciate the need for a new nation to have a robust central government. Democratic-Republicans were all too willing, according to Federalists, to use the worst techniques of demagoguery to whip up the uneducated masses into an uncontrollable popular frenzy that would ultimately result in anarchy, followed by tyranny.[3]

It was common rhetoric for Federalists to denounce the opposition party as "Jacobins," resembling the French agitators who partook in the bloody Reign of Terror that took place soon after France's revolution. The Jacobins began as a populist democratic movement that grew increasingly authoritarian. As far as Federalists in the United States were concerned, this was the perfect analogy: the Democratic-Republicans represented a combination of ignorance about human nature and dishonest motives about democracy. Democratic-Republicans were also labeled as anti-Christian, or even atheist—a curious line of attack given the many Americans of various Protestant denominations who preferred the Jeffersonian party. In the heat of Thomas Jefferson's reelection campaign of 1804, the pro-Federalist *Connecticut Courant* stated: "The Jacobins of the country believe that children should grow up without any acquaintance with religious truths. This is all wrong. Children should, must, read the Scriptures. None but a Jacobin with a most fixed hatred to Christianity and its Author, will question the propriety of the mode, or the importance of the end."[4]

Many Federalists were openly disdainful of the brand of democracy favored by Democratic-Republicans. The Hamiltonian party asserted that what the Jeffersonian team wanted was not a filtered democracy, governed by enlightened gentlemen, who were chosen by responsible citizens. Rather, Federalists contended that their opponents only sought a popular rule rooted in the bottom elements of society; Americans lacking in any level of education, property, life achievements, or civic maturity. A democracy of that sort was illegitimate because it would not produce a true manifestation of the public will and the people's needs. "A constitution never was, nor ever will be, preserved by a democracy," said Kentucky Federalist politician Humphrey Marshall, "which counts its majority from the nether end of society; whence is necessarily embraced, the greatest mass of ignorance, and the least attachment to good order, or constitutional restraint."[5]

Now this governing party was on the outside looking in. Since the pivotal 1800 race, Federalists were firmly entrenched in the minority in presidential and congressional politics. As is typical for a party that suffers from a disastrous election defeat, Federalists underwent a process of significant soul-searching. The key questions for Federalists to resolve concerned their attitudes about democracy and their willingness to engage in sophisticated techniques of party-building, organizing, and communication. While the idea of reaching out to ordinary citizens may have struck some Federalists as offensive, others in their ranks appeared ready to embrace their own version of grassroots politics. As state suffrage requirements still generally limited the vote to economically elite white males, Federalists could be well positioned to adopt an upper-class brand of populist messaging that stressed competence, moderation, and steady administration of the government.

In his comprehensive account of the Federalists in their opposition role in the Jeffersonian era, historian David Hackett Fischer revealed that there was a generational difference in attitudes about party organizing. Older Federalists, like New York's John Jay, held more closely to the Founding-era view of parties as disreputable organizations; that they would encourage unsavory citizens to be involved in politics, resulting in public servants who were men of low character and competence. They stressed the need for limitations to democracy. Conversely, Federalists of the younger generation were hardly pure democrats, but they demonstrated more readiness to accept the reality and necessity of political party organizing. Not only were parties not going away after two vicious presidential campaigns in

1796 and 1800, but these organizations were now permeating every level of American civic life as the nineteenth century began. Although they lagged behind the Democratic-Republicans in almost every key category, Federalists built sophisticated state and local party organizations in numerous states throughout the decade of the 1800s. That included locations where Federalists were firmly established in the minority of political life, although their groups were commonly weaker in southern states.[6]

As Fischer demonstrates, Federalists in various states created a hierarchical party arrangement of committees at the town, city, district, and county levels. In large cities like New York and Boston, committees were organized down to the ward level. Younger Federalists were at the forefront of these more systematic approaches to building an opposition party. No two states were structured identically, and some states maintained more centralized organization than others. Federalist committees raised money, disseminated publications, and produced nominations for various offices, while on other occasions local and state conventions were used to choose candidates. New England Federalists tended to employ caucuses of their members in state legislatures for the nomination function.

By the time of the 1812 election, the party was also actively holding public meetings in most states for citizens to engage in spirited debate and deliberation. In early 1800, party-themed clubs, known as Washington Benevolent Societies, surfaced. Beginning in Alexandria, Virginia, and eventually spreading throughout the non-southern states, these fraternal-political organizations promoted the Federalist message and aimed to recruit ordinary citizens as members.[7] Federalists were now publishing newspapers all over the nation, even in states where they found themselves in the political wilderness, and often featuring vituperative, sarcastic, and colorful rhetoric. As their party base was more likely to be literate and educated, the newspaper was an especially useful organ for Federalists to communicate with like-minded citizens, win over potential converts, and hold Democratic-Republican policymakers and politicians accountable.

At the national level, Federalists never really took to the congressional nominating caucus as a vehicle for choosing presidential and vice presidential candidates. The party did not use a formal congressional caucus in 1796, though John Adams was clearly most Federalists' preferred choice for the top job. Early in May 1800 they quietly held more of a formal congressional caucus proceeding, which resulted in the nomination of President Adams and Gen. Charles Cotesworth Pinckney, although exactly who was at the top and bottom of the ticket was not specified. His rupture with

Adams now complete, Hamilton made his preference for Pinckney well known (and then did so again in the general election campaign), but it was assumed among American political observers that the incumbent president was nominated for another term.[8]

Now with their numbers in the House and Senate diminishing, and their national appeal eroding, Federalists ended their brief flirtation with the congressional caucus. While some states were organizing robust party infrastructures, the national Federalist establishment flagged ahead of the 1804 presidential election. In spite of some previous efforts, interstate communication and organization between Federalists failed to launch in any significant way.[9] Party leaders formed a consensus around General Pinckney for president and New York's Rufus King for the vice presidency. The doomed ticket faced Jefferson when he was at the apex of his political authority and command over his party.

In 1808, with an unpopular embargo ravaging the economy, Federalists now mounted a more organized and spirited campaign. The absence of a popular sitting president running for reelection also created opportunities to rebuild their declining party. Without a congressional caucus, some kind of centralizing nominating device would be needed. The clumsy alternative the Federalists devised was a national meeting of party elites, which was organized by loosely constituted interstate committees of correspondence. First, on June 2, Philadelphia lawyer and local Federalist power broker Charles Willing Hare communicated with Harrison Gray Otis of Massachusetts, who was a prominent state legislator and former congressman. Hare encouraged Otis to round up support in Massachusetts for a multistate meeting to nominate a national ticket for 1808. Next, Otis and other Massachusetts Federalist leaders connected with additional New England counterparts to begin planning a national gathering in New York, with a tentative date of August 1.[10]

Otis was sometimes labeled as a member of Massachusetts's controversial Essex Junto, a group of prominent Federalist politicians and influencers within that state. The extent of the Junto's actual power has been debated, but fairly or not, by the 1810s the consortium had earned a negative reputation for extremism, elitism, and hostility to democracy. Otis seems to have kept his distance from the Essex Junto, maintaining a respected standing within the Massachusetts political establishment.[11] Realistically, if any Federalist nominee were to be perceived as tied to the Essex Junto, this would surely complicate any efforts to reach out to disaffected Democratic-Republicans, who still valued democratic principles.

Meanwhile, a New York Federalist committee got word of the proposed party huddle and assumed the task of inviting their cohorts from Connecticut and New Jersey. Another party committee in Pennsylvania, based in Philadelphia, reached out to associates in Delaware and Maryland. Efforts to fetch delegations from southern states were mostly unsuccessful. Federalists in Washington, DC, and the Philadelphia committee spoke with party members in Georgia, North Carolina, Virginia, and South Carolina, but only the latter state actually sent a delegation to the New York meeting. Kentucky, Ohio, and Tennessee were fully ignored in the nomination phase. In those corners of the country the party organization was so small and feeble that the New York committee lamented that "we have no means of Communication" with allies in the three states.[12] These ad hoc interstate committees were really more like a series of letters and individual meetings between influential Federalists across state lines, as opposed to an institutionalized national infrastructure. Consistent with the norms of the party system in the early republic, neither Federalists nor Democratic-Republicans maintained a permanent centralized body. In addition, Federalists aiming to hastily put together this meeting had no real authority to compel any state to send a delegation. Communication with various states was also incomplete and spotty, given the limitations of travel in this era.

These logistical challenges contributed to the meeting being delayed three times. Though the exact date of the event has never been determined, Federalists met in the middle of August to nominate Pinckney and King again. The conclave, held at an undisclosed location in New York City, was intended to be a secret, but word eventually got out after the fact. Historian Samuel Morison called the event "the first national nominating convention." About thirty-five delegates were reportedly in attendance from Connecticut, Maryland, Massachusetts, New Hampshire, New York, Pennsylvania, South Carolina, and Vermont. The national party appears not to have made rules concerning state delegation sizes or the selection of representatives. While not all delegates have been identified, this was not a gathering of back-benchers. Many of the gentlemen at the meeting were influential Federalists in their respective states, although mostly from the ranks of the younger generation. In addition to Hare and Otis, participants included John Rutledge Jr. of South Carolina, a future military officer in the upcoming war with Britain, and Maryland lawyer and brash populist Robert Goodloe Harper, a rarity among his party. A former South Carolina politician, Harper would later serve as a general in the war. Another prominent Federalist was Vermont's Josiah Dunham, who would become a major organizer and influencer of that state's party. In addition to Otis, Massachusetts sent Christopher Gore, who served on the state party central committee and would be a future governor. Also in the Massachusetts delegation was James Lloyd, that state's newly selected US senator.[13]

Alliance with the Clintonians was not a new idea in 1812. There was a mutual antipathy with the embargo policy, and the weakening Federalist Party might be able to revitalize itself through a fusion with a dissatisfied faction of Democratic-Republicans. If a Federalist/Clintonian coalition could succeed in a presidential election, perhaps the long-term foundation could be laid for a robust party alternative to Jeffersonian orthodoxy. Going into the 1808 cycle, Federalists considered a merger with Vice President George Clinton, as doing so might secure most or all of New York's electoral votes and block Virginia from further domination of the presidency. In the end, the delegates resolved that it was the "Correct and dignified Policy to afford neither Aid nor Countenance, direct or indirect, to any of our political opponents, but, holding ourselves perfectly distinct to nominate Federal Characters for the offices of President and Vice President."[14] Hence, Federalists avoided the risky politics of an alliance with the Clintonians and nominated their 1804 ticket once again. In addition, the Democratic-Republicans' January 1808 congressional nominating caucus had already selected Clinton for another term in the vice presidency, which would have made a sudden Federalist fusion candidacy awkward.

The New York City meeting was still an innovation for American politics, and the Federalist Party was not prone to doing new and different things in the first place. Any national political meeting in the early nineteenth century would also encounter scheduling and logistical problems. The party stronghold of Delaware declined to send a delegation due to the opposition of powerful senator James A. Bayard, who exerted significant influence over that state's Federalist politics. The senator even apparently tried to talk other Federalist leaders out of the enterprise. Rhode Island's participation was precluded by its domestic political campaign season. New Jersey also abstained for unknown reasons, but its proximity to New York City makes it unlikely that difficulties with travel and communication can be blamed. Additionally, the near total absence of southern and western states makes it hard to call this event a genuinely national meeting. Instead, this assembly only reflected the party's lack of a nationwide appeal.[15]

Both parties practiced limited democracy within their ranks, while criticizing each other for diverting from foundational American principles. They both maintained an elite-based method for nominating presidential and vice presidential candidates. While Democratic-Republicans continued to use the congressional nominating caucus (though not without internal controversy), Federalists utilized an incomplete and haphazard system of selection by party bosses and politicians that was similarly closed to public observation or participation. Federalists were embracing more democratic methods of party organization at the state and local levels in the Jeffersonian era, but elitism still prevailed on the national stage.

THE CLINTONIAN OFFENSIVE OF 1812

With the Madison administration's drive to push the nation into war, the Clintonians' patience was at its end. In contrast to other states, the New York legislature had little party support for the president. DeWitt Clinton huddled in Albany with his supporters in the legislature on March 16, 1812, to feel out his political standing. Allegedly, Clintonians wanted to avoid alliance with the Federalists if they could choose a nominee that would command support from Pennsylvania and states in the West. A committee of nine men was selected to investigate this possibility. However, this optimistic scenario was a political nonstarter, given Madison's recent strong showing in the Pennsylvania nominating caucus, as well as the pro-war sentiments in the West and general lack of Clintonian influence in that region.[16] Madison's sweep of the congressional nominating caucus later in the spring only enhanced his political momentum.

DeWitt Clinton certainly had his adversaries in the fractious world of New York politics. Within his party, Clinton's critics were known as the Martling Men, named after a tavern in Manhattan where they used to congregate.[17] Madison also enjoyed a minority base of support in New York that was strong. The president still had not only Governor Tompkins in his corner but also a handful of congressmen in the state delegation. In addition, House Foreign Affairs Committee chair Peter Porter was a solid New York Madison ally and advocate for war with Britain.[18] There was even a failed Clintonian effort to bribe New York's Abraham Lansing, a state-level Democratic-Republican politician who had ties to Vice President Clinton. Representative Thomas Sammons asked Lansing to endorse DeWitt Clinton for the presidency in exchange for an appointment as quartermaster general (the supply officer for the army). Lansing refused, however, later telling Madison that he "should by every means support your Re-election regardless of Interested considerations."[19]

Abandoning the caucus in Washington, DC, some Clintonian congressmen journeyed to Albany to promote their man. Among them was Rep.

Pierre Van Cortlandt Jr., a member of one of New York's prominent political families and the son of Governor George Clinton's longtime lieutenant governor, Pierre Sr. Congressman Van Cortlandt carried with him a letter of endorsement for Clinton's candidacy from long-serving postmaster general Gideon Granger. A native of Connecticut, and appointed to the job in the first year of the Jefferson administration, Granger continued holding his office into the next presidency, but as an opponent of the war he was now firmly disillusioned with Madison. Now providing assistance to the Clintonians, Granger increasingly became an ally of the incoherent Invisible faction. Madison's popularity was overblown, Granger claimed, and at least Clinton would be a stronger commander in chief if war was inevitable.[20]

Following Governor Tompkins's prorogation amid allegations of bribery, the New York legislature completed its passage of a charter for the Bank of America on May 24. With that matter resolved for the time being, Clintonian Democratic-Republicans in the legislature took the initiative and called a caucus at the state capitol on May 28–29. Approximately ninety of the ninety-five party members appeared and unanimously voted to confer the presidential nomination upon DeWitt Clinton. A vice presidential running mate was not selected. The caucus chose a committee of seventeen men from each congressional district "to promote the election of the Candidate nominated at the Capitol."[21]

The New York caucus issued a proclamation denouncing the congressional nominating caucus as unconstitutional, asserting that this function should be the proper domain of states rather than the federal legislative branch. The character of DeWitt Clinton was celebrated as his leading attribute for the presidency: "From our knowledge of his public virtues, eminent talents, and inflexible principles, we are satisfied that his elevation to that station will greatly promote the peace, the prosperity, and the permanency of the union." In the New York nomination proclamation, no mention was made of the imminent war that was about to take place, nor was there even any statement about foreign policy whatsoever.[22]

In the early years of the republic, state pride remained an important part of American political culture. The fact that a New Yorker had never served as president continued to be a sore spot for some of their politicians. Speaking at the caucus on behalf of the Clinton nomination, state senator Ruggles Hubbard bemoaned Virginia's long domination of the office, and of the nation more generally. "That irregular assumption of power," Hubbard said, "in which she perseveres grows alarming and dangerous: not only because it is contrary to the nature of a confederacy, but because the continuation of power in the hands of a few individuals from Virginia hath used the whole state to consider itself as the head of the Union." Clinton, Hubbard noted, was the "fittest character" to be chief executive. Seeming to concede Clinton's ambiguousness on issues, Hubbard cited it as a virtue that his candidate was "committed on no particular system either in diplomacy or in administration."[23]

Upon being told of his nomination, Clinton accepted, noting "that he sensibly felt and duly appreciated so distinguished a proof of their confidence."[24] The New York *Columbian* cheered the news: "In the selection of a successor, they have fixed their choice upon a man of tried and approved patriotism, of a profound and liberal mind, of unimpeachable integrity, pre-eminent for his talents, and greatly distinguished for the energy and firmness of his character—a man whom Heaven has reared to fit the occasion of the times."[25]

The *National Intelligencer*, in contrast, reacted with a snarky dismissal of its rival newspaper's fawning approbation, stating, "We only thank God we have no man-worshippers among the friends of the real Republican Ticket."[26] The *Albany Register* celebrated Clinton's overwhelming mandate while overlooking Madison's similar domination of the caucuses in Virginia, Pennsylvania, and Congress. "So full," the newspaper gloated, "so strong and so clear a testimony of confidence in the virtues and ability of the scholar, the statesman, the patriot and the republican, recommended to the suffrages of the Presidential electors, has not been witnessed in any other state in the Union."[27]

Meanwhile, Federalists reacted to the news out of Albany with a wait-and-see attitude. The *New York Evening Post*, a newspaper founded by Alexander Hamilton, was all too happy to point out the hypocrisy of Clintonians for deriding Virginia's early state caucus. The *Post* ambivalently stated, "On the relative merits of James Madison and Dewitt Clinton let the question stand; and to the people we cheerfully leave the award, with the single remark, that the mere pronouncing these names in the same breath forces on our observation a contrast so marked that we will not at present trust our pen to describe it."[28] As war commenced in June, the Clintonian offensive provided Federalists with an opportunity to rebuild and reshape their national coalition. Or the party of Hamilton could go it alone with its own candidate in a three-way race.

As a party faction, Clintonians represented a formidable force, but they controlled no levers of national power. That status was affirmed even more by Vice President Clinton's recent death. Their regional base was sparse outside of New York and almost nonexistent outside of the Middle Atlantic states. The Clinton wing needed to build a coalition with other actors that could make a national majority possible. Having been shut out in the state and national caucuses, Clintonians made the rational calculation to look outside of their party to advance their signature issues. The stakes were more urgent now, as compared to 1808, with the country about to embark upon a potentially disastrous war with Britain that could devastate the northern shipping and commercial interests that Clintonians championed. Federalists held a more skeptical view of democracy than the Clintonians, but they both deplored the war and promoted industrialization. War, however, disrupts equilibrium in ways that can bring disparate political factions together.

In addition to their critique of the war, the Clintonians sought to make character and process issues major parts of their campaign narrative. Before Federalists met to consider their options, a New York Committee of Correspondence working on Clinton's behalf published a manifesto promoting its candidate. Formal national party platforms were still at least two decades away, but the document articulated fundamental principles and grievances. Only one man on the committee was a member of the state legislature that picked the nominee, while the other gentlemen were politicians allied with the Clintonians. The document, dated August 17, relayed the familiar criticisms of Virginia's domination of the presidency, while pivoting to New York's rightful claim for a turn to hold the office. Predictably, the congressional nominating caucus was dismissed as illegitimate. The character and leadership qualities of the nominee were duly noted. The committee's statement framed the Clinton candidacy around an argument that emphasized an opposition to the war based on pragmatism, denounced the process of choosing a nominee, and condemned the Madison administration's mismanagement of events.[29]

The Clintonians' opposition to a possible Virginia presidential dynasty was part of a broader critique that promoted an integrated economy, harmony between the states, and a responsible national defense. The New York nomination was based on the principle that no state should enjoy perpetual control of the constitution's highest office. Such an arrangement undermined national unity among the states and aroused jealousies between them. Because of Virginia's presidential supremacy, "the agriculture and commercial states are beginning to be arrayed against each other, and to feel as if they were not connected by a common bond of interest." New York, in comparison, was the ideal state for the next president because it was in the Middle Atlantic region, with vital commercial and agricultural sectors of the entire economy. There was even a hint of criticism directed toward the drafters of the Constitution because they failed to provide for a regular rotation of the presidency between the states, based on their population.

Similarly, the caucus in Congress was brushed aside as an illegitimate cabal of Washington, DC, insiders. As the Constitution said nothing about the pre-selection of presidential candidates, the New York Clintonians asserted that such a process should rightfully belong to the people's democratically elected state legislatures. "The nomination of a candidate for the presidency of the United States, by an association of members of Congress, convened at the seat of government, is hostile to the spirit of the federal constitution, dangerous to the rights of the people, and to the freedom of election," their statement said. Members of Congress could and should only intervene under their constitutionally prescribed role of certifying electoral votes or, as in 1801, choosing a president in the event of a deadlocked Electoral College.

Consistent with a pragmatic, nonideological critique of the war with Britain, the Clintonians chided the Madison administration for failing to take appropriate military measures to prepare the United States for possible hostilities. "The probability of its taking place could not but have been anticipated; the resources it would require should have been maturely considered, and the means of providing them digested and arranged; the preparations to wage it with effect ought to have been seasonably made." In reading their platform in support of the nominee, one might be fooled into thinking it represented a critique from Democratic-Republican War Hawks. The manifesto pointed to a specific series of poor decisions and oversights that brought the United States into an economically damaging war that it was unlikely to win. Madison was attacked for leaving New York and the nation vulnerable by neglecting to strengthen the navy. In addition, the Clintonians argued, the commander in chief should have taken proactive steps to invade Canada and launch a full offensive in Florida. Why, they asked, was trade with Spain and Portugal allowed to continue? Britain would only be able to take advantage of this opening to supply its war machine; this omission was the equivalent of giving *"aid and comfort to our enemy."*

The Clintonians thanked Madison for his life in public service, but in their view the incumbent just didn't measure up to the greatness of Washington and Jefferson, who were far more deserving of two terms in office.

To reelect the president should not be a routine affirmation in American constitutional government, lest "we shall imperceptibly slide into an election for life, and perhaps towards an hereditary succession." Whatever political chaos brought the nation into this war, Madison must now face accountability for the emerging consequences. A war takes place on the commander in chief's watch, and he must bear the ultimate political responsibility; not the Cabinet secretaries, not the military commanders, and not even the European belligerents. "Either he directed the necessary preparations to be made," the platform said, "or he did not. If he directed them, he is responsible for continuing incapable men in office; if he did not, the blame attaches personally on himself." Such claims are not controversial today, but this was the first time the United States embarked upon a constitutionally declared war, and the Clintonians pledged to thrust the issue into the forefront of national debate in the coming months.

Pragmatists will also be inclined to sidestep ideological anti-war arguments in favor of budgetary critiques. If critics can make the case that war is too expensive, perhaps they can convince uncommitted citizens that the financial sacrifice will be harmful to the nation. Additionally, a country demonstrates its resolve and seriousness in confronting a foreign foe by showing that it is economically ready to do so. Before pivoting to the attributes of Clinton, the statement criticized the Madison administration for having "insulted the patriotism of the people" by failing to make appropriate fiscal preparations for armed conflict. Mounting debts and declining American credit would actually be a national security risk when tangling with the world's foremost military power.

The statement closed by making the pragmatic case for Clinton as the competent leader America needed. The candidate, his supporters claimed, was a man without dangerous ideological fixations, or prejudices toward particular European countries. The nominee would rescue the nation from "an inefficient administration, and of an inadequately conducted war." Far from an argument for pacifism, the statement praised his "vigor in war" and responsible foreign policy while drawing comparisons with his recently departed uncle. Finally, as a New Yorker, Clinton would be well positioned to restore the commercial prosperity of the United States, backed by a strong navy.

Mainline Democratic-Republicans, in contrast, rebuked the Clintonians for their obsession with trifling political matters in the middle of a war. Governor William Plumer of New Hampshire insinuated that the rebels in his party were unpatriotic. "Read the address of the New York Committee in favor of Clinton," the governor said. "In a state of war, it is an improper time to talk about Virginia influence, or, indeed, the influence of any other state. Our united energies should be directed against the common enemy of our country."[30] Madison supporters were already setting up to attack the Clintonians as shameless opportunists.

THE FEDERALIST DECISION

Lacking a consensus nominee of their own, Federalists had a choice to make. They could select an established figure, a rising star, or a man outside their party apparatus. Even though they had spent a decade exiled from the executive branch, there remained many elder statesmen to choose from. Pinckney was a decisive two-time losing candidate, no longer viable, and had in fact indicated that he would not accept a third nomination.[31] John Jay was a highly qualified New Yorker, with a distinguished résumé of experience that included tours as governor, Supreme Court chief justice, and various diplomatic posts. Although he did not attend the Philadelphia Convention of 1787, Jay had previously served in the Continental Congress, and had collaborated with Madison and Hamilton to vigorously defend the new Constitution in five of *The Federalist Papers*. A believer in a strong national union as a bulwark against foreign mischief, Jay was of an older generation of Federalists, politically washed up, and was ineffectively positioned to connect with younger party adherents.[32]

Some within their ranks mused about current Supreme Court chief justice John Marshall of Virginia. Arguably, he was now the most powerful Federalist in Washington, DC, following the party's three national electoral defeats and its steady erosion in Congress and state governments. From his position on the Court, he had already established himself as a stern defender of the federal government's constitutional supremacy over the states and localities. After serving a short tenure under John Adams as secretary of state, Marshall was elevated to the top spot on the Court as one of the outgoing president's last-minute judicial appointments. Although he was a Federalist, Marshall was not a Hamiltonian who was willing to support expansive interpretations of presidential discretion. In the 1804 case of *Little v. Barreme*, for example, the chief justice slapped down Adams for issuing orders to the navy that were not consistent with existing laws.[33] Marshall was also a war opponent and so could be appealing to Clintonians who favored a stronger central government for the promotion of commerce, even though he was a Virginian who would extend that state's domination over the presidency. Perhaps, some Federalists reasoned, Marshall could even take Virginia's electoral votes from Madison, and capture North Carolina.[34] The movement to draft the chief justice, however, did not produce a consensus, and it never evolved much beyond speculation and chatter among a few Federalist elites.

The notion of a current or former Supreme Court justice as a presidential candidate was apparently a respectable idea within the party, given its members' reverence for a strong and independent judiciary, staffed by men of character and detached from silly political jealousies. Another name that popped up among some leaders was Bushrod Washington, nephew of the first president and a fellow Virginian who served with Marshall on the Court as an associate justice. Washington's judicial voting record was almost identical to that of the chief justice. In addition, New York's Rufus King, now an influential Federalist at the national level, still had a base of supporters. Neither gentleman, however, was interested in being nominated for the presidency or the second job, though King would be very active in the selection process.[35]

For a party that had been on the outside looking in for many years, a fully deliberative meeting would present an opportunity to assess its future direction, choose new leaders, and fundamentally redefine what it could offer the American people. For the 1812 election cycle, the party refined its model from four years prior, as operatives in Philadelphia coordinated the gathering. Smaller meetings, some of which were quite informal, also preceded the culminating national event. Planning appears to have begun shortly after the war commenced, when a small group of Connecticut and Massachusetts Federalist politicians met at Saratoga Springs, New York. In an apparently impromptu conversation "into the neighboring woods," Boston lawyer and state legislator William Sullivan recounted that the men discussed aligning with DeWitt Clinton to defeat Madison's reelection. Together they agreed to help facilitate a national meeting in New York City in September with "as many states . . . as could be induced to send delegates."[36]

In an environment of discouraging battlefield developments for the United States, the national conclave of Federalist leaders met at Kent's Tavern on Broad Street in New York City on September 15–17. The assembly was late in the election cycle, but this time it consisted of about sixty to seventy delegates from eleven states. All participating states from 1808 sent delegations, as well as Delaware, New Jersey, and Rhode Island. North Carolina and Virginia sent no delegates but submitted letters endorsing the proceedings. Generally, state party committees chose delegates. There was some semblance of proportionality for state population this time, as larger states sent more delegates than their smaller counterparts. While a strong argument could be made that the 1812 meeting was more like a truly national convention, western and southern states remained absent, save for South Carolina. Once again, the proceedings were generally secretive, though some participants kept notes and correspondence that would later become public.[37]

Chairing this event was Elias Boudinot of New Jersey, whose credentials as a senior statesman were impeccable. A successful lawyer and devout Christian, his past tours of government service included the state Assembly and the old Articles of Confederation Congress, where he served for one year as president. That position carried little power beyond its role as a presiding officer, thereby familiarizing him with the task of moderating contentious debates between sometimes loquacious and egotistical politicians. During the American Revolution, he was appointed the Continental Army's commissary general of prisoners, where he held the rank of colonel. Boudinot continued serving in Congress under the new Constitution for six more years, followed by a decade as the director of the United States Mint. Like many venerable Federalists, he deplored political parties and believed in limitations on democracy, lest mob rule take over.[38]

Before the meeting began, a consensus appeared to exist among attendees that a true Federalist was unelectable. The party had no national leader or figurehead, and it was unclear who the rising stars were within its ranks. With the nation now engaged in a controversial war, Federalists had the opportunity to compensate for their unreliable national appeal by assuming the mantle of the peace party. As wars hold the potential to temporarily or even permanently alter partisan loyalties, this course of action could reverse a decade of decline. A coalition with John Randolph's small band of anti-war Old Republicans was a nonstarter, for Clinton was considered to be a man of suspect character by this group. Nor was it realistic to expect the party of Hamilton to make common cause with a political wing that saw something sinister in almost every action of the federal government. In addition, the unofficial organ of Old Republicans, the *Spirit of '76*, made no endorsement in the 1812 campaign.[39] Randolph was of limited value anyway, as he was now representing a faction within a faction, given that the war divided the already weakening Old Republicans.

As the nation moved into a war footing, Federalists began discussing an alliance with Clintonian Democratic-Republicans, with whom they shared a nationalistic ideology and an anti-war stance. However, this merger did not command universal support from the Hamiltonian party. Within the Federalist ranks, there remained some distrust of the former Jefferson allies, including Clinton. Furthermore, what about after the war? Could Federalists expect to rebuild in New York, and at a national level, with the Clintonians under their tent? Beginning on August 3, a three-day meeting took place between Clinton and a small group of New York's Federalist elites at Morrisania, which was the family estate of Gouverneur Morris, located in what is now the Bronx.

Like so many of the Federalist elder statesmen, Gouverneur Morris had his roots in the episodes of the American Revolution and the Founding era. Born into a prominent New York family that encompassed some who were loyalists to the British crown, he moved to Philadelphia as a promising young lawyer, politician, and businessman. Morris was a witty man, with experience that included a noteworthy role as a Pennsylvania delegate to the Constitutional Convention, and short tours in the US Senate and as minister to France. At the proceedings in Philadelphia in 1787, Morris distinguished himself as a man ahead of his time on the matter of slavery. Madison's detailed notes recorded Morris as stating that the institution was "nefarious" and "the curse of heaven on the States where it prevailed." Morris then called out the inconsistency and moral hypocrisy of treating slaves as property while counting them for the purposes of legislative representation, but affording them zero political rights. "Are they men? Then make them Citizens and let them vote. Are they property? Why then is no other property included? The Houses in this city [Philadelphia] are worth more than all the wretched slaves which cover the rice swamps of South Carolina."[40]

After New York's Democratic-Republican legislature declined to reelect him to the US Senate in early 1803, Morris never again held federal political office. He remained, however, an influential figure in New York's Federalist Party and was a major booster of the Erie Canal project. Now Morris, John Jay, and other Federalist power brokers discussed anti-war collaboration into a so-called Peace Party. They reviewed plans for an upcoming national "Peace meeting" in a few weeks, and chatted about the current state of political affairs. Clinton surmised that such an alliance could deliver New York, Pennsylvania, and even Massachusetts, in spite of Gerry's vice presidential selection. Rufus King, however, was skeptical of making a coalition with the Clintonians. Although he agreed to take this meeting with his colleagues, King could not be convinced that Clinton was a reliable ally, and he worried that the party would have to sell out its principles.[41]

As they moved toward considering an anti-war alliance with the Clintonians, New York Federalists met on August 18 in the city at Washington Hall, which was a common site for party deliberations. The assembly approved a set of public declarations, asserting that war was "unwise," due to the shabby position of the American armed forces and the weak financial situation of the United States. Even if unintended, making war on Britain was also likely to subordinate America to the French, "under the name and form of an alliance." In addition, the war would be injurious to economically diverse states like New York, which was compounded by the Madison administration's careless preparation for military action. Avoiding moralistic arguments in opposition, the New York Federalists reviewed the evidence, assessed the lack of American planning, and declared: "That a calm review of the conduct which has been pursued, and which is so utterly irreconcilable to the maxims of Common Prudence; so little commended by any facts which have been exhibited to public view, and so fatal to the dearest interests of this country, leaves no room to doubt of the alarming consequences to which it leads."

Furthermore, they mocked the notion that because the United States was now officially at war, somehow all criticism of the president's foreign policy must cease. David B. Ogden, a prominent lawyer, denounced "the danger, falsity & absurdity of this doctrine of passive obedience & non-resistance." Federalists in New York counties were encouraged to organize similar peace meetings and select representatives. Still, the Clintonian fusion was hardly a done deal, for there was no explicit language concerning Clinton or his faction in the resolutions, even as the New York Federalists urged citizens "to banish party feelings, to unite."[42]

New York's Federalist peace movement was just one example of a national party rallying cry that was replicated in other states—and it was not the first. Counterparts in New Jersey convened a statewide peace convention of their own on July 4 in Trenton. Present at the meeting were Federalist heavyweights that included Aaron Ogden, who was a future contender for selection as governor if his party should ever capture the legislature. Also in attendance was Richard Stockton Jr., son of a signer of the Declaration of Independence, and himself a former senator, US Attorney, and three-time candidate for governor. The convention's statement denounced any possible alliance with France and called for "the settlement of any differences with Great-Britain, on honorable terms, by *Negociation*." No mention was made of any Clintonian partnership, but the convention proclamation looked forward to the upcoming election as an opportunity "which may be of importance to the Peace."⁴³ Resolutions from Federalists in New Jersey's Somerset and Middlesex counties articulated ideological and economic arguments, lamenting the "destruction of our commerce and agriculture" and decrying the war "as pernicious to our morals and national character." A local gathering in Trenton bemoaned the higher taxes that war would surely bring, along with the great expense of military mobilization, "with all the attendant mischiefs to the morals and safety of the country."⁴⁴ Similar peace meetings were held in Pennsylvania and Massachusetts.⁴⁵

In Washington, DC, Federalists in Congress asserted their peace principles in a letter released in late June, just after hostilities commenced. Threading the needle gently between appeals to morality and practicality, they argued their case on several fronts. They fought on process issues, denouncing the secrecy of the congressional debate and consideration of the war resolution. They also took a swipe at the administration for deceptiveness in the Henry papers' affair. Whatever maritime offenses the British committed could be resolved by diplomacy, and simply did not rise to the level of acts of war. Additionally, Federalists warned that the United States was still a young nation, with "a form of government, in no small degree experimental." The country was not yet ready to tangle with the titans of Europe in frivolous wars, for that would endanger national security, especially with Americans so divided on the matter.⁴⁶

Moreover, the United States was militarily and financially unprepared to commit to a new Anglo-American war, which would only play into the hands of France. Federalists favored a strong national defense and held little regard for pacifist approaches to foreign policy, but to march headlong into war with Britain on the basis of perceived insults to American honor was simply reckless in their view. What the War Hawks called honor, the Federalists called bloodlust and ego, just to fulfill "a selfish vanity, or to satiate some unhallowed rage." Furthermore, they asked, what about the insults to American honor that resulted from French outrages at sea? The thrust of the Federalist congressional argument revolved around the practicality of a foolhardy American military campaign against the world's preeminent power, which the party deemed as neither "required by any moral duty, or any political expediency." Launching an unnecessary, long-shot war was itself immoral.⁴⁷

Even though he declined to be nominated for any national office, Rufus King played a vocal dissenting role in the national New York City meeting in September. A lawyer and a native of Massachusetts who later relocated to New York, King argued for a robust central government at the Constitutional Convention. A gifted orator, King was a latecomer to the nationalist cause and an opponent of slavery. At the age of fifty-seven, and with an impressive résumé of accomplishments during the formative years of the United States, King now found himself playing the role of an elder statesman for the Federalists. All healthy party organizations need such figures to provide sound judgment, cool temperament, and the wisdom that they can bring to political dilemmas, given their long record of achievement and experience with setbacks. King, however, was clearly not pleased with the direction his party was taking. While he was open to working with the Clintonians on issues of mutual agreement, King was critical of elevating the leader of a dissident Democratic-Republican faction to head the Federalist ticket. Arguing against an alliance with Clinton, King compared the former to another ambitious New York political schemer: Aaron Burr. King preferred a bona fide Federalist, stating, "I would have nominated a candidate, a respectable federalist from any quarter . . . for the purpose of keeping the federal body as entire in numbers and as unbroken in principle as possible."[48]

King was fatalistic, and he did not believe that Clinton could win, noting that "it was questionable whether any considerable portion of the Repubs. would follow him." Additionally, King held doubts that Clinton would even promote better policies than Madison. A genuine Federalist might still not win, King conceded, but a second Madison term would be survivable. Perhaps, King asserted, another four years with the incumbent would create the groundwork for a real Federalist resurgence with popular support, given the failing trajectory of the current administration's foreign policy.[49] Speaking at the national September meeting, King "pronounced the most impassioned invective against Clinton," denouncing the soon-to-be nominee as fickle and overly ambitious, "and was so excited during his address, that his knees trembled under him."[50]

The outcome of these proceedings was actually somewhat ambiguous, beyond a consensus to rally behind some kind of an electoral fusion ticket. Early on, a motion proposed by Robert Goodloe Harper was approved that deemed it "impracticable" to nominate an authentic Federalist candidate for the presidency. A second measure was agreed upon, "that it should be recommended to the Federalists to co-operate in the election of a President, who would be likely to pursue a different course of administration from that of Mr. Madison," with the understanding that this man would likely come from the ranks of renegade Democratic-Republicans. Lastly, the delegates resolved to create a five-man committee from the party in

Pennsylvania—which was clearly going to be *the* pivotal state in 1812—"to ascertain the result of the elections for Electors, and the Candidates whom they wd. be inclined to support, and to communicate the same as expeditiously as practicable to the Electors of the several States."[51] Like in 1808, Pennsylvania would again be selecting electors by way of a popular vote. At the very least, the Federalist high command could claim in some degree to be reaching out to operatives who were connected with rank-and-file voters in the state representing the most valuable electoral prize of 1812.

On the third day, Harrison Gray Otis made a vigorous defense of a Federalist/Clintonian alliance, delivering a stirring speech that appeared to persuade the vast majority of participants. After three days of lengthy debate, King and other dissenters were outnumbered by Federalists eager to build common cause with the Clintonians, defeat Madison, end the war, and promote similar commercial economic policy. Differences on other issues could be papered over so long as the United States was engaged in hostilities with Britain on American soil. The task of long-term party-building could wait until after the election and the conclusion of the war. Positive enthusiasm for Clinton, however, was not in abundance at the Federalist meeting. When the assemblage settled on a lukewarm and less than final consensus behind Clinton as their likely presidential nominee, it "was adopted with reluctance by some who were present," according to William Sullivan. "They could not overcome the repugnance which they felt," he continued, and cited Clinton's apparent weakness in New York as another matter of concern, for "there were others who feared that he had not strength and popularity enough in his own state to be successful."[52] Additionally, no official platform or statement of policy commitments was adopted, nor was there any formal public proclamation coming out of the meeting, thereby reflecting the event's ambiguity, secrecy, and lack of affirmative fervor for Clinton.

Also noting the mediocre energy for the nominee was lawyer Peter Augustus Jay—son of the Founding Father—who was active in New York state Federalist politics. In a letter to his father, the younger Jay called it "very doubtful" that Clinton would prevail, and expressed a fear that a loss would prolong the party's national decline. According to Peter Jay, who attended the deliberations, New England and southern New York delegates were initially most eager to forge an alliance with the Clintonians. The vast majority of other participants, in contrast, "consented to it very reluctantly." Additionally, Jay described the resolution supporting the nominee as "cunning" and "meant to recommend Mr. Clinton without saying so," over concerns that an overt Federalist endorsement would damage the candidate's prospects in Pennsylvania.[53]

Despite the organizers' intentions, word of the clandestine meeting circulated in the newspapers anyway, including the rival organs. In a short write-up of the gathering, the Jeffersonian *Boston Patriot* sarcastically labeled the group as "puissant patriots."[54] The *National Intelligencer* was also eager to reveal gossip from the opposition, and perhaps stir up just a little bit of acrimony within their ranks. Accusations were made that the Federalists collaborated with Clinton and his supporters, as if to insinuate this meant the anti-Madison coalition somehow lacked sincerity and conviction. Clinton, the paper said, had permanently severed ties with his party, and made the amusing claim that "this fact can be established in a court of law if necessary." Several weeks later, with balloting in the states already underway, the *National Intelligencer* doubled down, asserting that Clinton made a promise to end the war within twenty-four hours if elected. The paper reprinted a pamphlet inviting Morris to swear under oath that he played no role in forging an alliance with the Clintonians.[55] By now, the advocates for Madison had firmly established their general election narrative about Clinton and his supporters: the opposition coalition was dishonest, unreliable, and incoherent, which served as evidence that their nominee could not be trusted with a wartime presidency.

For his part, Morris disavowed the existence of a sophisticated Federalist/Clintonian fusion, and denied cooperating with the nominee. While he admitted attending the September national meeting, Morris claimed not to have met with Clinton anytime recently. "I have never been in company with, nor even seen, Mr. Clinton," he said in a written refutation to the *New York Evening Post*.[56] Similarly, Clinton's allies pushed back on the charges that their man was a turncoat, and affirmed in a statement that "his political sentiments are decidedly Republican." This proclamation, however, was silent on the matter of the nominee's war policy, thereby foreshadowing what would become a bigger problem in the campaign.[57]

Still, neither gentleman was being particularly honest about their communications. Clinton not only participated in the early August meeting at Morrisania but also conversed there with Morris on May 3, where the two men spoke about New York politics, the imminent war, and the upcoming presidential election. In his diary entry for that date, Morris struck a generally cynical tone. Clinton told his fellow New Yorker that the United States should sit down at the table and hammer out a peace treaty with Britain before hostilities might commence. Morris replied that such a course of action now seemed politically impossible, given the inevitability of war and nationalistic fervor sweeping the country. Achieving a peaceful settlement with Britain would result in "a speedy Ejection of him and his Friends from Power and a Return to the same base and dishonorable Course in which we are now engaged." Morris also lamented "that in the degenerate State to which Democracy never fails to reduce a Nation it is almost impossible for a good Man to govern even could he get into Power or for a bad Man to govern well." Furthermore, he doubted that a hypothetical President Clinton could choose "efficient Men" in his party to rectify the foreign policy crisis. Nor would it be practicable for him to rely on the opposition party for support, Morris said, lest Clinton become beholden to the forces that put him in office. In Morris's view, the excesses of Jeffersonian democracy, with all of its populist demagoguery and substandard public servants, had brought America to the brink of a foolish war with the world's mightiest power. In addition, Morris shared his views with Clinton on the matter of national unity. Still an opponent of slavery, Morris indicated his support for repealing the Constitution's three-fifths compromise, and if the southern states would not agree to that, then perhaps the Union would just have to break up.[58]

The Federalist strategy was apparently to disavow any overt collaboration with Clinton and his allies. Harrison Gray Otis publicly denied working with him to procure the nomination, as did Robert Goodloe Harper. In a long letter to Baltimore's *Federal Republican*, the newly transplanted Marylander argued that even though the Federalist meeting did not explicitly choose Clinton as their candidate, the renegade New Yorker's candidacy was the best means of ending a misguided war. Furthermore, if hostilities should have to continue while Clinton was commander in chief, at least he would act "with far more ability, and therefore with far more honor, and less injury to the country, than could be expected from the present administration." In addition, Harper argued, because the candidate was from a northern manufacturing state, he surely understood the economic consequences this war would bring. Rather than behaving as a pacifist ideologue, Clinton would responsibly end the fighting "on reasonable and honorable terms," at the right opportunity.[59]

The qualified and unofficial Federalist endorsement of a Clintonian Democratic-Republican on the grounds of anti-war pragmatism could have provided a chance for a major reorganization of the opposition to the Jeffersonian governing party. Under the most optimistic scenario, a full revitalization of robust two-party competition might have emerged and endured for years to come. Instead, there was lukewarm and contradictory messaging from Federalists, and the nominee himself. The case against Madison and the war was buried in a morass of confusion. In election campaigns, an approach like this does not communicate a signal of resounding confidence and support. Voters and other political actors will notice.

In contemporary presidential campaigns, candidates sometimes receive a burst of political momentum after they are formally nominated. Party factions will lay aside their internal squabbles in the interest of unity and defeating a common foe, as a general election narrative crystalizes. For Federalists and Clintonians in 1812, however, these phenomena failed to fully materialize. In a nascent party system that had yet to establish many norms, the secretive and ambiguous process by which Federalists made Clinton their nominee revealed the importance of openness in political meetings where major decisions will be made. Unsurprisingly, secret conventions and private conferences among powerful men will generate inaccurate information, conspiracy theories, gossip, and accusations that shadowy elites are cutting deals for their own benefit. These criticisms persist to the present day in presidential nominating politics, which is why transparency remains critical in this phase of an election campaign, if the party is to be successful.

Nor were all Federalists willing to accept a Clinton nomination. Madison's home state was never a realistic prospect for the opposition's fusion ticket, but its large size and influential position made it impossible to ignore disruptive developments there. Virginia did have an outspoken and functioning Federalist infrastructure, but its leading men were not ready to embrace an alliance with the Clintonians. After refusing to send a group to the national meeting, state party leaders sent eighteen county delegates to a gathering of their own in Staunton on September 21. Proclaiming "Peace, Union and Commerce, and No Foreign Alliance," their choice was Rufus King, despite his lack of interest in being nominated for national office in 1812.[60]

In a letter to the *Virginia Patriot*, an anonymous attendee of the convention was dismissive of Clinton, "whose chief virtue it permits us to understand, is derived from his birth." In addition, this delegate took offense at the Clintonians' inconsistent commitment to the cause of peace. He chided them for attacking Madison's insufficient military preparation in the invasion of Florida, and for criticizing the president's failure to plan for war in British Canada. Furthermore, the Clintonians were too open to restricting trade, even with nonhostile European nations, a course of action that was strategically nonsensical and economically disastrous—all while they let France off the hook for its behaviors. Ultimately, the Clintonians were still Jeffersonian Democratic-Republicans, and this statement revealed the Virginia Federalists' distrust of anybody who carried the ancestral banner of their enemy. The dissident wing from New York "extols very highly, the administration of Mr. Jefferson, in which the whole of our present calamities had their origin; while it finds no *just* ground to censure Mr. Madison, except that he is a Virginian."[61] Apparently the Clinton nomination was suspicious because it was all about New York state pride, even though these Federalists picked Rufus King.

Bizarrely, the convention's public report used up no ink to promote its own candidate, nor to denounce Clinton. Instead, it was merely an anti-war manifesto that repeated logical Federalist arguments attacking the Madison administration's string of careless foreign policy choices. Furthermore, this clash with Britain would only strengthen France. Their statement asked, "Why have we challenged for battle a nation most capable of injuring us at present, and whose destruction, could we accomplish it, would be but the prelude of our own subjection to her rapacious and insidious enemy?"[62]

For the vice presidency, their choice was William R. Davie of North Carolina, who held experience that would have been considered ideal if this was a serious candidacy. More of an old-fashioned Federalist, he frowned upon populist party organizing tactics. A British-born Princeton graduate, lawyer, and army officer in the war for independence, Davie went on to serve for over a decade as a state legislator, with a short tenure as governor. In the North Carolina General Assembly, his crowning achievement was to make possible the creation of the state's first public university. In addition, he had been a Constitutional Convention delegate and was one of President Adams's peace commissioners who helped to stave off war with France in 1800. Ironically, Davie also resented the outsized influence of Virginia over the nation, but this did not stop that state's Federalists from nominating him.[63]

Many of the Virginians appeared to have preferred John Marshall, who was also uninterested. Still, in following their course of action, there may have been a hope that presidential electors would act as independent agents and reject both major candidates, "in the enjoyment of that liberty of choice, for the exercise of which, the constitution seems to have created it."[64] This is a hard scenario to imagine, however, given Madison's strong position in his home state, and the failure of the King-Davie ticket to gain traction elsewhere. If it is to be deemed credible by voters and other key political actors, a fusion candidacy presents significant challenges revolving around crafting a unified message and strategy. Failing to secure a prominent state like Virginia only further confirmed the appearance of incoherence among the anti-Madison and anti-war forces.

STUMBLING TOWARD A FUSION: THE VICE PRESIDENTIAL SLOT

In spite of Madison's vulnerabilities, by early autumn Clinton's shortcomings at rallying the Federalists were all too clear. A fusion ticket requires the alliance to balance what is already an inherently risky enterprise. A renegade presidential candidate from a dissident wing of his party is likely to be the focus of considerable distrust from many precincts within the political universe, especially among his coalition partners. In an effort to smooth over tensions with loyal Federalists, Clinton was willing to yield to the party in the selection of a vice presidential running mate. National Federalists deferred that choice to their cohorts in the states, resulting in a stumbling process and an unhelpful delay soon before the general election balloting was to begin.

In fact, not all Federalists were insistent upon a purist for the second slot. Among the party's North Carolinians, conversations were held about installing a running mate from their state. As was common in presidential politics of the early republic and well into the nineteenth century, a North-South coupling was preferable, if not expected, in a nation where sectional prejudice was still very potent. John Steele, a former congressman, opposed pairing the presidential nominee with a full-blooded Federalist and argued in favor of two possible names, both of whom were strange picks that would have only further muddled the message of the Clinton campaign. Steele was known for his moderation and was now serving on the commission that sought to resolve the boundaries between southern states, but his electoral strategizing here was bizarre. He counseled delay in the choosing of a running mate, hoping that a second Democratic-Republican on the ticket would favorably tip North Carolina and Pennsylvania.[65]

The first of Steele's suggestions was Representative Nathaniel Macon, a nominal ally of John Randolph and the Old Republicans, who had voted for the declaration of war but also had a mixed roll call record in the House. Macon opposed several bills to fully fund and expand the wartime military, and he voted against the higher taxes that were needed to pay for everything. Nevertheless, Macon remained a Madison supporter, and this proposed candidacy never got off the ground.[66] To install as a Federalist running mate a Democratic-Republican congressman who was a partial supporter of the Old Republican wing, but then gradually moved in the direction of the War Hawks, can only be described as incomprehensible.

The other name Steele offered up was Governor William Hawkins, which was an even more inexplicable plan given that this pro-war Democratic-Republican was fully behind the Madison administration.[67] Accordingly, this idea also went nowhere. Other pro-Clinton operatives out of New York proposed David Stone, a former North Carolina governor and US senator. He too, however, was a Democratic-Republican, although he was a war critic and a former Federalist. In a letter to the president, Representative William Blackledge of North Carolina was dismissive of a potential Stone vice presidential candidacy, telling Madison that "the knowledge which we have however of Stones character I think will justify the Conclusion that he will treat the overture with the disdain it merits."[68] Indeed, like the other North Carolina vice presidential suggestions, this proposition was a nonstarter.

A partial Federalist victory here once seemed at least conceivable, given the state's model of split electoral votes and the fact that Madison only carried its popular vote in 1808 by about 7.5 percent. Late in 1811, however, a pro-Madison Democratic-Republican General Assembly had already changed the law for 1812 to provide for full selection of electors by the legislature. Even a Federalist-backed North Carolina running mate would have been of no value, unless their party also captured the legislative branch. Efforts to install a favorite son Democratic-Republican on the Clinton ticket may have been aimed at a long-shot attempt to convince the General Assembly to repeal the new elector selection law and restore popular allocation by district.[69]

Now attention moved toward Pennsylvania, where Madison had prevailed in 1808 with a resounding 78 percent of the popular vote. Clintonians had a base of support there, but they were no match for the large—albeit fractious—main Democratic-Republican organization. For their own part, Pennsylvania Federalists were badly outnumbered in the legislature and almost invisible in the congressional delegation. Still, they had a functioning apparatus in the state, with newspapers, party operatives, and senior political figures.[70] Even if carrying Pennsylvania was out of reach, adding a nationally well-respected Federalist without a reputation for bitter partisanship could perhaps make the ticket competitive, unify anti-Madison factions, and exploit the incumbent's vulnerabilities.

Dissident Democratic-Republicans took the lead by calling a small meeting in Lancaster on August 26. Presiding was Representative Joseph Lefever, who had voted for declaring war on Britain just two months prior. Now the congressman had become a critic of how the military campaign was being handled by the president, and some Madison supporters called Lefever "our unworthy representative . . . whom the intriguer (Clinton) had himself seduced from his political friends, at Washington."[71] The assembly's proclamation of support for Clinton celebrated his character and upbringing, and included the usual potshots at the legitimacy of the congressional nominating caucus. Now in the aftermath of the fall of Detroit, Madison and his War Department were criticized for "the incapacity of our administration for their present stations, from the total want of every means of efficient preparation." Pennsylvania, these delegates asserted, must take its rightful place on the presidential ticket after two decades of neglect. New York and Pennsylvania, in their view, should unite because they were two large states with similar commercial and agricultural interests. Plans were made for more local meetings to nominate a Pennsylvanian running mate for Clinton.[72]

The anti-Madison Democratic-Republicans of Pennsylvania got right to work. On September 4, a meeting in York County endorsed Clinton at the top of the ticket and the state's Federalist attorney general Jared Ingersoll Jr. for vice president.[73] Subsequent gatherings of the party's defectors followed in the coming weeks among supporters in Bucks, Lancaster, Luzerne, Lehigh, and Northampton counties and the city of Pittsburgh. A consensus formed in these meetings around a Clinton/Ingersoll ticket, although the Pittsburgh group endorsed a ticket of Clinton and Elbridge Gerry. Notably, in its formal statement, that assembly affirmed its approval of the decision to go to war, but stated "that there should be a change in the administration of the general government at this present time," and then provided no explanation for this argument. Nor were there any publicized nomination meetings of Clinton supporters in Philadelphia, which would prove to be a harbinger of the candidate's problems in that city in the general election.[74]

One could argue that Jared Ingersoll Jr. was a stereotypical classical Federalist, in the sense that he did not have a reputation as a fierce partisan, and he did not care for electioneering. Jared Jr. was born in Connecticut in 1749 to Hannah and Jared Ingersoll Sr. The elder Ingersoll was a British loyalist who held various positions in His Majesty's colonial government, including one as a collector of the hated Stamp Tax. Local antagonism toward the senior Ingersoll resulted in his being tarred and feathered by angry supporters of the Patriot cause. The junior Ingersoll was a Yale graduate, trained in law in Philadelphia, and was admitted to the Pennsylvania bar in 1773, just as tensions with the British were mounting. The young man's father, however, remained loyal to the Crown. Shortly thereafter, Ingersoll Jr. was sent to Europe to continue his law education, including in London, where he began to sympathize with American colonists and detach himself from the loyalist sentiments of his father.[75]

After his return to America, Ingersoll began a career in law and politics. He was elected to the Continental Congress in 1780 and later served as a delegate to the Philadelphia Convention. Ingersoll's view was that the Articles of Confederation required a stronger central government, but he initially favored their modification instead of their replacement. Playing a minor role in the proceedings, and only rarely speaking, Ingersoll went along with the rest of the Pennsylvania delegation and supported a full repeal of the Articles, in favor of a new Constitution. Being practical, Madison's notes suggest that Ingersoll "did not consider the signing, either as a mere attestation of the fact, or as pledging the signers to support the Constitution at all events; but as a recommendation, of what, all things considered, was the most eligible."[76]

Similar to many politicians with a law background, Ingersoll's talents took him through a variety of different positions at local, state, and federal levels. Ingersoll served posts on the Philadelphia Common Council, as city solicitor, and US district attorney for the Eastern District of Pennsylvania in the closing months of the Adams administration. It was in his capacity as a federal prosecutor that Ingersoll made the case for sedition charges against William Duane of the *Aurora* in 1800. As one of many questionable prosecutions under the 1798 Sedition Act, Duane was accused of printing content that was allegedly trying to incite public hatred against the Senate, where his criminal case had originated. Truth be told, Duane did publish some inaccurate information about a pending bill in the upper chamber concerning the upcoming presidential election of 1800. Federalist senators, however, simply aimed to imprison Duane because of his strong advocacy for Democratic-Republicans. In addition, the citizenship status of the ethnically Irish Duane was not yet a settled matter, making him even more of a political target. The new Jefferson administration dropped the sedition case against Duane the following year, and he submitted papers to become a naturalized American citizen in 1802. Duane seemed convinced that the whole episode was a vendetta, as he lamented Ingersoll's "most incurable hatred for me." The future vice presidential nominee had besmirched an otherwise distinguished career because he was associated with a politically motivated prosecution.[77]

As the outgoing President Adams was racing to fill up the judiciary with last-minute appointments, Ingersoll was considered for selection as a Supreme Court associate justice in late 1800. After much indecision and delay, the Pennsylvanian was passed over, in part because Adams could not get a solid commitment from Ingersoll that he would accept the appointment.[78] Nor did Ingersoll wish to serve in Jefferson's administration; he had accordingly resigned his position as a federal district attorney. By now, Ingersoll was experienced in litigating before the Supreme Court, although he argued on behalf of the losers in the landmark cases of *Chisholm v. Georgia* (1793) and *Hylton v. United States* (1796). In the *Chisholm* case, Alexander Chisholm, an executor of a deceased merchant's estate, was seeking payment for goods supplied to the state of Georgia during the Revolutionary War. Refusing to dignify the lawsuit as legitimate, Georgia was represented by Ingersoll though a written statement, as opposed to oral arguments in-person. Ingersoll asserted unsuccessfully that Georgia held sovereign immunity from lawsuits by private citizens. The Court's ruling in favor of Chisholm was later overturned by ratification of the Eleventh Amendment to the Constitution soon afterward. In the *Hylton* case, Ingersoll contended that the federal tax on carriages was an improper use of Congress's taxing authority under the apportionment clause of the Constitution. Although the tax was upheld, the case marked the first time judicial review of the Constitution was applied by the Supreme Court.[79] Additionally, Ingersoll served two separate tours as his state's attorney general, which was where he was stationed when his party and the Clintonians came calling.

Ingersoll's name may have come up at the New York national Federalist meeting. The pro-Madison *Public Advertiser* in the city reported as early as September 19 that he was chosen as Clinton's running mate. In their purported scoop of the event, however, the newspaper diminished its credibility with unsubstantiated claims about a possible Clinton administration. Still, it is entirely possible that the Federalist delegates raised the possibility of Ingersoll as vice president.[80]

Now in the twilight of a highly respected career that ranked him as one of many of the less well-known constitutional Framers, Ingersoll sent word that he "will not decline the call of his country in this gloomy and perilous hour" after he became the consensus choice of the Pennsylvania anti-Madison coalition. Clinton accepted the running mate from his new allies, and the ticket was now firmly in place.[81] There was just one month before the first major state—Pennsylvania, as a matter of fact—was to begin general election balloting. Meanwhile, a lot of time had been expended on choosing a vice presidential candidate. The delay gave further exposure to the difficulties of running a fusion ticket candidacy in an era when political parties were still decentralized and rather unsophisticated.

A vice presidential selection is more than just a strategic choice to curry favor in a particular state or region of the country, or to mollify a particular party faction. Then, just like today, the selection serves as one of the major ways in which the party defines the package of what it is offering the American people. The message that was communicated here was that there was an uneasy alliance between Clintonians and Federalists over the single matter of war with Britain. Not only was the office of the vice presidency of limited use in the early republic, but so too was the electioneering role of the aspiring candidate. Ingersoll followed the norm of other candidates of his era by remaining silent during the campaign and making no tangible effort to proactively line up support for his ticket. The stumbling process by which Clinton's running mate was chosen was indicative of the anti-Madison coalition's incoherence. In addition, the absence of healthy national party organizations was a liability in a context where the anti-Madison coalition could have badly utilized centripetal forces to cogently make an opposition argument and rally behind principal candidates. Moving into the general election phase, the problems associated with mixed messaging would continue to trouble the Clinton campaign.

5

THE CAMPAIGN FOR A WARTIME PRESIDENCY

The war was not off to a good start. On August 16, a few weeks before Federalist power brokers met in New York City, the United States was forced to surrender Detroit to the British. The small city in Michigan Territory was a key port location bordering Canada. Brig. Gen. William Hull relinquished Detroit in an act that can charitably be described as derelict, if not criminally negligent. Hull had served with distinction in many battles during the Revolutionary War and was at the time of the surrender the territorial governor of Michigan. The lackadaisical general was now in the twilight of his career, with his skills and motivation in decline. After His Majesty's army launched a siege of the city, Hull refused to engage the enemy with American forces and promptly turned Detroit over to the British. Sincerely believing that the strength of the British and their Shawnee allies under the command of Tecumseh were far larger than they really were, Hull refused to partake in what he was sure would be a fruitless American bloodbath. British Maj. Gen. Isaac Brock, however, militarily deceived his American counterpart into thinking that the combined forces were more numerous than the facts indicated. While the British shelling of the fort was taking place, Hull was reportedly intoxicated.[1]

For the first time in American history, a war was taking place in the context of a presidential campaign, and the results on the battlefield were generally disappointing. As this chapter will show, the presses on behalf of both candidates ramped up their hyperbolic messaging now that the shooting had started. Madison and his supporters combined jingoism with racist scapegoating of Native tribes, while Clinton's boosters struggled to get their tardy campaign off the ground. The challenger had a valid case to make against the incumbent president, but it was more nuanced and complicated than the simplistic arguments coming from backers of the wartime commander in chief.

When word of Hull's embarrassing surrender reached the Federalist publications, they did not hesitate to exploit the American setback for political gain. The *Trenton Federalist* took a mocking tone, exclaiming that the British army "were met by a flag of truce from Gen. Hull, AND TERMS OF CAPITULATION IMMEDIATELY CONCLUDED!!"[2] Labeling his actions "disgraceful" and "calamitous," the *New York Evening Post* hinted that the defeat would be politically costly for the Madison administration. "The American people will institute a most strict and severe scrutiny into the causes which have produced it," the *Post* forewarned, while making no mention of the upcoming election.[3] The Baltimore *Federal Republican and Commercial Gazette*, which had only weeks before been ransacked by pro-war mobs, pulled no punches in its criticisms. "The surrender of Hull is industriously attributed to personal defection and incapacity, by administration and their trumpets." The newspaper said that "whatever blame may attach to the gen'l, he must it is certain, share it in a certain degree with his superiors."[4]

Pro-Madison publications, however, depicted the loss of Detroit as a normal wartime setback, and if there was blame to be assigned on the American side, it should be focused on General Hull alone. Anti-Indian rhetoric was also deployed in response. The *National Intelligencer* assailed the general's "dastardly conduct" but wrote that attention should also be directed toward the victorious British and Shawnee forces for their "indiscriminate plunder of property" in Detroit.[5] The *Boston Patriot* reasoned that "this misfortune will in the end have a good effect by producing an indignation that will display itself in efficient exertions and a resolution to prevail."[6] The *New Hampshire Patriot* told readers that "while indignation enkindles in every American breast at the conduct of Hull," this setback would rally citizens against the British.[7] Calling the surrender an act of "treason," Lexington's *Reporter* denounced Hull for "shamefully, ingloriously and disgracefully" quitting without putting up much of a fight. The newspaper continued its critique by claiming that Americans on the frontier were now allegedly vulnerable to attack from "thousands of merciless savages."[8]

The disaster at Detroit came soon after a battlefield loss at Brownsville, located near the city. Similarly, US forces outnumbered Tecumseh's Shawnee men, but rather than engaging in a humiliating retreat, the Americans were routed in this skirmish. Militarily the small battle was not significant in the grand scheme of the overall American war objectives. Combined with the other shoe dropping that was the loss of Detroit, the potential for political damage to Madison was very real, given that this already began as a controversial war. New Jersey's Jonathan Dayton, who had once been involved in the Aaron Burr conspiracy but was now attempting to be an ally to the president, warned Madison that with the fall of Detroit his reelection was in jeopardy. "Your political enemies are taking every possible advantage," Dayton said, "to render your Presidency unpopular, & your cabinet Council odious & contemptible. This is not doing by *Federalists* alone, but with equal zeal, tho' greater caution by 'the *Democratic Republicans.*'"[9]

Now the British strategic position was stronger in the Northwest Territory and Upper Canada. Other defeats, setbacks, and losses on the battlefield accumulated in the first few months of the war, punctuated by the occasional American victory. Soon after hostilities formally commenced, the British captured and burned two American schooners in the St. Lawrence River. Fort Mackinac in Michigan Territory easily fell on July 17, leading General Hull to give up on plans to invade Upper Canada. Hull now called for an evacuation of Fort Dearborn in present-day Chicago because the loss of Fort Mackinac left the base in the Illinois Territory exposed. The commanding officer of the withdrawing American troops, Capt. Nathan Heald, negotiated with local Potawatomi leaders over a possible transfer of weaponry and alcohol, but their communications fell apart. On August 15 the Potawatomi forces mounted a surprise attack, resulting in dozens of American military and civilian casualties. Fort Dearborn was then burned to the ground.

With the Northwest Territory now more vulnerable to attack from Native militias, Democratic-Republican newspapers pivoted to exploiting anti-Indian sentiments as a means to rally war supporters. The *National Intelligencer* denounced the British as an "insidious foe which has let loose on our frontier vast hordes of prowling savages, the indiscriminate butchers of the human race!"[10] The *Richmond Enquirer* blasted the "INDIAN MURDERS" at the Pigeon Roost village in Indiana Territory, after Natives killed twenty-four American settlers on September 3.[11] The *Independent Chronicle* in Boston waved the bloody shirt, condemning Federalists for rooting for American failure on the battlefield, and labeling the Indian tribes as "SAVAGE ALLIES" of the British.[12]

The daunting task of what lay ahead for the United States was becoming a reality. Just weeks before the balloting began, the first major land battle took place in Queenston, Upper Canada, on the Niagara River. The British prevailed over the unseasoned American troops despite the latter's numerical advantages on the battlefield. The *United States Gazette* mocked Madison's wartime stewardship in a condescending diatribe. Recounting the recent losses, the newspaper exclaimed, "The loss of how many armies, and of how much territory will entitle him to the presidency for life?"[13] After the Queenston debacle, the *Trenton Federalist* ridiculed war supporters for failing to enlist in the armed forces, sneering, "How ready to promote a war—the toils—the sufferings—the dangers of which, they now throw upon others—but themselves *back out* in the time of trial and of danger!"[14] Federalists and Clintonians who opposed the war on practical grounds already had political material to use when the voting began.

The news was not all grim for the United States, as there were some land and naval victories. Still, there was no significant military breakthrough that definitively created major American momentum, and certainly not to the extent that anti-war advocates could be put on the political defensive. In Canada, Americans won some skirmishes near the Canard River on July 16, and a small battle in Gananoque on September 21. On July 19 the United States beat back an attack on Sacket's Harbor in upstate New York, which was a key center for shipbuilding. The American victory on August 9 at the Battle of Monguagon in Michigan was, however, of no real value. In that engagement, Lt. Col. James Miller's forces failed in their real objective, which was to provide supplies for Hull's troops in the soon-to-be captured city of Detroit.

At sea, there was some positive news that was still qualified by setbacks. The USS *Constitution* destroyed the HMS *Guerrire* on August 19, approximately 750 miles east of Boston. Near Fort Erie, Ontario, the American navy captured the HMS *Caledonia* and ran the HMS *Detroit* aground on October 9. Additionally, the HMS *Frolic* was taken on October 18 about 500 miles away from the Virginia coastline. Unfortunately, then the USS *Wasp*, which had seized the *Frolic*, was itself promptly grabbed by the British. In yet another reversal of momentum, the HMS *Macedonian* fell to the USS *United States* a week later. Meanwhile a major hurricane had ravaged the Louisiana coastline in mid-August, doing damage to the naval fleets of both countries.

While there were sporadic moments indicating that the United States could militarily prevail, the overarching early assessment of the war was that the critics were correct, and America was in over its head in an unneeded fight with a major European power. The *Connecticut Courant* bemoaned the war's cost, accusing proponents of fiscal dishonesty and political manipulation. "This war has been declared by the President to secure his place *four years more*," the newspaper complained, "and his democratic friends in congress refuse to grant taxes to support it, from the same motive."[15] In fact, customs duties had just recently been doubled. Secretary Gallatin's plan called for financing the war through borrowing and reviving the excise taxes that had lapsed with the Democratic-Republican takeover of the federal government a decade ago. The Democratic-Republican majority in Congress, however, was initially unwilling to commit to tax increases. The Federalists were all too happy to call them out for hypocrisy, inconsistency, and deception.

RALLYING AROUND THE SAGGING FLAG AND INDIAN-BASHING

Madison's political problems were not just confined to the uncertainties of the election and inconsistent progress toward battlefield objectives. The early months of a war should provide an opportunity for the commander in chief's associates to enjoy bursts of public approval and goodwill. Instead of that phenomenon, the Madison administration was beset by news of failed or incompetent commanders in the field, like General Hull. Similarly, ineffective and/or controversial Cabinet secretaries created unwelcome election-year headaches for Madison. While heroes from the war eventually emerged, none were of any value to the president's reelection.

A wartime president must maintain satisfactory relations with Congress. Should the legislative branch obstruct the chief executive's budgetary requests for the military, that will create an unneeded fight and the appearance of political division on the home front. The sluggish results on the ground, however, diminished the political standing of Secretary of War William Eustis in 1812. Although he performed the duties of his office in good faith, aiming to hastily prepare the military for war, Eustis had frosty relations with the officer corps. Key members of Congress were also lukewarm to Eustis's proposals for improving the army. Nor did some of the early victories at sea elevate the standing of Secretary of the Navy Paul Hamilton. With his alcoholism becoming more of a public spectacle, Congress was increasingly unwilling to work with Hamilton or consider his suggestions for naval improvements. The final straw may have come when the secretary showed up drunk at a celebratory reception after the *Macedonian* was captured. Eustis and Hamilton both resigned under pressure from the president and Congress once Madison's reelection was essentially secured in December.[16] As for Secretary Gallatin, he retained his job but continued to be a target of attack for his proposals to resurrect unpopular taxes, and allegedly hiding the true cost of the war until after the election.[17]

Two future presidents emerged as early possible stars of the war. Gen. William Henry Harrison was still riding a wave of popularity from his victory at Tippecanoe the previous year. Concluding on September 12 in Fort Wayne, Indiana Territory, Harrison led a successful reinforcement to push back an attack by British-supported Miami and Potawatomi militias. That same month in Indiana Territory, Capt. Zachary Taylor saved Fort Harrison (which was named after the Tippecanoe general) from attacks by four British-allied Native tribes. In response, Madison promoted Taylor to brevet major "for his gallant defence of Fort Harrison."[18]

Madison, however, embarked upon the 1812 campaign with many advantages in his pocket. Some of these factors were due to the systemic nature of politics in the early American republic, while other variables worked in the president's favor because the nation was at war and he was the incumbent. First, Madison presided over a messy and factional Democratic-Republican national infrastructure, which remained the overwhelmingly dominant party of America. Holding together this entire dysfunctional family was not even necessary for victory. The United States remained a nation in transition, moving slowly but surely toward a positive acceptance of political parties. The wartime campaign of 1812 took place within a system where two-party competition was still crude, decentralized, not fully embraced, and not even completely understood.

Second, Madison enjoyed the advantages of being the president of a nation in the early stages of a war, when feelings of nationalistic fervor, militarism, and hostility toward adversaries would be at high levels. Presidents of his era spoke from a far less powerful bully pulpit than we are familiar with today. At the same time, chief executives of the early republic still communicated on a highly visible stage, given that they were bound to be among the very few active politicians that would be nationally known to the general American public. The words of such presidents would only be amplified even more if they were to lead the country into a controversial war, as partisan newspapers intensified the exaggerated rhetoric and attacks on their respective domestic political opponents.

On two occasions in August 1812, Madison received Indian delegations from various tribes. There were pleasant exchanges of gifts, culture, and food, and the president spoke in a conciliatory tone—though he was also somewhat condescending toward "my red children," as he referred to them. As Madison urged the Indian peoples to stay out of this war, he said, "The British, who are weak, are doing all they can by their bad birds, to decoy the red people into the war on their side. I warn all the red people to avoid the ruin this must bring upon them." An American victory and Indian neutrality was of mutual interest, for "your father does not ask you to join his warriors. Sit still on your seats; and be witnesses that they are able to beat their enemies and protect their red friends."[19]

Diplomatic overtures notwithstanding, Native peoples were already being used by Madison and his supporters to achieve victory in the coming election. Rhetoric infused with anti-Indian tropes, degrading stereotypes, and demagogic fear-mongering was already shaping up to be part of the incumbent's reelection campaign. Framing the war as a fight against alleged Indian savagery could perhaps help rally the American people around a sagging flag—with Madison leading the charge. On November 4 Madison delivered the first-ever wartime Annual Message by an American president. In his written address, Madison tried to make the best of disappointing news from the battlefields, while also emphasizing the positive developments and urging continued vigilance against what he called "ruthless" adversaries. In the president's narrative, the British enemy was duping the Native peoples into aggressive actions against the United States. Madison referred to the Natives as "savages" seven times, labeling them "that wretched portion of the human race." The British-allied tribes were described as "merciless" and "blood-thirsty" fighters who had no respect for the rules of civilized warfare. They were responsible for "shocking butcheries of defenseless families," the president said.[20]

Amid an environment of mostly disappointments on the battlefields, in a war that was controversial from the start, now Madison had an even more politically potent enemy to use than the British. Well-publicized military engagements with Native tribes, alongside reports of civilian casualties and rumors of wartime atrocities, played into the hands of actors who were all too willing to exploit anti-Indian prejudices for political gain. A war against Britain could always summon some degree of American support in the early nineteenth century, given the prevalence of anti-Anglo sentiments that went back to the end of the colonial era. Britain, however, was now a vital trading partner with the United States, and that relationship was essential for the economic livelihood of many Americans employed in key industries. Even so, popular support could be rallied if the war was framed as a clash between Americans in opposition to hostile Indigenous peoples being egged on by scheming British officers.

Like future wartime presidents, Madison depicted the United States as the nonaggressor, and as reluctant combatants in an unwanted fight.

> Above all, we have the inestimable consolation of knowing that the war in which we are actually engaged is a war neither of ambition nor of vain glory; that it is waged not in violation of the rights of others, but in the maintenance of our own; that it was preceded by a patience without example under wrongs accumulating without end, and that it was finally not declared until every hope of averting it was extinguished by the transfer of the British scepter into new hands clinging to former councils, and until declarations were reiterated to the last hour, through the British envoy here, that the hostile edicts against our commercial rights and our maritime independence would not be revoked; nay, that they could not be revoked without violating the obligations of Great Britain to other powers, as well as to her own interests.

America, Madison claimed, was open to an armistice, so long as impressments were ended. The Orders in Council must also be repealed permanently without new blockades. Enclosed with the Annual Message, and in the coming days, the president sent to Congress diplomatic correspondence. Those documents portrayed the United States as seekers of peace. Among the papers were communications between the American ambassador to Britain (referred to as the Court of St. James), Jonathan Russell, and Britain's foreign secretary, Lord Castlereagh. The conversations revealed that Castlereagh rejected the armistice proposal and also declined an offer to convene peace commissioners to discuss a treaty to resolve differences between the two nations. Russell then returned to America, convinced that the war must be prosecuted and won.[21]

These diplomatic documents did not reach widespread public dissemination until after popular voting had already taken place in nearly all the key states. In a future era of speedier communications, a fair argument could be made that these papers would have served as a valuable refutation to critics who called Madison a warmonger. By mid-November, the Annual Message and the diplomatic documents would be just starting to circulate beyond the Washington, DC, area. There may have been realistic time for the communications to have had some impact on voters in Maryland, who would be going to the polls on November 9. Two days earlier, the *American and Commercial Daily Advertiser*, a Democratic-Republican newspaper in Baltimore, published some of the correspondence.[22]

As for the fiasco with General Hull and the loss of Detroit, Madison was unwilling to publicly defend the derelict commander, declaring that "the causes of this painful reverse will be investigated by a military tribunal."[23] It was incumbent upon the United States to stay the course and finish the tasks at hand. Madison said nothing about the election, which was—and still is—considered inappropriate for a president in this venue. The Annual Message is a constitutionally ordained report from the chief executive, intended to inform the public about the business of government; it is not meant to be a stump speech to curry favor with voters. Still, the messaging here echoed that of pro-war Democratic-Republican politicians and publications in the 1812 campaign.

In fact, pro-Madison newspapers had already begun the job of spreading anti-Indian propaganda. The *National Intelligencer* ran a headline that decried the " ANGLO SAVAGE HOSTILITY." The *Carthage Gazette* told readers, "You well know, from your contiguity to the scene, that the savage tribes, at the instigation of British agents, are now waging against us a cruel war, unknown among civilized nations." Reporting on the war in the West, the *New Hampshire Patriot* lambasted the tribes and accused them of barbarity. "The British had engaged as allies," the newspaper said, "the savages who are known to give no quarter, who are known never to refrain from pillage and murder," and who could not be counted on to respect any armistice in the fighting. The *Savannah Republican* ran an article waving the bloody shirt with the assertion that "it is no time, now, for temporising, when the tomahawk and the scalping knife of the murderous savage, directed by their still more murderous allies, are desolating our frontier, and we lie, through a shameful neglect, a helpless prey to their wanton depravity."[24]

Any rally effect for a wartime commander in chief is going to erode in the face of military setbacks, loss of life, or administrative bungling that complicates battlefield objectives. Demands for sacrifice from civilians on the home front will not be supported by the citizenry indefinitely. The speed and extent of this political decline will depend upon a variety of factors, but it can be mitigated through effective messaging from the president's team. That obligation became even more important decades later, when the presidency became a more personalized office, with an expectation of regular and direct communication before the American public. In Madison's era of slow and inconsistent communications, and a far less public presidency, the chief executive could politically get away with muddled messaging. By the autumn, a narrative was emerging from pro-war Democratic-Republicans that the British were up to their old tricks again, and this time they were encouraging the Indian tribes to sow terror on the frontier.

A FUMBLING FUSION AND A STUMBLING CANDIDACY

The incumbent may also be blessed to have an opposition party that struggles to justify its central argument in the election campaign. The Federalist/Clintonian coalition may have had an opening to critique incompetence in the Madison administration's prosecution of the war, but their own disorganization precluded them from making a coherent case. With balloting about to begin in Pennsylvania on October 30, the opposition coalition had barely emerged from a secretive national party conclave where Federalists could not even definitively state that they were nominating DeWitt Clinton. Following the New York meeting, rumors and inaccurate speculation circulated for weeks without a decisive confirmation from Federalists about who would be their candidate. Selecting a vice presidential running mate also frittered away valuable time and exposed the fragility of this anti-Madison coalition.

A failed effort to convince Clinton to drop out caused his candidacy an unneeded distraction in early October. Maj. Gen. William King of Massachusetts, a Democratic-Republican and half-brother of Rufus King, engineered the strange plan to sideline Clinton from the 1812 race. King was a large shipowner in the Maine Territory, who would become the first governor of that state eight years later. Along with judge Ambrose Spencer of New York, Clinton's brother-in-law, the two Madison supporters informed Clinton's agents that if he dropped out now, Massachusetts would be solidly in his corner for an 1816 run. King and Spencer also seemed to threaten Clinton, asserting that they would destroy his career if he remained in the race. Also involved in the King/Spencer withdrawal plot was John Tayler, Clinton's predecessor and successor as New York's lieutenant governor. Richard Riker, a Clintonian Democratic-Republican who was the district attorney for the area that now includes Manhattan, publicly rejected and denounced the idea on his candidate's behalf. Reelecting Madison would be "the ruin of the republican party," and it was Clinton's duty to answer his country's call to serve.[25]

The Clintonian faction of Democratic-Republicans made a comprehensive and articulate case for their candidate through the New York Committee of Correspondence on August 17. The alliance with Federalists, however, never gelled together for a unified drive against Madison and the war. In an era that still maintained an institutionally weak party system at the national level, executing a successful fusion between one party and a faction of the other party was a task that was fraught with even more challenges. When efforts to create a fusion ticket are carried out in a careless and confusing manner, its advocates will be vulnerable to ridicule, and their candidate will be mispositioned for the general election campaign. Even before the voting began, a few lessons emerged.

First, the logistics of a party fusion must be carried out with dispatch. Speed is necessary because of the election calendar, which had varying state-level dates in the America of the early nineteenth century. Nominees must be chosen promptly, as time will be needed to present a cogent case to voters, newspapers, and other key political players. Given that all communications moved slower in this era, it would have been even more essential for the Federalist/Clintonian alliance to be firmly in place earlier in the summer. The case must be made through all contemporary media organs that the unique circumstances of the present moment—a clumsy war with a major European power—require an unprecedented cooperation between old domestic political adversaries.

Second, the demands of the electoral calendar will create a tension with the imperative of efficiency. A party merger cannot be a sloppily done job, lest opponents find ways to easily exploit vulnerabilities. Candidates must be nominated with resolve and finality, which is exactly what did not happen within the anti-Madison coalition of 1812. A platform of issue positions and policy commitments must be distributed all over the country, stressing areas of commonality between the major partners within the coalition. Furthermore, all major actors within the fusion ticket should work together on messaging and campaigning, so that the public is hearing a consistent and persistent narrative.

Third and finally, presidential candidates have always been attacked on a personal level. The character of a fusion nominee, however, will be especially vulnerable to condemnation, which is why it will be necessary for campaign managers to minimize this potential weakness. DeWitt Clinton already held a reputation as a calculating and ambitious politician in an era that frowned upon that character archetype. Joining forces with a declining political party in his quest for the presidency could only give credence to critics who charged that he was a man without principles. As the standard-bearer of a hastily assembled fusion ticket, the candidate can expect to be criticized for political opportunism, dishonesty, and flip-floppery on vital contemporary issues. Predictably, partisan newspapers, pamphleteers, and essayists went on the offensive against Clinton, exposing his entire career and personal integrity to scrutiny.

Much of today's political discourse from ordinary citizens occurs through aliases on social media, where the rhetoric can be very vicious, petty, and personal. Similarly, anonymously written essays carried sharply partisan and vitriolic language in the early nineteenth century. Writing under the pen name of Milo, an essayist blasted Clinton in a series of letters. "He can flatter and betray," Milo wrote, "and still wheedle the victim of his perfidy." Through this unholy party fusion, the author alleged, Clinton would install the bitterly partisan Federalist Timothy Pickering for another term as secretary of state. The nominee was suspect because he flip-flopped on the embargo policy, and reversed himself into a supporter of the congressional war declaration once hostilities began. "That a man should present himself," Milo continued, "as a candidate for the chief magistracy of a great people without any known politics, is a very strange thing. For a nation to confide in such a character would be still more strange." Clinton was a man who was "one of the most unprincipled of the human race," and a "mock general" who deserved no accolades for serving in uniform because he was not a field commander. Instead, Clinton remained in New York City, "enjoying good dinners; and dispatching emissaries through the Union to intrigue for the Presidency."[26]

The mainline Democratic-Republican presses continued to deploy the character attacks on Clinton. The *Fredonian* in Chillicothe, Ohio, castigated him as the candidate of a lame, dying political party that was fomenting a "*monstrous* alliance with the apostate republicans." Clinton "appears, like Proteus, to have the faculty of assuming a new character on every occasion . . . one thing to one man, a different thing to another, and another thing to a third."[27] In an effort to make Clinton look two-faced, the *True American* in Trenton published the transcript of a speech he gave in 1809. In that address, Clinton denounced the Federalists in vitriolic language, labeling the party as pro-British, with designs on breaking up the United States. The newspaper sarcastically stated, "Now, FEDERALISTS, turn out to a man at the approaching election, and give a hearty support to DEWITT CLINTON, who has drawn such a flattering portrait of your party!!!"[28]

Through their affiliated newspapers all over America, both parties could be vicious in their published attacks. Even in the absence of swift and efficient communications across the country, consistent narratives emerged, though to a greater extent from Madison's supporters. For advocates of the president's reelection, Madison was the steady commander in chief, who only committed the nation to war after all options were exhausted. In their framing of events, several years of aggressive British behaviors and provocation of the Native peoples were making a mockery of American independence. Madison, the lifelong statesman who had devoted his life to the integrity of the national union, was just the man to defend American honor. DeWitt Clinton, in contrast, was a Machiavellian politician who was far less well-known to the common citizen and was easily prone to changing what he stood for depending upon the circumstances. Truth be told, his own Federalist supporters were coy about their endorsement of his candidacy, almost as if their party was acknowledging its own unpopularity. Perhaps he was a backdoor vehicle being used to divide Democratic-Republicans, so as to revitalize the discredited Federalist Party, and "paving the way for their own ascension to power," speculated the *New Hampshire Gazette*.[29] The *Rhode Island Republican* compared Clinton to another ambitious politician who had once tried—albeit under very different circumstances—to hastily build a fusion with Federalists: the disgraced Aaron Burr.[30]

Only President Madison could "maintain the republican institutions and character of our country," in the words of the Pennsylvania correspondence committee working on behalf of his reelection. Their open letter to that state's voters dismissed Clinton as a party turncoat and a useful idiot for the "*British party in America*."[31] In an open letter to New Hampshire voters, the *New Hampshire Patriot* praised "the amiable, the incorruptible MADISON . . . the man who nobly hazarded his personal popularity for his country's good." A vote for the incumbent was an endorsement of this war to reaffirm independence from Great Britain, and a commitment to stand up to their Indian "savage allies."[32]

For Clintonians and Federalists, their man was uniquely positioned to bring peace because of his linkages to both parties. Clinton would restore the smooth flow of commerce and dispense with destructive and confusing embargoes. He would break the Virginia dynasty of the presidency. He would end this immoral, misguided, and poorly executed war, but how he planned to do that was framed differently depending upon the audience. New Hampshire's *Concord Gazette* said that Clinton represented "the voice of peace, moderation and unity." As president, he would make America normal again, for "*we shall soon have an honourable peace, and restoration of commerce*, and all things return to their proper channels," as an essayist named Clintonian told the *New England Palladium* in Boston. The *Albany Register* warned that another term with Madison and war would mean "the country will inevitably become bankrupt in fortune as well as in fame." The *Trenton Federalist* played up the practical case against the war and defended Clinton supporters against accusations of disloyalty to America, lamenting "the amazing LOAD OF DEBT, and the HEAVY TAXES which will be the consequence" of the country's current situation.[33]

Some Clinton supporters asserted that their candidate would improve military preparations and reverse incompetent management of the war. An advocate labeling himself a Democrat wrote to the *Lancaster Journal* claiming that a President Clinton would "regain our posts; and conquer the Indians." Under his leadership, the writer argued, the United States "will soon have arms and ammunition provided," and military enlistments would increase accordingly. Another writer, with the pen name of Saratoga, pledged to vote for Clinton as the best option for achieving victory in the war. Another term of Madison will mean "we shall suffer the calamities of an ill conducted war, and of an abrupt dishonorable peace." Clinton as commander in chief, Saratoga argued, would rid the Cabinet of Gallatin and Eustis. Carrying out a war "requires practical skill and judgment," which demanded a man of Clinton's "prudence and strength." A Clinton supporter calling himself Americanus wrote that his candidate would strengthen the navy and "put us in the best situation to make an immediate peace; or to prosecute, if necessary for its attainment, an effectual war with England." An essayist calling himself Melancthon told the New York *Columbian* that Clinton would bring "success to our arms in war; prosperity to our negociations in peace; the upholding of our national honor under every circumstance," revealing the muddled messaging of the Clinton camp.[34] Clearly the coalition that frequently referred to themselves as the "Peace Party" was communicating nebulous justifications on behalf of their nominee.

Madison's critics tried to attack the president for shifting political positions and ideologies throughout his career. The *Baltimore Whig*, a dissident Democratic-Republican newspaper that was essentially a mouthpiece for the Smiths in Maryland, conceded that Madison was a man of strong intellect who championed the federalist cause of ratifying the Constitution. Then, however, he gingerly moved into the Jeffersonian party as a member of the House, and strenuously opposed Hamilton's national banking system. Now, as president, he "urged congress to revive and continue the Bank of the United States, unconstitutional as the institution had been proved to be by his own arguments." Furthermore, he had opposed internal taxes as a congressman, but as president, his treasury secretary was now recommending their reinstatement.[35]

Perhaps the president's reputation for great intellect was overrated, and he wasn't up for the job because he didn't understand the complexities of European affairs. "He has shewn himself a completely bewildered politician," an essayist named Thousands told the *Charleston Courier*. The author blasted Madison as aloof, indecisive, and lacking in pragmatism.[36] A Madison reelection would undeservedly vindicate a man "whom the strongest inducements could not make favorable to *peace*—altho' he was proved utterly incompetent to carry on *war*," the *New York Evening Post* claimed.[37] Denouncing Madison for perpetuating Virginia's "Jeffersonian aristocracy," the *Connecticut Courant* charged on September 29 that this president had been a disaster for navigation and commerce. Without mentioning Clinton, whose candidacy was still ambiguous at this point, the newspaper implored voters to choose "a *practical statesman*; a man of enlarged views, and inflexibly firm and independent; a friend to the commerce of these states—we ask no more."[38]

President James Madison. Beset by the squabbling of his own political party and a war his country was not prepared to fight, the incumbent faced a tough reelection race in 1812. James Madison, by Thomas Sully, derived from Gilbert Stuart, 1809. National Portrait Gallery, Washington, DC.

New York City mayor and New York lieutenant governor DeWitt Clinton. The unique circumstances of the War of 1812 created a pathway to the presidency for the ambitious Clinton, but an alliance between his wing of Democratic-Republicans and the Federalists was tenuous. DeWitt Clinton, by Rembrandt Peale, c. 1823. National Portrait Gallery, Washington, DC.

Vice President Elbridge Gerry. Fairly or not, he became the namesake for the political practice that is known as gerrymandering. Gerry's presence on the Democratic-Republican ticket produced no gains for Madison in Massachusetts. Elbridge Gerry (1744–1814), American statesman, by James Bogle after John Vanderlyn, 1861. Independence National Historical Park, Portrait Collection (Second Bank of the United States), Philadelphia.

George Clinton. Until his death, he was the leading figure behind the New York–based Clintonian faction. Vice President Clinton was DeWitt's uncle and an enduring public servant to his state. George Clinton, *engraved by Peter Maverick from a painting by Ezra Ames, 1816. National Portrait Gallery, Washington, DC.*

John Randolph of Roanoke. The eccentric congressman from Virginia was a fierce opponent of the war and the leading figure in the Old Republican faction. By 1812, however, his influence was declining. John Randolph, *by John Wesley Jarvis, 1811. National Portrait Gallery, Washington, DC.*

Brig. Gen. William Hull surrendered the city of Detroit to the British on August 16, 1812, thereby handing President Madison a battlefield defeat just as the presidential campaign was intensifying. William Hull, by Gilbert Stuart, c. 1823. National Portrait Gallery, Washington, DC.

Federalist Rufus King was skeptical of making a coalition with the Clintonians. Nor was he much interested in running for president himself, in spite of his nomination in Virginia. Privately he told a confidant that he would reluctantly support Madison's reelection. Rufus King, by Gilbert Stuart, c. 1820. National Portrait Gallery, Washington, DC.

William Duane. As editor of the Aurora in Philadelphia, Duane was a persistent critic of Madison, but he voiced his support for the president's reelection late in the campaign. William Duane, *by Charles Balthazar Julien Févret de Saint-Mémin, 1802. National Portrait Gallery, Washington, DC.*

Albert Gallatin served honorably as Madison's secretary of the treasury, but he was also a major target for critics of the president and the war. Albert Gallatin, *by Thomas Worthington Whittredge, after Gilbert Stuart, c. 1859. National Portrait Gallery, Washington, DC.*

6

IN THE HANDS OF THE LEGISLATORS AND SOME VOTERS

With growing intensity, partisan newspapers blasted away at each other and their respective presidential candidates in the final weeks of the campaign. Rumors, gossip, and hyperbolic attacks spread throughout the print media. The principals themselves, however, adhered to the protocol of the era, which frowned upon any personal campaigning from an aspirant of the nation's highest office. Party surrogates from state and local committees, as well as partisan publications, trumpeted the arguments for the presidential contenders. The election was a civic event within the context of the early American republic, alongside nascent signs of greater democratization to come in the future.

One of those features of early American elections was the presence of alcohol. Civic norms dating back to Colonial America freely mixed booze with the act of voting for public officials. These practices continued well into the nineteenth century. Political meetings, most notably the Federalists' big September national gathering, were frequently held at taverns, along with the accompanying beverages. Polling places were also commonly located at bars, thereby facilitating a potentially festive and rowdy atmosphere on election day. In New York City, elections in April saw at least two of the ten ward precincts stationed at taverns.[1] Given that taverns were understood to be a social space for men, and voting excluded women, such an arrangement is understandable.

As this chapter walks readers through the race, observers of the 1812 presidential contest should not be surprised to see how disorganized and decentralized everything appeared to be in hindsight. Campaign organizations, messaging, and tactics reflected the playing field of competition. The election for president occurred on different calendar dates in the states, just as contests for other federal, state, and local offices were often held separately from the presidential race. States maintained varying modalities of selecting electors, which frequently shifted every few years. Some states still assigned this responsibility to the legislature, meaning which party controlled that institution was paramount. Other states entrusted the voters with choosing the electors. If voters were given the choice, some of these states prescribed an at-large system, where the winner would take all electors. A state might utilize a popular vote but allocate electors on the basis of the winner in specific districts, giving each candidate an opportunity to at least win some electors in their geographical areas of political strength.

For all of his troubles, James Madison went into his reelection cycle with an advantageous base of states in his corner. Just like in contemporary presidential contests, many states provide no mystery or suspense as to how they will behave on election day. Newspapers across the political spectrum were aware of this fact in 1812, as they commonly predicted results and engaged in their generation's version of political punditry. As Madison himself assessed his prospects in various battleground states, he told Jefferson that "the other States, remain pretty decided on one hand or on the other."[2] The incumbent was assured of victory in the southern states of Tennessee, Georgia, South Carolina, and the newly admitted Louisiana. The western frontier states of Ohio and Kentucky also seemed a virtual lock for the wartime president. Party control of the necessary legislatures in those six states, as well as public opinion, both augured well for Madison. Virginia was also considered safe, for Madison could expect a favorite son advantage, given Clinton's absence and Rufus King's desultory single-state candidacy. North Carolina had recently switched to legislative selection of electors, giving the president a big boost in a state his party controlled. In the North, Madison could count on Vermont, where mainline Democratic-Republicans held strong control of the legislature. In total, Madison could be said to have a firm lock on at least 98 electoral votes, out of the 110 needed to win.

Clinton could certainly bet on the Federalist bastions of Delaware and Connecticut. The war was very unpopular in Rhode Island, a generally Federalist state, where all indications pointed to him winning big. Next door in Massachusetts, the war and embargoes were reviled, but the state would be choosing its twenty-two electors this year by way of a popular vote in special districts. Clinton was likely, if not guaranteed, to fully sweep the state, for accomplishing this task would be a necessity if he was to prevail. Then there was the candidate's home state of New York, where the legislature would be allocating its haul of twenty-nine electoral votes. Barring a spectacular failure to cement the Federalist/Clintonian alliance in the state where it began, New York could be counted as a safe state for the challenger. Due to recent changes in the political climate of New Jersey, as well as last-minute alterations to its elector selection rules, Clinton was likely to add eight more votes to his total. A fair observer could say that the challenger probably had at least seventy-six electoral votes in the bank before the balloting commenced.

New Hampshire, where the balance of power between the parties was tightly contested, would be a battleground for Clinton and Madison. That state by itself was too small to determine the outcome, but it might provide clues as to how well each campaign's messaging was resonating throughout the Northeast. Maryland was also a politically divided state, beset by pro-war riots in Baltimore for weeks that summer. Matters were further complicated by its mode of popular selection of electors by district. Neither candidate was likely to take all eleven electoral votes, but Clinton needed to at least hold his ground here. The brass ring of the election of 1812 was Pennsylvania, which created the illusion of being an extremely competitive fight.

THE LAY OF THE LAND: CAMPAIGNING AND THE VOTE

Developments in Pennsylvania worked in Madison's favor going back to the early weeks of 1812. The president's reelection campaign slowly but surely achieved a successful navigation of the state's bloated, fractious Democratic-Republican organization. After mollifying his differences with Governor Snyder, earning a unanimous stamp of approval from the party's legislative caucus, and benefiting from the opposition coalition's lumbering fusion efforts, the president's Pennsylvania momentum became impossible to stop. Enough of the regular Madison skeptics were on board, as his critics generally lost strength there.

The troublesome senator Michael Leib ended up endorsing Clinton, after having previously given token support to Madison in the congressional nominating caucus. In spite of that reversal, Leib's move only seemed to reveal the lack of grassroots backing for the Invisible faction. Similarly, Representative Joseph Lefever, who had tried in vain to rally other dissident Democratic-Republicans, declined to run for reelection. Another party rebel in the Pennsylvania US House delegation, the anti-war William Rodman, switched to the Federalist side of the aisle. Then he went down to defeat in the state's October 13 congressional elections. Pennsylvania's only other Federalist congressman, James Milnor, did not seek another term. Charles Jared Ingersoll, son of the Federalist vice presidential nominee, was elected to the House from the First District as a pro-war Democratic-Republican. There were some minor Federalist pickups in the legislature, but they remained well entrenched in the minority. When the dust settled, the House results produced Democratic-Republican victories in all but one congressional race—a bad omen for the opposition presidential ticket a few days later.[3]

In more good October news for Madison, William Duane and his cantankerous *Aurora* finally proclaimed their support for the leader they had been undercutting for months. The newspaper's indifference to the presidential election was increasingly criticized by Madison's supporters. On October 24, Duane declared his support for the commander-in-chief in a public statement, arguing on the basis of wartime national unity. Madison must be reelected, so as to leave "the enemy no pretence for saying there was a British party in America—that no differences should be countenanced which would lead the enemy to believe the people of this nation were divided on a question of public right or national independence." Clinton was the candidate of "toryism," and Duane made it clear that he wished to have no part of any alliance with the nominee and his Federalist allies. Clinton's supporters, furthermore, were men of "insincerity or treachery," who seemed to favor dissolution of the union and did not value representative democracy.[4] It is also difficult to imagine Duane ever supporting the Clinton ticket, given Jared Ingersoll Jr.'s prosecution of the publisher under the now discredited Sedition Act.

Carrying Pennsylvania was already going to be a reach for the Clinton camp, and their campaign's organizational tardiness handicapped that goal. Philadelphia Federalists, for example, did not endorse Clinton until October 17. They met and adopted a resolution asserting that their candidate would bring "an honorable and speedy peace" and "protect commerce." The conferees resolved to disseminate their message to all newspapers. In Pennsylvania, however, time was running out, which was compounded by the era's slow pace of communications. Furthermore, the designated slate of electors for Clinton was repeatedly changing as the days ticked away prior to voters going to the polls. Some of the men who were nominated as electors declined the assignment: not a good sign of an energized and unified base of support.[5]

Clintonian Democratic-Republicans hastily threw together their own Pennsylvania organ to communicate with party cohorts who might be amenable to an anti-Madison message that came from outside of the Federalist camp. Based in Philadelphia, the *Whig Chronicle* debuted on October 14. Trumpeting the Clinton candidacy, the publication asserted that Clinton, not Madison, was the genuine Democratic-Republican, and a "sterling democrat." Other talking points included standard complaints about the congressional nominating caucus, attacks upon Gallatin and Eustis, General Hull's failures, and the Virginia presidential dynasty. The *Chronicle* was supportive of the war effort but denounced the Madison administration for poor preparation and incompetent execution. "The constitutional remedy is at hand," the newspaper implored readers, "and it is in the power of the people to correct the procedure." After Madison secured another term, the *Chronicle* quickly faded out of existence.[6]

The state's pro-Madison Democratic-Republicans were quarrelsome but ultimately better organized and considerably larger in size than their opposition. The urgency of winning the Keystone State could not be minimized—not only because twenty-five electoral votes were at stake, but also due to the importance of building momentum elsewhere as the Pennsylvania results started to filter out to the rest of the country. An underwhelming victory, or even an unexpected loss, could create a slow-moving negative news cycle that might spread nationwide. The statewide reelection committee for Madison included John Binns, the Irish-born editor of Philadelphia's *Democratic Press*, revealing the nexus between the political parties and journalists of this era. The president's Democratic-Republican boosters mobilized their infrastructure of newspapers and local party committees to circulate supportive essays and messages, as well as holding pro-Madison meetings to adopt resolutions. The *Whig Chronicle* mocked the Madison committee as being "an orchestra of limping fiddlers!!!"[7]

The Association of Democratic Young Men was a political club aimed at promoting party messaging and candidates for office. Shortly before the presidential balloting, it released a statement to the *Aurora*. President Madison, it said, was a statesman whose views "have been marked with mild firmness, and integrity has always governed his actions." Clinton, however, was criticized as an undistinguished public servant, who was most noteworthy for his naked ambition and for holding opportunistic and slippery positions on the war. The critique from the opposition coalition was incomprehensible, the association stated, and only played into the hands of the enemy. Supporters of the fusion ticket were labeled as the "British party," and their candidate was compared to the seditious schemer Aaron Burr.[8]

The incumbent's advantage in Pennsylvania, and other states, was ironically aided by poor and inconsistent enforcement of the British trade embargo that the president himself supported. Inevitably, a war will disrupt markets and crop prices, as uncertainty percolates through the economy. Prior to the war, American corn and flour were being shipped overseas to the British armies of Sir Arthur Wellesley, later to be known as the Duke of Wellington. Now with exports to the enemy banned, these sales were technically illegal, thereby hurting the bottom line of American farmers and shippers in an election year. The policy drafted by Congress, however, did not permit the United States military to enforce the prohibition. Evaders quickly took advantage of the porous embargo, as Madison and his administration looked the other way.

In a letter to his successor after war was declared, Jefferson hinted that letting flour and other produce through would pay good political dividends. "To continue the war popular," Jefferson counseled, putting a stop to "Indian barbarities" was necessary, as well as capturing Canadian territory, and maintaining the flow of flour. "It would be mortifying to the farmer," the former president continued, "to see such an one rot in his barn. It would soon sicken him of war." Then Jefferson gave Madison some frank advice, saying, "For carrying our produce to foreign markets our own ships, neutral ships, & even enemy ships under neutral flags, which I would wink at, will probably suffice."[9] How seriously Madison took these suggestions is a matter of conjecture. Still, he must have been aware of the politically beneficial option of passively allowing certain produce to be sold to British armies in Europe, so as to keep prices competitive for American farmers. Congress had been out of session since early July and could address the issue when it convened in November—when balloting would be conveniently well underway or completed in the states.

Acting without the formal authorization of British minister Augustus Foster, at least one of his colleagues granted licenses to ships of the United States to transport flour to Spain and Portugal, where Wellington's forces were fighting the Peninsular War against Napoleon. Later in the summer, Jefferson told Madison that "our farmers are chearful in the expectation of a good price for wheat in autumn," which was right in time for the presidential voting. "To keep open sufficient markets," he continued, "is the very first object towards maintaining the popularity of the war which is as great at present as could be desired." Middle Atlantic states like Virginia, Maryland, and Pennsylvania responded favorably to the unofficial carve-out for shippers and producers of corn and flour.[10]

Federalists, in comparison, could sense the sticky fingers of politics messing with the inconsistent trade policies. As the *Lancaster Journal* observed, the current good prices for flour would surely not last; it predicted that Congress would fix the loophole soon. "Those at present in power," the newspaper reminded farmers and millers, "wished to be re-elected before the eyes of the people could be completely opened."[11] The willingness of the Madison administration to countenance corn and flour shipments to the enemy in wartime for electoral advantage seemed to give credence to the orthodox Jeffersonian creed that protectionism is susceptible to political manipulation and tweaking on behalf of favored constituencies. Like Jefferson before him, Madison was all too disposed to lay aside his principles on the trade issue. Meanwhile, high prices for various crops buoyed Pennsylvania farmers, and the state's manufacturing was humming along nicely, thereby undercutting a key argument from the Clintonian coalition.[12]

Results trickled in to the newspapers over the coming days and weeks, but a clear trend emerged. Central and western counties delivered robust support for Madison, revealing a mandate for the war in the frontier. Closer to Philadelphia, where shipping and commerce were more significant elements of the economy, the outcome was more nuanced. In 1808, Madison won 60 percent of the vote in the city proper of Philadelphia, with 40 percent for Charles Pinckney. The two candidates split the fourteen city wards evenly. Four years later, each ward voted for the same party as it did in 1808, but the president's overall support eroded to some degree. Now Madison's citywide majority was a mere 5 percent margin. Slightly farther out in Philadelphia County, Madison won by a large amount, but with a reduced spread of victory as compared to four years prior. Clinton showed strength elsewhere in southeast Pennsylvania, carrying Delaware County and flipping the counties of Bucks, Chester, and Lancaster. Additionally, he decisively flipped Adams County, which includes Gettysburg, as well as Luzerne County, where Wilkes-Barre is located. The final state popular vote was nearly 63 percent for the incumbent and over 37 percent for Clinton.[13] If Madison's Pennsylvania victory was not quite as overwhelming as in 1808, it was still a resounding success.

Mainline Democratic-Republican newspapers jumped at the chance to crow when it became clear that their man was going to win Pennsylvania convincingly. "The result of the late election has exceeded our most sanguine expectations," the *Commonwealth* said from Pittsburgh. With great confidence, the *National Intelligencer* proclaimed "the re-elevation of James Madison to the Presidency of the United States beyond a doubt." The *Whig Chronicle*, in contrast, continued to rage against the administration's mismanagement of the war, but acknowledged that "with what gloomy apprehensions must we look forward to the reelection of James Madison."[14] By no means was this election over, but the incumbent was now in a commanding position to prevail, and an emerging media narrative of momentum toward Madison became difficult to ignore as the other states shared their results.

Like in so many other states, the Democratic-Republicans of Ohio were rife with factions and rivalries, rendering the Federalists into a token opposition status. The Jeffersonian party in the state was divided between supporters of the weakening Tammany societies, and critics who regarded the clubs as elitist. These social, fraternal, and political associations originated in New York City as far back as 1786 and spread to other states, including Ohio in 1810. Tammany societies were dedicated to professionalizing and organizing state and local Democratic-Republican parties, as well as providing networking opportunities for affiliated politicians and insiders. In Ohio the Tammany societies were now becoming controversial. Skeptics denounced the clubs for holding secret meetings and serving as the vehicle for the state's most powerful politicians, such as Senator Thomas Worthington.[15]

Ohio's Democratic-Republican divisions over the Tammany clubs did not prove damaging to Madison, given the war's popularity in the western frontier. Demagogic attacks on Indian peoples would play well in this state. "It is a fact ascertained beyond refutation," a speaker told a Fourth of July gathering in Chillicothe, "that the British government have contributed by active measures, to excite against us the hostility of the savage tribes upon our defenceless frontiers."[16] Nor was the overall outcome ever in doubt, as the state had voted overwhelmingly for Democratic-Republicans since its admission to the union in 1803. Due to the decennial reapportionment after 1810, Ohio's electoral votes increased by five, to a total of eight for 1812, which could only benefit Madison. In congressional races on October 13, Democratic-Republicans won five of the six House seats. Pro-Madison governor Return J. Meigs Jr., a Democratic-Republican opponent of the Tammany societies, was also reelected by a convincing margin. Clearly General Hull's loss of Detroit did not negatively impact the political standing of the neighboring state's chief executive.[17]

Most county-level returns from Ohio are lost to history; however, in balloting for the presidency on October 30, Madison was the clear favorite, capturing just over 69 percent of the reported statewide vote. Clinton's campaign found very little grassroots support in this frontier state. Some candidates for elector ran as pro-Tammany men pledged to Madison, while other supporters of the incumbent ran on an anti-Tammany label. In addition, the overall influence of the Tammany societies was now in decline anyway, due to the war subsuming most of the state's political landscape. Results came out of Ohio slowly, but they confirmed the president's continuing momentum, as the *National Intelligencer* gloated that "the Madisonian Ticket is believed to have succeeded by a large majority."[18]

As Democratic-Republicans had been making steady gains in Vermont over the past decade, Madison was well positioned to hold that state's eight electoral votes. Due to the absence of ocean-based ports that would otherwise be injured by trade embargoes, any backlash against the war would be of reduced scale in Vermont, as compared to the rest of New England. Early balloting worked to the advantage of the incumbent president, given the model of elector selection in the Green Mountain State. Conversely, the Clinton campaign might have been able to credibly target Vermont had it been organized sooner. Results from the September 1 state government elections pointed to Democratic-Republicans maintaining their majority status. Governor Jonas Galusha, a loyal Madisonian supporter of the war, was comfortably reelected. The Jeffersonian party's long-time lieutenant governor Paul Brigham was also returned to office by a solid margin. The Governor's Council, a twelve-person elected body charged with diffusing the chief executive's powers, was swept by Democratic-Republicans. Finally, and most directly important to Madison, was the voters' continued affirmation of a Democratic-Republican majority in the legislature. The *Green Mountain Farmer* in Bennington exclaimed approvingly that the results were "PROOF That Green Mountain Boys Prefer War to Submission." Meanwhile, Clinton had not yet even been nominated.[19]

These races for down-ballot offices left no doubt that Madison had Vermont in his corner when the unicameral General Assembly and the Governor's Council chose electors on October 30. The *Washingtonian*, a Federalist publication in Windsor, could see the writing on the wall after the party's disastrous showing in the September balloting. The newspaper ranted that the outcome assured "the continuance and permanent establishment of BONAPARTE'S *dreadful system* of WAR, CONSCRIPTION TAXATION, and NO COMMERCE." As expected, the incumbent was awarded the elector slate, although "about 12 or 14" Democratic-Republicans reportedly voted with Federalists for the Clintonian ticket.[20]

The trend continued into the December 7 at-large elections for the US House of Representatives, although Federalists proved to be competitive opponents. Democratic-Republicans achieved a unanimous victory, but the margin was quite close. The combined vote for Democratic-Republicans was less than 1 percent greater than the aggregate Federalist total. The lone Federalist seat in the delegation was lost, as Congressman Martin Chittenden was defeated in his House race, which came two months after his unsuccessful campaign to unseat Governor Galusha. A year later, however, Federalists captured the legislature, and Chittenden won the governorship in a disputed election that had to be resolved by the General Assembly.[21]

In Connecticut, there was no suspense. The Constitution State was a rock-solid base of Federalist power, and so the political gains Democratic-Republicans achieved during the Jefferson years were not experienced there. Even in Jefferson's 1804 landslide reelection, Connecticut was not on board. The state-established Congregationalist Church also held roots in the Federalist Party.[22] As Connecticut was highly dependent on shipping, the war would make it impossible for Madison to be a serious contender there anyway. Federalist critics repeated the accusation that the war would only strengthen France. A letter writer to the *Connecticut Courant* under the pen name True American claimed, "Mr. Madison in all probability had pledged himself to Bonaparte. . . . It is in fact Bonaparte's war; and our president, in pressing it on, acted as the humble tool of that cut-throat."[23]

Roger Griswold, one of the New England Federalist governors who would not cooperate with the Madison administration's war preparations, was reelected with about 84 percent of the vote on April 13. The entire delegation of Connecticut congressmen was Federalist in 1812, and on September 21 they were all sent back to Washington, DC. On the same day that Madison was decisively winning Pennsylvania and Ohio with large popular vote totals, Clinton secured an easy victory in this New England fortress of Federalism. The mode of elector selection in Connecticut was by way of the legislature, which was strongly under the control of Federalists. Unsurprisingly, nine Clinton electors were chosen on October 30, but that did not generate any new national momentum for his candidacy.[24] Similar to election campaigns today, there is little to be gained from simply meeting expectations.

The same thing could be said with regard to New York, the state that acquired more new House seats than any other in the federal census of 1810.

Now empowered with ten additional congressmen and a larger slate of electoral votes, the home base of DeWitt Clinton was better positioned to challenge Virginia's domination of national politics—if not in 1812, then soon into the future. Since the Constitution's creation, New York law called for presidential electors to be chosen by the legislature. While Clinton's candidacy originated in that institution, political calculations were complex, especially given the nature of the clumsy Federalist/Clintonian fusion. The state's pro-Madison Democratic-Republicans still remained a relevant political force that could take advantage of squabbling within the opposition coalition.

The *New York Evening Post* told its Federalist audience what was at stake in the legislative elections scheduled for April 28–30. The newspaper reminded readers that these results would determine who chose electors in the fall, thereby making these elections a proxy for the presidential race. It was a choice between "the death-doing conduct of the present rulers at Washington" and the responsible gentlemen who embodied the true spirit of George Washington. Voters delivered and produced a Federalist takeover in the Assembly. The Senate remained technically Democratic-Republican, but the Clintonians were the controlling faction. If all of New York's twenty-nine electoral votes were to be carried by Clinton, the alliance of at least some Federalist legislators would be necessary. Even a mere partial victory here could doom his campaign, unless Pennsylvania generated a favorable result. No Federalists formally participated in Clinton's legislative nomination in May, but the party's vague fusion with his candidacy at September's New York City national meeting seemed to assure that he could count on the state's full support. Still, the skepticism of Rufus King and Peter Jay served as just two examples of elite Federalist figures that were unenthusiastic about Clinton. On October 23, King confided to his brother William by telling him, "It is well known that I do not approve of Mr. Madison's administration—but between him and Mr. Clinton for reasons which in my judgment deeply concern the public liberties, I prefer the election of Mr. Madison."[25]

The legislature began the business of selecting presidential elector slates on November 2. The first canvass generated a result that was essentially along party and factional lines. Each chamber commenced with its own vote, which would then be reconciled in a joint ballot of the full legislature. Initially, Federalist purists appeared not to have a preferred alternative to rally behind. In the Assembly, the approximate tally was twenty-three for Madison, twenty-eight for Clinton, and fifty-eight for Federalist electors pledged to an unspecified presidential candidate, although there were a few minor variations in the totals for certain elector candidates. In the Senate, the roll call was a solid win for Clinton, with his electors usually taking seventeen or eighteen votes. Madison electors captured anywhere from five to eleven senators each, and the Federalist slate won eight votes.[26]

On the November 9 joint ballot of all legislators, Clinton electors prevailed with seventy-four votes, to forty-five for an unnamed Federalist, with reports of anywhere from twenty-three to thirty-three blank ballots that were generally cast in protest by Madison supporters. Freshman Democratic-Republican senator Martin Van Buren asserted that a majority of Federalists voted for the Clinton elector slate on the joint ballot, although their exact number is not discernable. Indeed, Clinton would obtain the twenty-nine electoral votes that he needed from his home state, but the fusion could only be described as just barely successful, given that so many Federalists continued to resist voting for their somewhat official nominee. The skepticism of King and Jay seems to have been shared by other Federalist office-holders in their state.[27]

In securing New York's electoral votes, Clinton received some help from the young Senator Van Buren of Columbia County in the Middle District. A future president and builder of the national Democratic Party around the ideology of Andrew Jackson, Van Buren was just beginning his career as a power broker in the New York legislature. He actually gave his support to the war effort, but felt himself compelled to defer to the will of his state party before the national Democratic-Republican organization. In recent years, he had also formed an alliance with the Clintonians, as he was seeking to detach himself from the toxic Aaron Burr faction.

Leery of too much overt cooperation with the Federalists, Van Buren was confident that the other party would line up behind Clinton without direct pandering. In the joint meeting of legislators, Van Buren reached out to the pro-Madison men with an offer to share part of the elector ticket in a number congruent with the incumbent president's supporters in the full legislature. When one considers the proportion of Madisonians in the legislature, this arrangement could have given Madison four to six electors at Clinton's expense. Even with this concession, everything really did hinge on Pennsylvania for both candidates, and the early results were looking very good for the president. Losing about half a dozen New York electoral votes would not matter to Madison if Pennsylvania was secure, while an unexpected Clinton win in the latter state would then turn the election into a razor-close tossup. Cutting a deal with the Clintonians in New York might well also backfire among War Hawks, among whom Madison had worked so hard to build trust over the previous two years. Van Buren's offer was not accepted.

Following a period of debate that went nowhere, the politician who later became known as the "Little Magician" was done being conciliatory and motioned for a vote on a full slate of Clinton electors. The joint legislative meeting approved his proposal. Van Buren reported thirty-six Federalists voting for the Clintonian elector slate, while the *Public Advertiser* in New York City claimed thirty-nine Federalist crossovers. The pro-Madison newspaper identified the legislators who abstained as "honest blanks," and raged against the process in the legislature as being rife with "iniquity, fraud and depravity" as well as a "hydra of corruption." Still, with a kernel of truth the *Public Advertiser* pointed out "that notwithstanding the federalists had set up a ticket of their own, it was not their intention to support it. They stuck true to their *pledge*, and loaned from their stock a sufficient number to carry the point, and keep up appearances."[28]

In his posthumously published autobiography, Van Buren defended his advocacy of Clinton but also conceded that his course of action was ultimately mistaken:

> The rejection by the People of the President who had recommended the War, in the absence of any act to show his incompetency, would have done more injury to the public service than could have been counterbalanced by the alleged superior qualifications of Mr. Clinton for the crisis. This consideration should have induced Governor Clinton to decline the State nomination, after the declaration of War, notwithstanding the ground upon which he had been put forward, and to unite with his friends in the support of Mr. Madison. His failure to do so was fatal to his national aspirations, and many of his friends destroyed their political influence by adding disparagements of the War to their opposition to the candidate by whom its declaration had been recommended.[29]

After the election, relations between Clinton and Van Buren deteriorated. The two men became political rivals, although they achieved some reconciliation when they mutually backed Andrew Jackson's 1828 presidential candidacy.[30]

Congressional elections for New York proved to be a mess. Initially, balloting was scheduled alongside legislative races in late April. Redistricting for the state's enlarged US House delegation, however, had not yet taken place, which may have been a consequence of Governor Tompkins's

March 27 order to prorogue the legislature. Still, some counties held congressional elections anyway under the existing boundaries. The next legislature subsequently created new congressional districts and scheduled balloting for December 15–17. The April US House elections were nullified. After several more months of mostly bad news from the battlefield, and with many new candidates on both sides running in December, Federalists achieved an overall successful outcome. Democratic-Republicans lost four seats while Federalists gained fourteen, putting them in control of the delegation. Taken as a whole, the split between Clintonians and Madison supporters was harmful to New York Democratic-Republicans and allowed a Federalist comeback that proved to be short-lived. As for Governor Tompkins, a loyal Madison ally, he survived his reelection contest in April 1813 with just over a 4 percent spread.[31]

The more pivotal state was New Hampshire. On August 5 the self-identified "friends of Peace" held a rally in the town of Brentwood, in Rockingham County. There was not yet an official Federalist nominee to run against Madison, but the assembly was reported to be in excess of two thousand people. Several speakers, including the promising young lawyer Daniel Webster, addressed the crowd. Leaders of the meeting resolved to draft anti-war resolutions and endorse New Hampshire candidates for Congress and presidential electors. The event became known as the Rockingham Convention, and it revealed the intensity of New England's opposition to the war. Soon before the election, the *Portsmouth Oracle* denounced the American incursions into Canada as an "unblessed War" and "a miserable and *wicked* attempt to invade, to kill and to destroy those who owe us no enmity, nor wish us any evil."[32]

In fact, Federalists had reason for optimism in this state. Prior to the outbreak of war, Federalists actually won the popular vote in the March 10 gubernatorial election. The state constitution, however, called for the General Court (the name of the legislature) to make the selection when no candidate for governor prevailed with an absolute majority. Democratic-Republicans remained in control of the General Court, and they chose their candidate, William Plumer. The political pendulum then moved sharply in the Federalists' direction by that autumn, when war was a reality. In at-large voting on November 2, the party swept all New Hampshire seats in the US House of Representatives, for an impressive net gain of five. Federalist candidates took a combined 54 percent of the vote. Daniel Webster's illustrious career in public office also began in 1812 with his election as an anti-war congressman.[33]

Throughout the Jefferson years, Democratic-Republicans had been making gradual gains in the state and building a strong party apparatus. In the 1808 presidential race, New Hampshire was closely contested, but Federalists held on, as Charles Pinckney prevailed by a 5 percent margin. The unpopular war disrupted this trajectory and seemed to kick New Hampshire back into being a Federalist stronghold. Presidential electors for 1812 were chosen by the voters in a winner-take-all ballot on November 2, alongside their congressional elections. New Hampshire was clearly competitive, but it was also needed by Clinton more than Madison, given the latter's stronger base in more and larger states.

Clinton achieved the win he required and carried New Hampshire's eight electoral votes with over 54 percent of the popular vote, as compared to nearly 46 percent for the president. Some Federalist newspapers started to show overconfidence as the numbers were reported. Bragging over the state results, the *Constitutionalist* in Exeter proclaimed that "nothing has yet transpired to cloud the prospect of a change of rulers." A headline in the *Concord Gazette* called "Clinton's Election Sure," right above a letter containing several erroneous predictions about its candidate's prospects in other states.[34] The optimism of Clinton's boosters in the press proved to be ephemeral, if not naïve.

Still, the challenger did attain some success at persuading at least a few of 1808's supporters of Madison. Clinton flipped Rockingham County, which includes the seaside towns of Hampton and Portsmouth. Strafford County also flipped to the anti-war candidate, with a drastic loss of support for Madison in the seaport town of Dover. In 1808 Madison carried Dover with 172 votes, to 133 to Pinckney; four years later the president earned only 75 votes, to 229 for Clinton. Other patterns of New Hampshire's voting continued along the general equilibrium of 1808. Notably, Madison carried Coos County, which bordered British Canada, by a slightly larger margin than four years before.[35] The argument can be made that voters situated in a location like this one may have been very conscious of the threat of a foreign attack, which could have worked to the incumbent's advantage to some degree.

Clinton's boosters made opposition to Virginia's dominance of the presidency a major issue in their campaign. Federalists in this state declined to endorse him, and his dissident wing of the Democratic-Republicans had no real base here either. Nor were John Randolph and the Old Republican faction of much use anymore, given that they were themselves divided on the war. The limited Federalist organization advocated on behalf of Rufus

King's candidacy, but its members were easily overwhelmed by the mainline Jeffersonian party, which fully supported an aggressive war upon the British. In addition, as Jefferson predicted, strong prices for corn and flour provided a political lift to the incumbent president.

The *Richmond Enquirer* defended its state from attacks. The newspaper ran a letter from an author calling himself Pelopidas, who responded to the committee out of New York that nominated Clinton. Virginia, the writer reminded readers, voluntarily ceded territory after the Constitution was adopted. The state had no uncontrollable ambition to dominate the nation. Rather, perhaps New York was the real state that aimed to consolidate power. Pelopidas warned that "the desire of conciliating the imaginary feuds of the American Republics, is the plausible pretext now urged by the state of New York." Any alleged friction between commercial and agricultural states was minimal, and New York's claim to be a mediator between the two was laughable, especially when the messenger was a calculating politician like DeWitt Clinton.[36]

Madison supporters also criticized King's credibility as a potential commander-in-chief who couldn't be trusted to handle adversaries of the United States. The *Farmers' Repository* in Charles Town printed a resolution signed by King in 1806 that denounced British impressment of American sailors. The candidate concurred with signatories who demanded that the Jefferson administration take warlike measures in response to outrages as sea. In a mocking introduction to the six-year-old anti-British resolution, an anonymous writer stated, "The Staunton Convention of Delegates, after much ponderous consideration and puzzling hesitation, had pitched upon one RUFUS as a fit person to be their KING."[37]

Federalists called out the Madison administration for politically motivated manipulation of flour prices for electoral gain. The *Alexandria Gazette* asserted that "surely the *intelligent* farmer will not be so easily duped," for the good times were likely to be temporary, and predicted that Gallatin's higher taxes would result as the war continued. If the farmer wanted four more years of Madison, "then let him go to the poll and vote for *war and double taxes.*"[38] These criticisms may have been sound on the merits of policy, but they smacked of desperation and an implicit concession that the president was unstoppable in his home state.

The war was in fact popular in Virginia overall, and the statewide presidential results confirmed that verdict on November 2. Congressional races in April 1813 provided further vindication for the pro-war Democratic-Republican wing. Madison and his boosters lost very little ground here from 1808, as compared to other states, and the dominance of his party meant that he could shed some support and still be in a commanding position. The Madison vote was 73 percent in 1812; only a loss of about 5 percent from four years prior. Rufus King's total amounted to about 27 percent, though he showed pockets of local strength.

In the southside counties, Madison achieved a full sweep. In contrast to some other states, he saw no significant loss of his previous support from the seaside counties and port cities. The incumbent actually flipped Princess Anne County, which today includes Virginia Beach and in 1808 had voted for (the by then Madisonian) James Monroe. In the city of Norfolk, which had also voted for Monroe, Madison carried this port location by a big margin. On the Eastern Shore, the counties of Accomack and Northampton both voted massively for King, similar to their spread in favor of Monroe four years earlier. Elsewhere, King performed well in scattered inland counties, a few of which had voted against Madison in 1808. Most of the far western part of the state went solidly for the president. The capital city of Richmond also remained a Madison stronghold.[39]

As part of their Fourth of July celebration, citizens in Goochland toasted to the president, Congress, and Secretary Monroe. Then they burned John Randolph in effigy. The pro-war momentum continued into Virginia's April 1813 congressional elections, which were comparatively late in the cycle. Redistricting and the addition of one new seat meant that many congressmen would be running for reelection under new boundary lines. The overall outcome to the state delegation left the hawkish, pro-Madison majority intact, though with some key distinctions. Old Republicans continued their political death spiral, especially if they found themselves on the wrong side of the war issue for Virginia. Most notably, Randolph went down to defeat against John W. Eppes, a son-in-law of Thomas Jefferson and a fellow Democratic-Republican running on an explicitly pro-war platform. Randolph allies Edwin Gray and Matthew Clay, who both skipped the final roll call vote on declaring war, also were denied reelection by Democratic-Republican opponents.[40]

Like other northeastern states, New Jersey had been slowly but surely moving in a Jeffersonian direction for a decade. In 1808 Madison prevailed in New Jersey by a 12 percent popular vote spread over Pinckney, taking all eight electoral votes. Even amid Jefferson's embargo, the backlash from port communities remained limited. A peacetime embargo was one thing, but that on top of an Anglo-American war was clearly not well received there, especially as the economic damage piled up. Democratic-Republican senator John Lambert was a Clintonian opponent of the war, and four of the party's six New Jersey congressmen voted against the formal declaration. The outbreak of war disrupted this state's political equilibrium, bringing out hardball tactics from Federalists, and great outrage in response from mainline Democratic-Republicans.

New Jersey Federalists used the war to revitalize their party by way of some of the populist mobilization tactics they once disdained. They organized Washington Benevolent Societies, which were already up and running in New York, Maryland, and most of New England. Town hall meetings and rallies to oppose the war also provided a great venue for party-building, where Federalists advertised themselves as the "Friends of Peace." In an effort to make common cause with Clintonians, they formed a fusion with Democratic-Republican congressmen who had voted against the final war resolution. On September 15 Democratic-Republican representatives Adam Boyd, Jacob Hufty, and Thomas Newbold were nominated with the blessings of New Jersey Federalists for the congressional elections of 1812, which were scheduled for November 3–4. On these dates, voters were also slated to choose presidential electors.[41]

First, however, were the state legislative elections on October 13–14, which Federalists framed as a referendum on the war. "At no election since the war of the revolution, has so momentous a question been submitted to our suffrages," the *Trenton Federalist* told readers just before they went to the polls. The results represented a stunning reversal of the Democratic-Republicans' decade-long growth in New Jersey, as Federalists took control of both chambers of the legislature. "The late election has evinced that the people of New-Jersey are not the advocates of the present war," the newspaper bragged after the outcome was revealed. Expressing bewilderment at the voters' verdict, the Democratic-Republican *True American* in Trenton seemed to acknowledge the Federalists' spirited campaign, as well as the overconfidence of the Jeffersonian party. "Meantime the Republicans have this consolation," the *True American* said, "that the temporary change in this state, cannot alter the General Government," in an apparent reference to the presidential race.[42]

New Jersey Federalists, however, were determined to try their best with the limited window of time they had left. The new legislature convened on October 27, and they got right to work at maximizing their party's advantage and attempting to throw Clinton a lifeline. The Federalist majority took actions that delayed and curtailed democracy, while also sowing confusion and further inflaming partisan tensions. Pursuant to their constitution, they were first tasked with picking a governor, and their choice was Aaron Ogden. A respected leader in his party, Ogden was a lawyer, Revolutionary War veteran, and assemblyman, who had also done a brief stint in the US Senate a decade earlier.

Then the Federalist majority set out to postpone the congressional elections, scheduled to be held in just a few days, to the new dates of January 12–13. In the same year that Massachusetts Federalists mocked their opponents for gerrymandering, now New Jersey's Federalists did exactly just that. The state was reorganized into three districts, with each having two congressmen. Democratic-Republicans were packed into a single district in the northern counties. Perhaps owing to the slow spread of the news that the congressional balloting had been postponed, or even due to acts of protest by some Democratic-Republican voters, some counties held outlaw elections anyway on the original November date. Virtually no Federalist voters participated. As expected, Federalists took four of the six seats in the official January races.[43]

As for the presidential electors, the state promptly changed the law to shift New Jersey away from popular at-large selection to appointment by the legislature, thereby canceling the voters' opportunity to have their say in just a few days. On November 5 a joint session of both houses appointed a group of Clinton electors, handing the challenger the state's eight electoral votes and keeping his tenuous prospects alive. The legislators voted twenty-nine for Clinton and twenty-three for Madison. Similar to the recently postponed elections for the US House, citizen balloting for the presidency (originally scheduled for identical dates) was simply canceled. The *True American* reported dozens of rebellious voters showing up to polling places to cast ballots anyway, even in the face of sometimes uncooperative local officials.[44]

The Democratic-Republican *Centinel of Freedom* in Newark screeched to voters that their right of suffrage had been "snatched from you." Democratic-Republican legislators published an open letter calling their opponents' actions "a result, tyrannical in its operation, insulting to the liberties of every freeman in the state, and which may be attended with consequences disastrous to our country." Federalists defended their maneuvers on the grounds that holding elections for federal offices so soon after the legislative races was impractical. Furthermore, if appointment of presidential electors by the people's representatives in the statehouses was appropriate to choose George Washington, it should be good enough for the present circumstances. "Ever since this mode was departed from, the country has been going down hill to ruin," the *Trenton Federalist* opined, as it unapologetically endorsed the abrupt transformation of election laws, procedures, and calendar dates.[45]

The recent Federalist sweep of the legislative elections makes it puzzling to understand why the party endeavored so arduously to take away the ability of voters to cast what very likely would have been a strong anti-war mandate from the people in November. Such a possibility could have given the old Hamiltonian party the ability to reposition itself as a grassroots coalition centered on peace and commerce. Madison's double-digit win in 1808, however, may have made that hypothetical scenario a risky proposition for New Jersey's Federalist power brokers. Instead, by subverting the scheduled electoral processes, their party got their desired outcomes, but at a long-term cost. Once again, it became easy for adversaries to label Federalists as anti-democratic elitists who held the common people in contempt. Even before the war's conclusion, Democratic-Republicans resumed their climb back to dominance in the state.[46]

New Jersey's transient Federalist majority engaged in tactics that political scientists would later describe in other contexts as examples of *constitutional hardball*. Methods deployed are technically legal under state and national constitutions, but are clearly aimed at achieving a distinct political advantage for a ruling party or regime. Actions brush aside established norms of democratic behavior, in favor of the more immediate objectives of winning, consolidating power, and capturing institutions.[47] Still, the New Jersey Federalists of 1812 were hardly the first or last majority party to alter election laws to their own advantage, given the politically motivated changes being made in other states within this cycle.

In Tennessee, reapportionment added three new safely Democratic-Republican electoral votes, bringing the state's total to eight. The home base of War Hawk congressmen Felix Grundy and John Sevier was never in doubt. Governor Willie Blount was also a strong supporter of a military resolution of American conflicts with the British. As early as November 15, 1811, the legislature affirmed its full endorsement of Madison's leadership as the nation steered ever closer to war. Praising the president for his handling of the Anglo-American crisis, the legislature's official statement asserted, "We have much pleasure in assuring you, Sir, that we feel the fullest confidence in the wisdom and firmness of that administration which you have conducted so beneficially for your Country and honorably for yourself." The letter also applauded Madison's leadership of the fragile situation in Florida. As he carefully worked to court War Hawks well before the election, the president thanked Governor Blount and the legislature on December 10. "The wrongs which have been so long borne by our Country," Madison said, "are persisted in, with aggravations which leave to a nation, determined not to abandon its rights, no appeal but to its own means of vindicating them."[48]

Tennessee was divided into eight geographical districts, with each one allocating a single elector. On November 5–6, eligible voters chose a full slate of pro-Madison electors. The outcome here was assumed in the newspapers, as greater attention was paid to the incoming returns from Pennsylvania and other states. Official tallies from Tennessee's 1812 presidential elector races are lost to history, but there is no reason to speculate that Clinton made any headway here. War Hawk momentum continued into 1813, as Democratic-Republicans swept all six congressional contests, including the overwhelming reelections of Grundy and Sevier. Governor Blount was reelected nearly unanimously.[49]

In Georgia, where hawkish, Madisonian Democratic-Republicans held commanding control of government and political life, the General Assembly unceremoniously chose eight electors for the incumbent on November 9. Reapportionment gave Georgia two new House seats in Congress, and on October 5, Democratic-Republicans took the whole delegation. The Federalist vote was negligible. Similarly, legislative elections that same day revealed no noticeable breakthrough for Federalists in the port city of Savannah and Chatham County, where any wartime revival for their party would have needed to succeed.[50]

Kentucky's developments were somewhat more interesting, even though the final results were entirely predictable. Reapportionment gave Kentucky four new seats in Congress. Democratic-Republicans maintained their hegemony over the state, sweeping all House races on August 3. In the intraparty gubernatorial election on the same day, Democratic-Republican Isaac Shelby prevailed by a large margin. Shelby, a popular Kentucky military hero and former governor, answered demands from citizens to return to public life now that America was on a wartime footing once again.[51]

Support for the war here was intense, and appeals to anti-Indian sentiment ran strong as well. Senator John Pope stood out as a lone voice of opposition in a very hawkish congressional delegation led by Speaker Clay. Prior to the escalation into war, Pope was generally supportive of the Madison administration. Acting in concert with the president and Secretary Gallatin, he voted to renew the National Bank charter in 1811, but in defiance of the instructions from his state legislature. Pope disobeyed legislative orders again the following year, when he voted against the key roll call for unrestricted war upon Britain exclusively. He did, however, cast an unsuccessful vote for a triangular declaration of war on Britain and France. That nuance in the senator's position was subsumed by the jingoism in Kentucky, as the outbreak of hostilities brought about celebratory cannons in Lexington and Frankfort. Pope was burned in effigy in Nicholasville and Mount Sterling by warmongering mobs. Upon hearing the news, the *Trenton Federalist* called the perpetrators "ruffians." Bowing to the obvious political winds at home, Pope declined to be considered by the legislature for reelection the following January.[52]

Eligible voters chose twelve electors across three special districts on November 9. Each district awarded four electoral votes, and the results matched expectations. As the returns came in, newspapers reported overwhelming margins for Madison in county after county. "We are informed that in some counties the Clinton ticket has not received a single vote," the *Reporter* declared on November 14. Somewhat more specific district results became public on November 25, revealing that Madison prevailed with near unanimity. For example, in the Third District, which included Lexington's Fayette County, the lowest vote total for any of the official Madison electors was 4,942 whereas the highest tally for a Clinton elector was just 289. County returns from Kentucky's 1812 presidential elector races have been mostly lost, with only a few scattered exceptions. Popular vote tallies for two of the three electoral districts are currently in existence.[53]

No state's popular vote was tighter than in Maryland. In 1808 Madison won the state by a resounding margin of over 26 percent, which reflected Democratic-Republicans' majority status at the time. Federalists, however, remained resilient and competitive in legislative elections throughout the 1810s. Madison's feud with the Smiths tore at Democratic-Republican unity in this state. Opinions on the war were passionate and divided, as hawk-oriented citizens sometimes resorted to violence to assert themselves. Maryland maintained a method of allocating electoral votes on the basis of a special elector district map, which was different than congressional district boundaries. Splitting the state up in this way rendered it unlikely that either party would gain a major advantage from Maryland's voters. In 1808 Madison carried nine of its electoral votes and Pinckney secured two. In a campaign marred by violence, results were expected to be closer this time around.

Alexander Contee Hanson, a twenty-six-year-old publisher from a prominent Maryland family, used his *Federal Republican and Commercial Gazette* in Baltimore to make vitriolic attacks on Madison, Gallatin, and supporters of the war effort before and after hostilities had commenced. "TAXES! TAXES! UP TO THE EYES," the newspaper exclaimed in response to the treasury secretary's proposals. Frequently mocking "poor Madison," Hanson's publication predicted that "his name will sink with odium into oblivion, or only be remembered in the annals of intrigue and corruption, as an example to excite the scorn of posterity."[54] Upon learning of the declaration of war, the *Federal Republican* made no pretense of a call for national unity. Warning that civil liberties were in danger, and that America was not financially or militarily ready for this clash with Britain, the newspaper confidently asserted on June 20 that a majority of citizens agreed with their stance: "We are avowedly hostile to the presidency of James Madison, and we never will breath under the dominion direct or derivative of Bonaparte, let it be acknowledged when it may. Let those who cannot openly adopt this confession, abandon us, and those who can, we shall cherish as friends and patriots, worthy of the name."[55]

The match was lit, and now matters took a much darker turn. The city of Baltimore was a Democratic-Republican stronghold, including sizeable immigrant communities of German, French, and Irish stock—who had no love lost for the British. The populist energy unleashed by the outbreak of war, combined with several weeks of the *Federal Republican*'s slashing anti-Madison, anti-war diatribes, produced conditions ripe for violence. On June 22 an angry mob beset Hanson's office as he fled for his life. The crowd burned the newspaper's building to the ground. Democratic-Republican mayor Edward Johnson and other city officials were less than vigilant in their efforts to contain the rioters. Destruction of the *Federal Republican*'s headquarters was apparently a preplanned action following a series of meetings at local watering holes. Meanwhile, Hanson vowed to continue spreading his message, and he resolved to relocate his publication as soon as possible.[56]

Sporadic violence continued, however, for the next several weeks. Suspected British sympathizers were targeted, including African Americans. Ships in the harbor, allegedly carrying materials that could aid Britain, were also singled out for attack. Another inflection point came on July 27, when the *Federal Republican* attempted to resume operations at a private residence on Charles Street, this time with armed guards for protection. Included among Hanson's protectors was Henry Lee III, or "Light-Horse Harry," a hero of the Revolutionary War and father of future Confederate icon Robert E. Lee. Defiant against the "mobocracy," Hanson's newspaper picked up right where it left off, castigating the Madison administration for "fatal impatience" and denouncing War Hawks in Congress as "terrorists." The rioters were "implicitly sanctioned if not originated by the highest authorities in the country," the July 27 editorial claimed, and the mob proved itself to be the real enemy of the republicanism its members claimed to favor.[57]

The mob still wasn't finished with the *Federal Republican*. That same evening, rioters attacked the Charles Street house with rocks, which resulted in a doctor being shot and killed by guardsmen, along with several other rioters who endured wounds. The next morning a growing angry crowd returned with artillery equipment, which was not used due to the intervention of Mayor Johnson. Hanson and his contingent were evacuated from the house and escorted by city officials and an ad hoc local militia to the county jail for their own protection. Thugs subsequently ransacked the Charles Street house and continued to pelt the Federalist citizens with rocks and other objects. Meanwhile the *Baltimore Whig*, an anti-Madison—but also pro-war—newspaper, was egging on the rioters with supportive rhetoric and blaming the Federalists for the violence.[58]

The mob then broke into the county jail and began assaulting the *Federal Republican* men, including Hanson and Lee. Some of the Federalists escaped, but others were beaten, stabbed, and doused with hot candle wax. One man in their protective detail was tarred and feathered, an old mode of vigilante punishment for men labeled as pro-British. One of the protectors was killed by these pro-war "patriots": a former Revolutionary War officer named James Lingan, now a brigadier general in the Maryland state militia. Lingan, a former prisoner of war, had distinguished himself by refusing the British offer of release if he would just abandon the American cause and accept a commission in His Majesty's army. Lee was badly wounded in the head and died six years later, having never fully recovered from that evening's attack. The drunken crowd continued to celebrate their violent assaults all night.[59]

Hanson, himself suffering multiple injuries, moved his operations to Georgetown, where he began publishing again on August 3. "The history of barbarians scarcely affords a parallel in perfidy and cruelty to the late transactions at Baltimore," the newspaper stated in its account of the recent political violence. Not content with having forced the *Federal Republican* to flee the city, the mob tried to attack the Baltimore post office when the newspapers arrived by mail for subscribers. The local militia was activated, and despite some resistance in the ranks to defending the hated Federalist newspaper, Johnson was able to convince the rank-and-file men to at least protect the integrity of the post office. The rioters were broken up, but an uneasy peace settled over the city. Hearing about the violence in Baltimore, Mayor Clinton took steps to prevent the effusion of blood in New York City streets. Claiming that threats had been made against anti-war residents, Clinton preemptively called for peace and ordered the city's police force to prepare. No riot occurred.[60]

Madison did not condone the actions of the murderous mob, but he viewed the episode as a generally local problem. "I never considered an assault by the mob on the post office as probable," Madison wrote to Maryland attorney general John Montgomery, "nor allowed myself to doubt that, if made, the local authority was both able and willing to crush it." Curiously, the president was skeptical that he had the authority to provide federal protection for the US post office and left the responsibility to state and city officials. There was no public statement from him denouncing and repudiating the criminals who attacked freedom of speech, destroyed property, terrorized innocent citizens, and murdered a distinguished American war hero.[61]

Secretary of State Monroe told the president that while riots "must be prevented," the *Federal Republican* bore some of the responsibility for encouraging the violence with inflammatory rhetoric and arming in selfdefense. "Nothing can be said in favor of a party," Monroe told his boss, "organised for the purpose of its combating the mob unknown to the law, equally in defiance of it, and which could not fail, by the excitement it was sure to produce, to bring on the contest." Worrying about possible civil war, Monroe wished to see the newspaper survive, but also hinted that "the punishment even of such men as the Editors of that paper must be inflicted by law, not mob movments."[62]

To be fair, presidents were not expected by that era's contemporary norms to publicly denounce every act of citizen violence, even when it came from a politically motivated mob. Such a standard will be unfamiliar to the American people in the twenty-first century, when there is a demand for presidents to comment on every major news event. Still, Madison's silence revealed the indifference with which Democratic-Republicans treated this shameful series of incidents. The *National Intelligencer* made it clear that the violence in Baltimore was "disgraceful to all concerned," but pivoted to criticizing Federalist publications, particularly in Boston, for inaccurate and provocative rhetoric. Using a tactic of argument that is today known as whataboutism, the newspaper then raised the matter of Representative Charles Turner Jr., a Massachusetts pro-war Democratic-Republican. The congressman, who also served as a local judge, had very recently been grabbed and beaten by a Federalist mob in Plymouth.[63]

Federalists and their publications claimed the riots were evidence of the moral bankruptcy of the administration's rush to war. A Fourth of July celebration in Dedham, Massachusetts, made a mocking toast to "Mr. Madison's Mob at Baltimore," for when citizens resort to violence on behalf of the government, "they exhibit at once the badness of their cause, and the weakness of their means." The *Trenton Federalist* made a martyr of General Lingan, who was killed by "inhuman butchers," and saluted Lee's bravery against "cannibals" in the city. *Poulson's American Daily Advertiser* in Philadelphia also called Lingan a "martyr for the liberty of the press." Meanwhile, an effigy of the murdered general was burned on Capitol Hill late in the summer. One of the perpetrators was a navy midshipman; he was subsequently dismissed from the military.[64]

Maryland's congressional contests were held on October 5, producing no net change to the party equilibrium in the state's delegation. Most notably, Hanson was easily elected to the House from a Federalist district based around Frederick and Montgomery counties. That same day's elections for the House of Delegates generated a sweeping Federalist takeover of the chamber. The Senate was not elected by the people directly but was instead chosen by Maryland's own electoral college. The Senate remained in Democratic-Republican hands, but the raw total of Federalist legislators was larger, enabling their party to appoint the next governor.[65]

Popular voting for presidential electors took place on November 9. Two years earlier, a state constitutional amendment was approved to lift property qualifications for presidential and congressional elections. Given that this revision could have allowed much more Black male suffrage, the legislature also enacted a law to formally deny voting rights to African Americans, regardless of their status concerning slavery. Seven of the nine special electoral districts each held one electoral vote, while two of the districts (Three and Four) were worth two electoral votes each. The Third District was generally based around the city of Baltimore, while the Fourth District was mainly based around Allegany, Frederick, and Washington counties. Clinton easily prevailed in the overwhelmingly Federalist stronghold of District One, which took in Charles, Prince Georges, and St. Mary's counties, and took home a solid win in District Two, which included Calvert County and portions of Montgomery and Prince Georges counties. District Nine was also an overwhelming win for the challenger, which included the counties of Somerset, Worcester, and parts of Dorchester.[66]

In District Five, centered around Baltimore County outside of the city proper, Madison beat Clinton by a 70–30 percent margin. Although this was a resounding victory for the wartime president, it was also quite a bit below his 94–6 percent win over Pinckney there in 1808. In the double-elector Third District, Madison's base of support held, as he carried all eight wards in Baltimore, plus the Anne Arundel County portion. Clinton comfortably took the Montgomery County segment, but the incumbent still captured the district by a nearly two-thirds margin. Four years prior, Madison's vote total there was about 95 percent, indicating that while the war and the riots did damage him to some degree, the party's dominance in Baltimore was simply too significant. Madison also locked up a comfortable win in District Six, which included Cecil and Harford counties.

For his own part, Clinton secured an important win by about 120 votes in the double-elector District Four, and a flip for the Federalists from four years earlier. That key victory, however, was offset by Madison holding Districts Seven and Eight, where he had prevailed in 1808. District Seven, including Kent and Queen Anne's counties, was a comfortable Madison win. Similarly, the incumbent retained District Eight, including Caroline, Talbot, and parts of Dorchester counties, by a razor-thin margin. The final Maryland total stood at six electors for Madison and five for Clinton—a virtual draw in a state that had been so fiercely and bloodily contested. The popular vote was just shy of 52 percent for Madison and just over 48 percent for Clinton.[67]

Clinton failed to achieve the gains he required in the necessary districts and was unable to politically capitalize on the violent behavior of some of Madison's supporters. Maryland's Democratic-Republicans were a fractious bunch, just as their cohorts were in Pennsylvania, but they were also highly motivated around the rallying cry of war and a domestic opposition that was easy to label as pro-British. Assessing the results coming in from Maryland and other states, the *Richmond Enquirer* declared victory on November 20, proclaiming that the outcome "will show the determination of the majority of this nation to support their government in the grounds which they have taken." Madison's reelection would "abate though not silence that clamorous spirit of opposition to the war."[68]

In neighboring Delaware, Democratic-Republicans had made only a little headway during the Jefferson and Madison years. The Federalist Party was already tightly organized and well entrenched here, even before the war. Joseph Haslet, a Democratic-Republican, was a deviation from this trend. A planter from the southernmost Sussex County, he prevailed in a narrow election as governor in 1810, even amid the early ramp-up to war. Haslet's government cooperated with the Madison administration, and he worked with the General Assembly to improve the state militia and appropriate funds for military preparedness. During his three-year term in office, Federalists otherwise maintained firm control of the state's political establishment. Haslet was limited to a single nonconsecutive term, and Federalists captured his office in October 1813.[69]

In the arguably safest state of all for the presidential challenger, Delaware Federalists maintained their commanding control of the General Assembly in elections on October 6. At the federal level, the 1810 reapportionment gave Delaware an additional congressional seat and electoral vote. By comfortable margins, Federalists won both at-large House races. On November 10 the legislature unceremoniously voted 19–6 in favor of Clinton over Madison, and four electors were designated for the winner. These results were far too little and just a bit too late for him, as returns from neighboring Pennsylvania began trickling in, thereby making a Madison victory more likely by the day. "All hopes of DeWitt Clinton succeeding are now extinct," the *New Hampshire Patriot* declared on November 10, as the newspaper reviewed the incumbent's victorious achievement in Pennsylvania.[70]

Clinton needed a major win in Massachusetts, but even accomplishing that would only allow him to tread water. "I see no prospect of Uniting this Nation in any other Man better than in Madison," John Adams wrote to his son-in-law William Smith. "To turn him out, at this time would be such a Wound to all the Southern and Western States," the former president said, "who are now the great Sufferers by the War, and in the most distress and danger, that I know not what would be the Consequence." While Smith was a successful Federalist candidate for the US House of Representatives from New York in 1812, Adams broke with his party to not only endorse Madison's reelection but also serve as an elector for the incumbent president. The only real suspense, however, was if Madison could win any electoral votes in Massachusetts at all, and whether it would even matter.[71]

Federalists were on offense in New England's largest state. The *Repertory* in Boston attacked the Madison administration for letting flour slip through the embargo. "It cannot be pretended now, that a trade so profitable to the Southern States has unexpectedly grown out of the war," the newspaper declared, claiming that the policy was an act of cynical election-year pandering to cover for an incompetently managed war. France was the real beneficiary of a British war with America, the *Repertory* asserted, and Napoleon Bonaparte needed Madison to stay in office. If that meant Wellington's army had to be fed by farmers from the United States in the short run, then so be it.[72]

Congressional elections on November 2 generated major Federalist gains in the House. Congressman Turner earned no sympathy from his recent assault and was defeated by double digits amid an anti-war electoral wave. Federalists now held a 16–4 advantage in the Massachusetts delegation, which was enlarged by three due to reapportionment. In spite of the Federalist momentum, Clinton's hopes were in steady decline by the time of the presidential balloting on November 12. While the war and embargoes were polarizingly unpopular there, even a full sweep of all twenty-two electors would only allow him to maintain his losing pace. After Governor Gerry's reelection defeat in April, and the infamous gerrymandering that forever tarred his name, Federalists continued to show major revitalization in the war's early months. Although the creatively shaped state senate districts kept Democratic-Republicans in power in that chamber, Federalists took control of the Massachusetts House in May 1812. In tallying up the results in two separate columns, the *Columbian Centinel* in Boston referred to Federalists as the "Washingtonian" party, while Democratic-Republicans were labeled as "Commerce-Haters."[73]

In the short history of the Electoral College, Massachusetts had already changed modalities several times. In 1808 the Federalist-dominated legislature had unsurprisingly chosen Pinckney. Now matters were more complicated with a split statehouse. Democratic-Republicans had little chance to earn more than a few electoral votes here, while Governor Strong and other Federalists aimed to maximize their ability to achieve a full sweep. A general-ticket referendum of the full state would have surely resulted in Clinton taking all twenty-two electors, while some kind of district vote might have given Madison a fighting chance for a handful of electors. Brushing aside their recent criticisms of the other side's naked manipulation of political districts, Federalists intervened at the last minute to give their candidate as great an advantage as possible. After much haggling between the two chambers of the legislature, on October 22 a model was adopted that provided for popular selection in six districts, each with varying numbers of electors. Federalists remained confident that they could carry the entire state.[74]

Federalist optimism proved to be well founded. Madison's best opportunity may have been in the Maine districts near British Canada, but while he did run somewhat competitively there, it failed to yield him any electoral votes. Clinton prevailed in the Eastern District One, which encompassed the Maine counties of Cumberland, Oxford and York. Madison's only county victory in the state was in Oxford, which shared a border with Canada, but Clinton carried the district with nearly 56 percent of the vote. Nor was Maine's Eastern District Two any better for Madison. Clinton carried all three counties, for a win with nearly 57 percent of the vote. Similarly, Maine's Eastern District Three produced an even greater margin in favor of the challenger.

In the quintuple-elector Middle District, Clinton pulled off a full-on blowout. Powered by an overwhelming win in Boston, Essex County on the North Shore, and a narrow victory in Middlesex County, Clinton won with more than two-thirds of the vote. The Southern District (including the counties of Barnstable, Bristol, Dukes, Nantucket, Norfolk, and Plymouth) delivered an easy Clinton win. Likewise, the sextuple-elector Western District (including the counties of Berkshire, Franklin, Hampden, Hampshire, and Worcester) resulted in the challenger taking in excess of 72 percent of the vote. When everything was tallied up, Clinton pocketed all the twenty-two electors that he needed, and 65 percent of the Massachusetts popular vote. It was a resounding victory for the challenger that delivered no new momentum outside of New England.[75]

Going back to 1808, Massachusetts was the epicenter of fervent opposition to the war and embargoes. The Federalist/Clintonian fusion functioned smoothly and effectively there. A robust Federalist infrastructure was already in place, along with an eagerness among the state's party leaders to reach out to Clintonians, even though Clinton himself did not have a major Democratic-Republican following in Massachusetts. Two dissident Democratic-Republican newspapers under the same editorial control, the *Yankee* in Boston and the *Boston Pilot*, blasted away at Madison, revealing his unpopularity in most of New England. The *Yankee* was noteworthy for the fact that in September it abruptly flip-flopped from its former support for the president and the war, while the *Pilot* was a new newspaper that ceased publishing a few months after the election.[76] Gerry's vice presidential candidacy, meanwhile, added nothing to the ticket in his home state, given the mockery that his name still evoked.

Following the pattern of most New England states that had been drifting toward Democratic-Republicans in varying degrees during the first six years of the Jefferson presidency, Rhode Island was now experiencing a strong Federalist revival. Democratic-Republicans lost their rising momentum amid an environment of war and embargoes in a state whose economic livelihood was so tied to its coastal location and ports. Democratic-Republicans remained competitive, but in 1808 Pinckney still carried Rhode Island with over 53 percent of the vote while Madison earned nearly 47 percent.[77]

Four years later, the war's unpopularity put Rhode Island out of competition. The legislature declared July 23 a day of "fasting, humiliation and prayer" in protest. Federalists retained their solid legislative majorities in 1812, and their man William Jones was reelected to the governorship on April 15 by about a 3 percent margin over the former governor, Democratic-Republican James Fenner. Jones was a war opponent who would not proactively cooperate with the Madison administration once hostilities began. Along with Governor Strong of Massachusetts and Governor Roger Griswold of Connecticut, Jones was fiercely protective of his state militia's autonomy. The party's momentum continued on August 25, as both Federalist congressmen, Richard Jackson and Elisha Potter, were reelected by comfortable margins.[78]

Rhode Island did not gain any new House seats in Congress from the decennial reapportionment, thereby depriving Clinton of any additional electoral votes. The popular balloting for electors on November 18 produced no surprises, as the Federalist nominee swept all counties, with Madison only taking a few scattered towns. The cities of Providence and Newport both gave overwhelming majorities to Clinton, as he beat the president 66–34 percent statewide. Rhode Island was a coastal wall of political support for the challenger, but one that proved to be very small and inconsequential in the end.[79]

Consistent with the pattern of states manipulating their elector selection processes, procedures, and districts, North Carolina acted early to secure a full victory for Madison. Democratic-Republicans commanded a majority in the state, although Federalists held the offices of attorney general and treasurer. Lest the Federalists be able to obtain a few electoral votes by way of a district selection mechanism, as was the case for Pinckney in 1808, the General Assembly enacted a new measure in December 1811 providing for appointment of the full slate by joint legislative session.[80] Unless Democratic-Republicans lost control of the legislature the following summer, Madison now had a clear path to the state's fifteen electoral votes, which was an increase of one due to reapportionment. The failure of North Carolina Federalists to install a home-state running mate for Clinton also worked to the benefit of the incumbent.

The General Assembly's repeal of the district elector law proved to be controversial across the political spectrum, and contrary to the Jeffersonian party's identity as the populist champions of democracy. Eligible voters in

North Carolina had been electing the president by way of popular choice since 1796 but would now see that power taken away by a Democratic-Republican legislature. At least in New Jersey, it could be said that similar actions by Federalist legislators were consistent with their reputation for antidemocratic elitism. North Carolina county grand juries assembled to denounce this curtailment of citizens' voting rights. The new law was "inconsistent with the spirit of the constitution, and the rights of the citizens," the grand jury of Lincoln County declared. Johnston County's grand jurors demanded the law be repealed and replaced with "the restoration of the inviolable right of suffrage in the election of Electors." The Richmond County grand jury called the new law a "most unauthorised and dangerous innovation on our rights." Wayne County's grand jury attacked the law as an "unwarrantable assumption of power, and hostile to the principles of Republicanism."[81]

Legislative elections in August revealed a limited backlash against Democratic-Republicans, but not enough to dislodge them from the statehouse, thereby keeping North Carolina safe for Madison. Although they remained well in the minority in both chambers, Federalists gained ten seats in the House of Commons and two in the Senate. They showed strength in coastal counties around Newbern, the northern Piedmont, and the Fayetteville area, while losing some seats elsewhere in the state. The elector law continued to be a source of division for Democratic-Republicans, as some in the majority party defected in the November 16 House vote for Speaker, producing a surprisingly close 64–59 tally in their favor.[82]

Federalists and some Democratic-Republicans pressed for a special session of the General Assembly to repeal the elector law and restore popular balloting for 1812. Governor William Hawkins did not call a special session, but he did propose a long-term solution of a federal constitutional amendment to standardize modes of elector selection across the states. Efforts to repeal the law in the regular legislative sessions sometimes came close to success but failed before the election. After North Carolina's Democratic-Republicans had been able to use the law to secure Madison's reelection, they repealed the measure in December and restored popular elector selection. Voters in the future would choose by way of an at-large general ticket, which still put Democratic-Republicans at a significant advantage.[83]

Madison remained in good shape in North Carolina for the 1812 election, as Federalist support for Clinton was slow to materialize, given his lack of an organization and a following in the state. Rumors circulated about a possible bribery plot to buy off legislators for Clinton, with accusations of agents carrying money between New York and North Carolina. The *National Intelligencer* printed a letter from a man in Raleigh claiming that "we have had two men here from New York of rather suspicious character, but they have decamped" after realizing that "their scheme will not answer here." A joint session of the General Assembly met on November 21 and delivered 130 votes to Madison and 60 to Clinton. A handful of Federalists did not support their nominee and voted for the Democratic-Republican president, either because they were repulsed by the alleged New York bribery scheme or felt a genuine disdain for Clinton.[84]

In yet another state, Democratic-Republican divisions created headaches for Madison's boosters, but the party's overwhelming dominance, combined with the bungling Federalist/Clintonian fusion, did not prevent the incumbent from securing North Carolina's full electoral support. Congressional elections the following April 30 resulted in no overall change to political equilibrium, with one Federalist pickup and one Democratic-Republican gain, but opponents of the war could count a few victories. John Randolph's ally Richard Stanford won with over 60 percent of the vote in his district, centered around Orange and Wake counties. Pro-war William Blackledge was resoundingly defeated for reelection by a Federalist in his district, which was based around the port city of Newbern. Even in the South, anti-war sentiment could still be found, albeit to a reduced degree when compared with northern and Middle Atlantic states.[85]

In Congress, some of the most influential War Hawks came from South Carolina. The state was never competitive in the presidential election, and its small but occasionally vocal Federalist Party never mounted a major threat to Democratic-Republican supremacy in 1812. Although the entire congressional delegation voted for war, three freshmen congressmen stood out. Representative John C. Calhoun was at the beginning of an impactful national political career but was already a leading voice for military confrontation with the British. The states' rights militancy that he was so well known for would come later in Calhoun's life. Representative Langdon Cheves had yet to reach the prime of a career that would later include the presidency of the Bank of the United States. He too promoted war, and as an ally of Speaker Clay, Cheves was installed as chair of the Select Committee on Naval Affairs. In April 1812 he became the acting chair of the tax-writing Ways and Means Committee. Joseph Lowndes, who was frequently in poor health, was the final component among the most prominent South Carolina War Hawks.[86]

On August 29 the state legislature adopted a full-throated resolution of support for the war, and for Madison's stewardship of the crisis. "It is a war of right against lawless aggression, of Justice against perfidy and violence," the statement declared. The South Carolinians called the British in Canada a "barbarous Neighbor" who must be stopped. Echoing racist themes that Madison would repeat in his November Annual Message, the legislature accused Great Britain of "secretly fomenting by her emissaries, divisions and factions among us; and who has at no time ceased to direct the tomahawks and Scalping knives of her fellow Savages, the indians against the defenceless women and Children of our frontier." Madison was praised for his "patriotism and wisdom," as South Carolina pledged its full support in the war effort.[87]

As Madison and fellow mainliners in his party gradually moved toward an indistinguishable position from the War Hawks throughout 1812, the commander in chief promoted the morality of American principles. In a written response to the South Carolina legislature on October 10, he stressed that the United States was engaged in a defensive struggle, "having its origin neither in ambition, nor in vain glory." Hinting at the war's popularity among the citizenry, he declared that "having been called for by the public voice, every motive ought to be felt, to bear its necessary pressure with cheerfulness, and to prosecute it with zeal to a successful issue." Madison was practicing smart politics by using his wartime presidency to directly address the same legislators that would soon be choosing electors. Even though South Carolina was safe for the incumbent, his words would be disseminated in newspapers across the nation, right about at the time many voters were going to the polls. Without mentioning his own election contest, Madison was reminding like-minded War Hawks all over the country that the president was an unambiguous advocate of their cause.[88]

Federalists made a gallant effort to defeat Congressman Cheves in his Charleston-based district. John Rutledge Jr., whose family name still held great value in South Carolina, was nominated to run against the incumbent. Congressional and legislative elections on October 12–13, however, delivered a mandate for pro-war Democratic-Republicans. Cheves was reelected with nearly two-thirds of the vote, as anti-war sentiment did not gain traction in Charleston. Lowndes faced only token opposition, and Calhoun ran unopposed. Democratic-Republicans swept the rest of the delegation's remaining six seats. The *Investigator* in Charleston rallied the party around a bloody shirt-waving message that depicted a vote for Democratic-Republicans as a poke in the eye of the British, who were allegedly riling up the "savages" to slaughter innocent South Carolinians. The so-called friends of peace were really just subversives, "and the man who now temporizes is no FRIEND, but a TRAITOR to his country." Meanwhile, an effigy of John Randolph was hung in Charleston, alongside a label calling him a "British agent." The *Charleston Courier* scolded its city for this deed: "We blush . . . when we reflect that it contains wretches capable of such disgraceful conduct."[89]

State legislative and congressional elections were the true proxy of the people's will in South Carolina and several other states in 1812. Property qualifications for white males were liberalized in 1810, resulting in more economically downscale voters, who would be ripe for Democratic-Republicans to cement their control of the state. Federalists, as the party of well-to-do planters and merchants, made a game effort, but they lost ground in the legislature. National issues revolving around the Anglo-American clash loomed large in these contests, given the legislature's role in appointing presidential electors there and elsewhere, as well as Congress's role in authorizing this controversial war. Overwhelmingly Democratic-Republican legislators assembled on December 1 to select a slate of eleven electors for their president, at which point the election was effectively over. Out of 159 participating legislators, Madison electors earned anywhere from 139 to 153 votes. No tally for Clinton electors was reported. South Carolina persisted in choosing presidential electors by way of the legislature as late as 1860.[90]

Last and least was Louisiana, and its results were never in doubt, but its lengthy delay created chatter that its electoral votes would not be counted in time. The legislature of the newly organized state took its time to devise a method to choose electors. "It appears that its suffrage will be lost, owing to the want of a law for the appointment of Electors," the *Richmond Enquirer* surmised in its assessment of the incoming election results on November 20, which was otherwise rosy for Madison. Pro-Clinton newspapers speculated that Louisiana's absence might open a narrow pathway for their man to win, although that was contingent upon unexpectedly carrying North Carolina and one of the three districts in Kentucky. After North Carolina voted in line with expectations, Boston's *Columbian Centinel* ran a headline entitled "BAD NEWS" on November 28, but still clung to the hope that Louisiana might have to forfeit its electors and Kentucky might produce a partial surprise.[91]

Louisiana did eventually get its affairs in order, although word of its legislators' action moved slowly to the eastern newspapers. On November 30, a joint session of the legislature voted 23–16 in favor of Madison over Clinton, adding three more electors to the incumbent. The tally for the challenger was surprisingly high in a state where pro-war Democratic-Republicans dominated, though Clinton supporters made a game effort to spread their message in New Orleans. According to Governor William C. C. Claiborne, a Madison supporter, "The Clintonians were numerous & active" in the city, where they pitched their candidate as a friend of sugar and cotton planters. Surely, such persons might be amenable to arguments on behalf of reducing trade barriers, securing stable markets, and peace. Those appeals were insufficient for victory, but the results were indicative of a limited degree of skepticism toward Madison in southern coastal states.[92]

FINALIZING THE OUTCOME

Meetings of electors in state capitals, scheduled for Wednesday, December 2, produced no faithless defectors in the presidential race. The absence of a few Madison electors raised false hopes from Clintonians, but these vacancies proved to be either temporary or irrelevant. The president won reelection with 128 electoral votes to 89 for Clinton. Ohio only submitted seven of its eight electoral votes due to the nonattendance of elector David Abbot, apparently due to illness. In a closer election, the unforeseen absence of an elector could have been critical to the outcome, which is why it remains vital today that the men and women chosen for this task be reliable people. The balloting for vice president totaled 131 for Gerry and 86 for Ingersoll. Two Clintonian electors from Gerry's home state of Massachusetts, as well as one from New Hampshire, defected in his favor. Another sign of a leaky party fusion is the failure to line up all electors behind the ticket.[93]

The national popular vote for 1812, and any other presidential election through at least 1820, is much more complicated to assess. The large number of states that denied the direct ballot to their citizens, as well as the disenfranchisement of women and persons of color, makes it hard to assert that the popular vote represented the true will of the people. Although New York would not allow voters to directly choose electors until 1828, one can conjecture that Clinton would have bolstered his national tally if his home state had been permitted the same popular right of suffrage as Madison's Virginia. New Jersey's last-minute shutdown of citizen ballots may have impacted the final numbers in either direction. Had North Carolinians been allowed to go to the polls, Madison's total surely would have been larger. Missing vote counts from Tennessee and Kentucky also detracted from the president's final tally.

Historical narratives of the 1812 election provide slightly varying popular vote totals, perhaps due to the aforementioned absent returns. In addition, in some states each elector who was pledged to the same presidential candidate frequently carried very slightly different popular vote tallies from their cohorts. A negligible handful of voters in every state would surely split their presidential elector tickets, perhaps because of some animus toward one or a few individual electors. Other accounts of this contest wrongly lump Rufus King's votes—all of which were from Virginia—into the final tally for the Federalist/Clintonian coalition. All of these caveats aside, in the assessment of this researcher, Madison's recorded popular vote total stood at approximately 140,730 (52.64%), to 121,021 (45.27%) for Clinton, and 5,584 (2.09%) for King.[94]

After Pennsylvania's results were widely disseminated by mid-November, and it became clear that there would be no surprise Clinton wins in states outside of his base, the prospects of a second Madison term grew ever more realistic. "I am happy, extremely so, in the prospect of your re-election," vice president elect Gerry wrote to Madison, "for the reverse of this would, in my mind, have given to G Britain, a complete triumph over our most meritorious administration, & Legislature, & Would have been considered by her, & probably by all Europe, as a sure pledge of the Revocation of our Independence." The *Public Advertiser* hailed the victory against "the British peace ticket." Some Clintonian newspapers, however, started to grasp at straws, given the uneven reporting of results. Perhaps, they told themselves, there was a pathway for Clinton due to the lost elector from Ohio. Additionally, the fact that Louisiana had not yet been heard from could deprive Madison of three electoral votes. There were also overly sunny claims that their candidate might capture one of the Kentucky districts.[95]

A problem with the selection of the gentlemen slated to be Pennsylvania's electors caused some pro-Clinton newspapers to indulge in wild hypothetical scenarios. Four of the Keystone State's twenty-five electors failed to report to the capital on the scheduled date for them to cast their ballots. The legislature promptly replaced them with Madison men that same day, and the delegation proceeded to give their votes to the incumbent president. Clintonians, however, cried foul, claiming that Pennsylvania was in violation of the 1792 law governing elector selection and voting. That statute, the Presidential Succession Act, explicated that electors from the states must be chosen during the thirty-four days preceding the first Wednesday in December. According to New York's *Statesman*, because the four substitute electors were chosen *on* Wednesday, December 2, rather than beforehand, this should therefore void the entire Pennsylvania elector slate. Such a scenario could have been disastrous for Madison, although the law did not really authorize the full disenfranchisement of a whole state under these circumstances. Still, pro-administration Democratic-Republicans controlled enough state delegations in the House of Representatives to ensure his reelection if the lower chamber had to choose the president in accordance with the Constitution's Twelfth Amendment. The *Statesman* called upon "eminent jurists" and congressmen to challenge the credentials of Pennsylvania's electors, lest a dangerous precedent be set. Other Clintonian newspapers asserted that at least those four electors should be disqualified, although such a penalty would not have damaged Madison in any significant way.[96]

The newspapers' claims about Pennsylvania's alleged violations of the letter of the law accordingly went nowhere. Clinton supporters in the House and Senate were not interested in pursuing these desperate demands on behalf of a candidate that generated little enthusiasm within their ranks. At a joint session of Congress, Federalists and Clintonian Democratic-Republicans made no recorded objections to the official certification of the results on February 10, 1813. The following day, a congressional special committee was appointed to formally notify Madison and Gerry of their election.[97]

Federalists had a little more to cheer about in Congress, though they remained deep in the minority. The election cycle netted Federalists thirty-two new seats in the House, which would be expanding in membership due to reapportionment. Democratic-Republicans gained only seven seats, revealing that Madison's win did not carry coattails at a national level. Selections for the Senate reflected the prevailing political winds in each state's respective legislative elections for the year. Federalists gained two, and Democratic-Republicans lost two. The overall electoral cycle of 1812 strengthened the Federalists in Congress, weakened Clintonian Democratic-Republicans, and left Randolph's Old Republicans almost completely decimated. At the beginning of the new Thirteenth Congress, the House party composition stood at 114–68 in favor of Democratic-Republicans. The Senate remained even more dominated by Democratic-Republicans, with a 28–8 spread.[98]

Madison was about to enter his second term with his same large fractious majority in Congress, alongside an emboldened Federalist minority. America's first wartime presidential election was concluded.

7

MADISON AND CLINTON THE WAR OF 1812 AND THE BALLOT BOX

On March 4, 1813, James Madison was once again sworn in as president of the United States. In spite of a war on domestic soil with a major European power, all of the major celebratory features of this quadrennial American event took place. There was a military escort of the president to the Capitol, followed by Chief Justice Marshall's administration of the constitutional oath, and a speech by the chief executive—who was known more for his intellect and written words than his oratory. Foreign dignitaries were in attendance among the large crowd, though notably not the French ambassador. President Madison and the first lady then appeared at an inaugural ball at the Davis Hotel in Washington, DC.[1]

In the early republic, inaugural addresses were among the very few times when presidential speeches before a general audience would be considered appropriate and befitting the dignity of the office. After his wartime reelection, Madison's remarks were short, as he repeated common themes about British aggression and the enemy's alleged manipulation of "savage" Indian peoples for their military conquest. "As the war was just in its origin and necessary and noble in its objects," the president told the crowd, "we can reflect with a proud satisfaction that in carrying it on no principle of justice or honor, no usage of civilized nations, no precept of courtesy or humanity, have been infringed. The war has been waged on our part with scrupulous regard to all these obligations, and in a spirit of liberality which was never surpassed." In a speech that mentioned no other issues than the war, Madison praised the citizenry for their commitment to the task ahead: "When the public voice called for war, all knew, and still know, that without them it could not be carried on through the period which it might last, and the patriotism, the good sense, and the manly spirit of our fellow-citizens are pledges for the cheerfulness with which they will bear each his share of the common burden."[2]

Similar to other presidents who were reelected in the context of a controversial war, Madison used his inaugural address to affirm his belief that he was sent back to the White House with a mandate to finish the job. As he hailed the successes of the American navy, Madison concluded his speech by referring to the ground campaign, where the good news had been sparser. The president saluted the service of the army and militias, but also hinted that more grueling days could be in the future: "If the reputation of our arms has been thrown under clouds on the other, presaging flashes of heroic enterprise assure us that nothing is wanting to correspondent triumphs there also but the discipline and habits which are in daily progress." These words proved to be prophetic, as events on the battlefield waxed and waned for the United States during the next two years.[3]

In this concluding chapter, readers will see the impact of the wartime 1812 presidential race on the party system, as well as the leading figures of the election. Much of what is to be found in the Madison/Clinton matchup was decentralized, confusing, and chaotic. In addition, the election revealed the challenges that come with trying to build a coalition between a declining minority party and a regionally based faction of the governing party. In looking at 1812's electoral landscape, close observers can also see small steps toward a more populist brand of politics that would burst on to the American scene within less than twenty years.

WAR AND NATIONALISM: A DEMOCRATIC-REPUBLICAN TRANSFORMATION

Victory in the election did not preclude the continuation of political and military problems for the Madison administration. Although the president had established some degree of control over his bloated, fractious party majority in 1812, a national Federalist resurgence remained a threat. The Clintonians may have been weakened as a faction, but their absorption into a reinvigorated Federalist Party was a realistic prospect if the war descended into a catastrophic defeat. Should matters on the battlefield take an especially negative turn for the United States, Federalists would possess the tools they needed to rebrand themselves as the party of peace, commerce, and prudent foreign policy. Now with the election resolved in their favor, Democratic-Republicans politically owned the war, along with all the benefits and consequences it was sure to produce.

Madison's troublesome Cabinet continued to complicate his administration. After being exited from his position, William Eustis was replaced at the War Department with James Monroe, who served on an interim basis while still secretary of state. Hoping to put on his uniform again and take the field with a commission, Monroe declined to take the job in a long-term role. Madison, however, needed his future presidential successor in the Cabinet. The new permanent secretary of war was John Armstrong Jr., a New Yorker who was known as a political schemer and author of the Newburgh Letters, which encouraged the Continental Army to mutiny in 1783. After limping to a Senate confirmation by a vote of only 18–15 in January 1813, he proceeded to create more headaches for his president. Armstrong bickered with Monroe and Gallatin and gave an army staff position to William Duane, who remained a critic of the administration in spite of his reluctant endorsement of the president's reelection. More importantly, Secretary Armstrong failed to prepare Washington, DC, for the British siege that would burn the city on August 24, 1814. The Capitol, the White House, and other government buildings were torched. The Madisons, along with their household staff and slaves, fled the capital. The furious president then fired Armstrong and replaced him with Monroe, who was already well positioned to continue the Virginia dynasty in 1816.[4]

Incompetent generals also continued to plague the commander in chief. Most notable was General James Wilkinson, a manipulative and scandal-ridden officer who had a knack for worming his way out of trouble in spite of doing considerable damage to other people. In 1809 Wilkinson lost about a thousand of his men from malaria, dysentery, bilious fever, or desertion in the swamps near Natchez, prompting Madison to order a military court of inquiry. Secretary Eustis had ordered Wilkinson to encamp on higher ground, which would have been safer for the troops. The negligent commander was also suspected of being a paid spy for Spain, though this clear conflict with his duty to America could not be definitively proven at the time. Wilkinson was exonerated by the court-martial, promoted to major general, and returned to the field in March 1813. Past his prime and in poor health, Wilkinson commanded two more losing battles: at Crysler's Farm, Upper Canada, in November 1813, and then again at Lacolle Mills, Lower Canada, in March 1814. Wilkinson was subsequently relieved of command, and his military career was effectively over.[5]

The war that was known for impressive battlefield victories at Baltimore and New Orleans, as well as the inspiration of Francis Scott Key's *Star-Spangled Banner*, also produced a litany of embarrassing defeats that revealed America's lack of financial and military preparation for a clash with a European superpower. First, however, the current conflict had to be brought to an honorable conclusion. Russia, a British ally that also imported American tropical produce, appealed to both countries to convene peace negotiations. Despite some successes on the American continent, the conflict was a drain on British security resources on the European front, given the continuing Napoleonic Wars. The French emperor was temporarily forced to abdicate in April 1814, however, and the American war was responsible for higher taxes and economic consequences due to the closing of trade with the United States.

Madison appointed a distinguished delegation of peace commissioners. John Quincy Adams effectively led the team. He was now the American minister to St. Petersburg and would be an important voice for New England, where opposition to the war had been so intense. Second, there was Secretary Gallatin, who would at long last leave his post at the Treasury Department after over a decade. Federalist senator James Bayard of Delaware resigned his seat to serve on the commission. Although he opposed the declaration of war, Bayard fully supported the military campaign once it began; he had a reputation as a moderate and a pragmatist. Speaker Henry Clay also resigned his House seat to participate, thereby giving a stamp of War Hawk credibility to whatever emerged from the proceedings. Jonathan Russell, the recently departed pre-war ambassador to the Court of St. James, also joined the commissioners.

The British were slow to begin negotiations, but direct talks commenced in Ghent, Belgium, on August 8, 1814, and a treaty was hammered out by December 24. The signature American issue of the war—impressment—was negotiated away with the blessing of the Madison administration. The final defeat of Napoleon at Waterloo in June 1815 ultimately ended the British incentive to use this practice as a means of conscription, just as many American policymakers had hoped. The treaty was generally a standoff, with provisions to return prisoners of war, captured wartime property (including slaves), and promises of peace to impacted tribes of Indigenous peoples. Both sides were required to remove themselves from territory controlled by the enemy. The only land issue that the treaty resolved called for appointing a commission to determine ownership of the Passamaquoddy Islands, which are between New Brunswick and Maine.

While some Britons wanted a renewed commitment to defeat America, most elements of the country's leadership establishment were happy to extricate themselves of the war overseas, so as to free up military resources that could be used in Europe. Indeed, just a few months later Napoleon emerged from exile and attempted to resume his conquest over the continent. Britain ratified the Treaty of Ghent on December 27, but not wanting to let their guard down, the British insisted that the document not become effective until both countries exchanged ratification papers. They had no way of knowing if American politicians might become mired in debate, or perhaps even demand changes to the treaty.[6]

Those fears were put to rest, as Americans across the political spectrum were eager for a peace agreement. The treaty, and the British ratification documents, arrived in New York on the evening of February 11. The city erupted into great celebration, and word of the treaty spread quickly down the eastern coast and inland. Upon receiving the treaty, Madison quickly sent it to the Senate, where it was unanimously ratified on February 16. The next day, Secretary Monroe, now serving in two Cabinet positions, exchanged ratification papers with Anthony St. John Baker, a British diplomat who had made the trip to the United States bearing the documents that ended the war.[7]

The *National Intelligencer* claimed vindication, claiming that "the treaty is thought in all respects to be honorable to the nation, and to the negociators." The *Connecticut Courant* applauded the agreement, noting that "as for party spirit, which has so often before unhappily infused bitterness into the cup of our public pleasures, it seemed now to have followed after 'the shades of departed Time,' and was no where to be found." Both major Clintonian newspapers in New York also cheered the Ghent accords. In an editorial from the *Columbian* that also ran with the endorsement of the *Albany Register*, Charles Holt proclaimed that America successfully stood up to the "Invincibles of the eastern continent" and hailed the "honor and justice" of the peace deal. In the aftermath of the jingoism unleashed by the victory at New Orleans, the pro-Clinton organs shifted to celebrating military success.[8]

While the Ghent peace agreement was on a ship at sea, matters were about to culminate as part of the British campaign in the Gulf of Mexico. On January 8, Brevet Major General Andrew Jackson commanded a motley and outnumbered force in defense of New Orleans, resoundingly defeating the enemy. Euphoria from this impressive victory, combined with upcoming news of the peace deal, unleashed a wave of nationalistic energy. The

Ghent agreement did not give Americans everything they wanted, but at least the war's last major battle was a decisive win for the United States. Citizens and their elected representatives could tell themselves that the war marked a triumph for America, even as the capital lay in ruins. More significant in the long run was the beginning of Jackson's rising stardom, which would one day push American politics in a more populist direction.[9]

Now that the war was over, Madison steered in the direction of some measures that were more characteristic of Federalist and Clintonian policies, perhaps tacitly acknowledging the nation's ill preparation for the recent conflict. In his penultimate Annual Message, submitted on December 5, 1815, the president called for steps to improve military readiness:

> The character of the times particularly inculcates the lesson that, whether to prevent or repel danger, we ought not to be unprepared for it. This consideration will sufficiently recommend to Congress a liberal provision for the immediate extension and gradual completion of the works of defense, both fixed and floating, on our maritime frontier, and an adequate provision for guarding our inland frontier against dangers to which certain portions of it may continue to be exposed.

America's first wartime president urged Congress to enhance the military academy, better organize the state militias for national defense purposes, and strengthen the navy. If the United States was not yet destined to be a superpower, at the very least it would be ready and able to defend its interests from the titans of Europe. Additionally, Madison seemed to complete his evolution on the national banking issue, as he opened the door to this possibility if the state banks should prove to be inadequate. Congress obliged, and the president signed into law a new charter for the Second Bank of the United States in April 1816. Even on the protective tariff Madison was ready to embrace some level of proactive federal action to safeguard vulnerable American industries. The federal government could also provide support for internal improvements under some circumstances, given the relationship between interstate commerce and transportation projects. That said, Madison the strict constitutionalist suggested that an amendment to the document might be necessary to legitimize a robust national internal improvements policy.[10]

In contrast with so many future presidents who greatly struggled with the legislative branch in the latter months of their second terms, the solidly Democratic-Republican Congress was generally willing to follow Madison in the direction in which he wished to take the country. Not only was a new bank chartered, but a modest protective tariff was instituted, most wartime taxes were maintained, and the armed forces remained staffed and funded so as to provide for a credible national defense. There was no internal improvements bill until early 1817, which Madison vetoed on constitutional grounds on his last full day in office. The legislation would have set aside surplus revenue from the Bank of the United States into a fund for internal improvements.[11]

War Hawks and mainline Democratic-Republicans were in firm control of their party, in spite of Madison's slow embrace of some policies that were more characteristic of a Clintonian or Federalist vision for America. The president's emphasis on taking military preparations more seriously was certainly more reflective of the War Hawks' preferences, albeit without their belligerence. The old Jeffersonian party had now come a long way from the days when it was an agent of fiscal thriftiness, low taxes, humble foreign policy, free trade, and states' rights. To be sure, many Democratic-Republicans still believed in these principles and spoke of these platitudes, but at a national level they had to temper ideas with the reality of governing. As factions multiplied, mutated, and reorganized, the task of rallying around a unifying governing philosophy only became more complicated after the war's conclusion and Madison's departure.

As for the Invisible trio in the Senate, they were diminished after the war, but neither did they become totally irrelevant. Samuel Smith, who served as a major general in the Maryland militia, contributed to the defense of Baltimore while he was a sitting US senator. In early 1816 he moved over to the House of Representatives, but he returned to the Senate in late 1822, where he eventually became president pro tempore of that body. William Branch Giles was not reelected by Virginia's legislature in 1814, and he subsequently returned to political affairs in his own state. The legislative body selected Giles three times for one-year terms to the governorship between 1827 and 1829. After being selected for a fourth term, Giles declined to serve and retired. Michael Leib was removed from the Senate in February 1814 by way of his appointment to the powerful postmastership in Philadelphia. Postmaster General Gideon Granger chose Leib for the job, along with other Madison critics in additional cities. The following month, an annoyed president fired the long-tenured head of the postal system, but the hiring of Leib at least extricated from the chief executive a major nuisance in the Senate. Madisonians reassumed control over the Post Office in due course anyway, for Granger's replacement was Ohio's Governor Meigs. Accordingly, Leib was exited from his position within a year.[12]

As a faction, the Old Republicans may have been obliterated by the war and election of 1812, but their influence diffused throughout the political landscape in future decades. John Randolph was unfazed by his defeat in 1813, and in April 1815 he won back his old House seat in a rematch against John Eppes. Still as eccentric as ever, his political career was revived, though Randolph continued to suffer setbacks as he transitioned into a Jacksonian Democrat and an apologist for slavery. Purist Old Republican ideas were certainly influential on some of the principles of Jackson's Democratic Party. Doctrinaire advocates of states' rights, later embodied by John C. Calhoun, could also point to Old Republican values.[13]

As secretary of state, James Monroe held the office that was most likely to position him as the next Democratic-Republican presidential nominee. At a well-attended congressional nominating caucus on March 16, 1816, Monroe prevailed 65–54 over William H. Crawford of Georgia, Madison's current secretary of war. The Virginia dynasty endured, as Monroe was easily elected later that autumn. New Yorkers took a consolation prize by regaining custody of the vice presidency, as the nomination went to Governor Daniel Tompkins. While the Democratic-Republican competition was spirited in 1816, the caucus itself remained a source of controversy, as the impulses of Jacksonian democracy showed early signs of emerging. The party aborted its caucus in 1820, and four years later this congressional nominating event was poorly attended and carried a badge of illegitimacy and elitism. The caucus was discontinued for the 1828 election cycle.[14]

Clay's resignation from Congress was temporary, for even before he returned to America he was reelected to his seat and reinstalled as House Speaker in the autumn of 1815. From that position, he continued to establish his political significance as a major national party leader. Clay became identified with his advocacy of what was called the American System of robust internal improvements, as well as a national bank. Like many Democratic-Republicans of a nationalist orientation, Clay moved into the Whig Party in the mid-1830s. In the House and the Senate, Clay was known for his legislative craftsmanship and ability to achieve compromises, especially on sectional issues. Making three separate unsuccessful runs for the presidency, he was arguably the most famous national politician of his time who had not served as president. In the multi-candidate presidential election of 1824, which was thrown to the House of Representatives, Speaker Clay was a key kingmaker that helped hand the office to John Quincy Adams over Andrew Jackson. The new chief executive then chose Clay as secretary of state, prompting unsubstantiated accusations from Jackson supporters of a crooked deal. As a party, Democratic-Republicans by 1824 were so large, so ideologically diverse, and so ubiquitous over the country that the label no longer meant much of anything. A new party system was already evolving, with Jackson as its leading actor, although Clay would play a major role as an antagonist.[15]

MADISON AND GERRY

Madison left office with the bulk of his policy objectives fulfilled, even though he presided over a governing party that was splintered into multiple factions. Returning home, he resumed life as a Virginia plantation owner. Consistent with many of the men who once held the job, Madison was not in great financial shape once he departed from the presidency. His Montpelier plantation was struggling and in debt, and the former president sold land and slaves to make ends meet. Like Jefferson before him, he would continue to be an active participant and commentator on public affairs, while still showing respect to subsequent chief executives.[16]

As a believer in public higher education, he assisted Jefferson with the creation of the University of Virginia. After the passing of his presidential predecessor on July 4, 1826, Madison took over as the university's rector (the equivalent of the chair of the governing board), a position he would hold for the next eight years. As Jefferson's heir apparent in the presidency, and now as his heir apparent in the early leadership of one of today's great public universities, Madison assumed an active role in all campus affairs. Both men worked hard to develop the curriculum, recruit distinguished professors, and maintain the barrier between enlightened scholarship and religious dogma.[17]

Virginia also called upon Madison's expertise when the state set about writing a new constitution. A convention was held in Richmond between October 1829 and January 1830, with Madison in attendance for three months. Also at the gathering were Monroe, Randolph, and Chief Justice Marshall; the latter's presence would today be regarded as a completely inappropriate conflict of interest for any sitting US Supreme Court justice. Among the issues the convention handled were the matters of apportionment and the possible liberalization of suffrage for white males. Although loosened property qualifications in Maryland prior to the 1812 election arguably benefited Madison by opening the polls to many working-class white men, Virginia took a slower approach toward universal white male suffrage.[18]

As an elder statesman, he was also a voice for compromise on the matter of legislative apportionment, an issue on which he spoke at the proceedings. The current state constitution favored counties with large numbers of slaves to the detriment of the western region, which had few persons in bondage. Acting rationally, western counties wanted only the white population to count for the function of apportionment. Madison argued in favor of counting slaves as three-fifths of a person for the purposes of drawing up legislative districts, just like the United States Constitution, and still very beneficial to slaveowners. Other delegates respectfully listened to him but then adopted a constitution that maintained representation based on counties and districts, thereby keeping the center of Virginia's political power in the slavery-heavy eastern and Tidewater regions.[19]

Still commanding significant respect, but with his influence otherwise waning, Madison denounced the advocates of nullification that were slowly taking over South Carolina politics in the early 1830s. Vice President John C. Calhoun, once a firm nationalist, now threw himself in with the constitutional troublemakers from his state. Their argument revolved around the theory that a state's political leadership held the authority to deem null and void any federal measure that they found to be unconstitutional and harmful to their people. If, after all attempts at resolution were exhausted without success, then it was a state's right to nullify the law in question, or possibly even secede from the union.[20]

The policy at stake here was the high tariff of 1828, which hit South Carolina planters especially hard. The nullifiers contended that the tariff was well beyond the nation's budgetary needs to raise revenue, and only served to protect northern industries at the expense of southern planters. In their view it was unconstitutional for Congress to use its power to tax in such an egregious way. On the merits of public policy, they had a serious argument to make, but nullification was another kettle of fish. Madison rejected the analogies being used by the nullifiers to compare their philosophies with the concepts he once put forth to oppose the Alien and Sedition Acts. States were well within their right to challenge and oppose measures they felt were unconstitutional or bad public policy. Madison long ago argued in the Virginia Resolution that states could "interpose" themselves against the central government, but in his view, this vague language should not be interpreted as meaning that any state had the authority to declare a federal law null and void, much less secede. One or a few disgruntled states should not be able to dictate terms and conditions in a system of constitutional government. In a letter to Congressman Edward Everett of Massachusetts, Madison asserted that "to establish a positive and permanent rule giving such a power, to such a minority, over such a majority, would overturn the first principle of free government, and in practice necessarily overturn the government itself."[21] Cooler heads ultimately prevailed as President Jackson, the nullifiers, and Senator Clay achieved a carefully crafted compromise to lower the tariff, and South Carolina repealed its ordinance of nullification. In the coming years, however, states' rights extremists increasingly appropriated Madison's principles to defend secession and armed resistance to the federal government.

His health finally in decline, Madison increasingly retreated inward to life at Montpelier, and his personal correspondence became less frequent. On June 28, 1836, the fourth president of the United States died at his Virginia estate of apparent heart failure. At the age of eighty-five, Madison was the last of the living Constitutional Convention attendees. The copious, meticulous notes he took of the proceedings first became public four years later, thereby providing a long-awaited record of one of America's most pivotal chapters. Madison's notes, as well as *The Federalist Papers*, are certainly valuable tools that allow us to see the intent of the Constitution's architects. The documents also reveal how much these gentlemen were skilled agents of compromise, reducing every contentious issue down to a subject that could be negotiated away.

One of those matters was slavery, which was absent from the conversation in the 1812 campaign. Otherwise, Madison tended to treat slavery as just another nettlesome political issue, like internal improvements or national banking. Far from being an affirmative defender of the institution, Madison handled slavery the way a calculating politician would navigate a divisive controversy that held the capacity to upend other policy priorities. At the time of his death, Madison had been serving as the president of the American Colonization Society. The organization was not dedicated to abolitionism or racial equality, but rather, promoting the settlement of free Blacks into Africa. To clear their conscience, some southern planters—including John Randolph—freed slaves in their wills. None, however, were manumitted in Madison's will. Dolley Madison took possession of Montpelier, along with the men and women who were held in bondage.[22]

Now recognized as one of the most well-liked First Ladies in American history, Mrs. Madison financially struggled in the remaining years of her life. She moved to Washington, DC, on a part-time basis the year after her husband's death and relocated to the capital permanently in 1844. That same year, the Madison plantation was sold, as her alcoholic son, Payne Todd, proved to be incompetent at running Montpelier. Although Dolley maintained an active social schedule, given her widespread and bipartisan popularity, she remained generally impoverished. Following Dolley's death on July 12, 1849, the capital went into a full mourning mode. The eighty-one-year-old former first lady was honored with a large funeral and was remembered as a social bridge builder between Americans of differing political ideologies.[23]

Vice President Gerry was well positioned to revitalize his career after taking the oath of office. Not wishing to travel in the winter, he did not make the trip to the capital for the inauguration, and instead was sworn in at his Elmwood home in Cambridge. By the standards of an early nineteenth-century vice president, Gerry took an active role in the Madison administration. Acting as a sort of secretary on matters of patronage, Gerry tried to ensure that Massachusetts got its fair share of federal jobs. However, efforts to procure positions for relatives were unsuccessful. In his short tenure, the new vice president partook in the Washington, DC, social scene, which was surprisingly robust until the British invaded and burned the city. Gerry died in his boardinghouse in the capital on November 23, 1814, making him Madison's second vice president to pass away in office.[24]

FINISHING OFF THE FEDERALISTS

The war provided the declining Federalist Party with a jolt in the arm, producing electoral gains in New England and, to a lesser degree, the Middle Atlantic states. Through a coalition with Clintonian Democratic-Republicans, the fundamentals were in place to enable Federalists to reposition their party as the boosters of commerce, evidence-based trade policies, and a foreign policy that balanced diplomacy with strong military preparations at home. Unfortunately for Federalists, pulling off a successful reorganization of a party within this context seems to almost require rooting for the war to go awry, or fail outright. A political party that revolves around the principle of opposition to an existing war has chosen to stake its fortunes on public opinion souring on the conflict. That phenomenon may be dependent upon the country suffering defeats on the battlefield or heavy casualties. Fairly or not, this puts the anti-war party in the situation of appearing to side with the enemy, which was manifested in 1812 through the common attacks on the Federalists as the "British" or "Tory" party. In fact, many Federalists served in the officer corps, but such epithets and accusations can be very hard to refute within a climate of nationalism, militarism, and jingoism.

The 1814–1815 congressional election cycle was mostly disappointing for

Federalists, especially in New York, where in April 1814 the party lost thirteen House seats. Their national loss was three seats, and they remained buried deep in the minority in the Senate. The momentum that Federalists showed in 1812 was starting to peter out even before the conflict with Britain was over.[25] Two-and-a-half years of war disrupted political equilibrium, generating an awkward alliance with the Clintonians while revealing Federalist opportunities and occasional electoral victories. When peacetime returned, their identity as a party dominated by New England was firmly restored.

The other shoe to drop came in the form of the Hartford, Connecticut, convention that took place between December 15, 1814, and January 5, 1815. An objective observer could fairly call this gathering just an assembly of disgruntled New England Federalists airing out their grievances with the Constitution and the current direction of the United States. Harrison Gray Otis and his colleagues held meetings and adopted a series of resolutions that called for constitutional amendments to end the three-fifths compromise, limit the president to one term, require that no president be from the same state as his predecessor, and limit trade embargoes to sixty days. The Federalist delegates also demanded requirements to mandate a two-thirds congressional vote to declare war, to admit a new state, and "to interdict the commercial intercourse between the United States and any foreign nation or the dependencies thereof." All of these reforms were aimed at halting the decline of the Federalist Party, ending the Virginia dynasty over the presidency, and weakening the chief executive office. Interestingly, it was their party that had favored a stronger president in the early years of the republic.[26]

The political context, however, took place within the wartime news cycle of the early nineteenth century. Word of the Hartford Convention's proceedings competed with the joyful news of Jackson's smashing victory at New Orleans. On top of the documents from overseas about the Ghent peace deal, Federalists were now on the defensive, and their convention resolutions were discredited. Democratic-Republican critics accused their opponents of promoting disunion and secession in a moment of nationalistic fervor. A letter carried by the *Boston Patriot* decried "The Internal Enemy," as the writer denounced "the tories and traitors among us."[27]

The truth is that the convention did not advocate secession, although the matter was clearly discussed at some of the meetings. The final report actually dismissed the notion of a New England secession from the union as premature and impractical. Still, the conclave became tainted as a mischievous event that ran counter to the current mood of the country. At a Fourth of July celebration in Union Village, New Jersey, citizens made a mocking toast to the Hartford Convention: "The hopes of men void of understanding are false and vain—and dreams lift up fools." Regardless of what the facts on the ground indicated, Americans were convinced that they had just defeated the British in war for a second time. Federalists were politically mispositioned, and their party's decline accelerated; however, Federalist policy ideas remained viable among Whigs and Republicans throughout the remainder of the nineteenth century. Those parties of the future did a far better job of blending elements of the Hamiltonian program into a more populist brand of politics.[28]

Other Federalist statesmen from the 1812 election cycle went into the twilight of their distinguished careers. As Federalists were currently enjoying a brief revitalization in New York, Rufus King was sent back to the US Senate by the legislature in early 1813, where he would serve until 1825. His second round of service in the Senate was defined by his opposition to expanding slavery westward. In April 1816, King challenged Governor Tompkins for reelection and was defeated by a solid margin. Following King's Senate assignment was a brief stint as the American ambassador to Great Britain, before retiring due to deteriorating health.[29]

King was once more called upon by Federalists as a stand-in candidate for president in 1816, which resulted in his resounding defeat against Monroe. Only the states of Massachusetts, Connecticut, and Delaware were carried by the token Federalist ticket. This time Federalists held no formal nominating meeting or anything resembling an organized convention. Nor did King and his party aggressively promote his candidacy. Democratic-Republicans were hardly unified, but there was no longer a war to aggravate their divisions. Another coalition with aggrieved Democratic-Republicans was a nonstarter, especially given how poisoned the Federalist label had become. By 1816 the party's national infrastructure had regressed backwards on the road to irrelevancy.[30]

Jared Ingersoll Jr. was a logical and safe choice for the vice presidential nomination, although his presence on the ballot failed to bring in large numbers of dissident Democratic-Republicans in Pennsylvania. Opposition campaigns can aggressively pounce on a vice presidential nominee who has vulnerabilities, but in 1812 the office was treated as if it was insignificant. Even so, Ingersoll's candidacy brought no real harm to the fusion ticket's efforts. Pro-Madison newspapers tended to ignore Ingersoll, preferring to make attacks on Clinton and the entire Federalist Party. Consistent with many losing vice presidential nominees, Ingersoll did not bring in significant numbers of new voters to his ticket. Meanwhile, Ingersoll was still the Pennsylvania attorney general, an appointed job, which he concluded in December 1816. On October 31, 1822, the Federalist elder statesman died at the age of seventy-three.

Gouverneur Morris was a supporter of the Hartford Convention and was sympathetic to the idea of secession by New York and New England. That stance would not be helpful to any public figure after the war, but he could properly foresee the growing power of the slave slates to dictate foreign and domestic policy. Nor was he a fan of the American policy of displacement and slaughter of Indigenous peoples. Morris, who died on November 6, 1816, established a positive legacy as a rare leader from the Founding generation who warned against slavery and cruelty to the Native population.[31] As more of these Federalist elder statesmen passed away, the party was poorly situated to compete in an increasingly populist era of American politics. Their failed fusion with Clintonians in 1812 serves as a prime example of a declining party's inability to adapt to an emerging new era.

DEWITT CLINTON AND HIS FACTION

Some failed presidential candidates thrive after losing the election. For others, their defeat is the inflection point at which their career, and possibly even their personal life, goes into a tailspin. Just shy of forty-four years old, DeWitt Clinton generally falls into the former category, as he continued to rack up achievements in New York and has left a legacy that remains impactful to this day. Although Mayor Clinton was a nominal opponent of the war, he took seriously his responsibility to prepare New York City's defenses from British attack. Clinton took a hands-on approach to supervising the construction of fortifications to protect his community.[32]

First, however, there were setbacks, as the war's conclusion and word of the Hartford Convention turned momentum against the Federalist Party. As their most recent presidential nominee, Clinton was vulnerable to being a casualty of the fallout. Like many losing candidates for the presidency, Clinton's political capital was initially diminishing, with old allies deserting or distancing themselves from the defeated nominee. Right after the presidential election, his fragile alliance with Martin Van Buren was already fraying. The state senator who only months before had labored so hard to deliver New York to Clinton was now angry with him. Van Buren's chosen candidate for the US Senate was not selected by the legislature, and the Little Magician blamed Clinton for Rufus King's victory. Never mind that Clinton was not a King supporter, but Van Buren now intended to deny

Clinton the nomination for another term as lieutenant governor. That effort was successful, as Democratic-Republicans pushed Clinton out of the office and replaced him with a pro-Madison candidate in 1813.[33]

The next humiliating blow was when the increasingly powerful Council of Appointment removed him—again—from the New York City mayorship in March 1815. As Federalists and Clintonians in the state weakened in 1814, state elections resulted in the council being composed of a majority of men loyal to Van Buren. Clinton's opposition to the war and alleged lack of patriotism were cited as the reasons for firing him from the mayorship.[34] Having lost his father in September 1812, then the presidential election, followed by the lieutenant governorship, and finally his mayor's office, Clinton appeared headed down a path of misfortune that would end his tenure in government.

As it turned out, New York still needed DeWitt Clinton. His pet project, the Erie Canal, still had yet to come to fruition. After Tompkins departed the governorship for the vice presidency, a special gubernatorial election was held in accordance with the state constitution. The only real contest was for the Democratic-Republican nomination, which would be decided by a special convention of legislators and party activists in Albany on March 25, 1817. This format, rather than a caucus in the legislature, favored Clinton, for Democratic-Republicans from the Federalist pockets of the state were likely to favor the 1812 presidential nominee. Van Buren's men in the legislature, now known as "Bucktails," put up Peter Porter—the former War Hawk congressman—as their candidate. The convention's tally was 85–41 in favor of Clinton, who went on to win a basically uncontested election later that spring. The decimated Federalist Party did not even choose a nominee, although the Tammany Society printed some ballots for citizens in New York City who wished to vote for Porter.[35]

Clinton's comeback was underway. Before he even took office, the legislature enacted a measure that became law on April 15, 1817, authorizing construction of the Erie Canal. Cognizant of the project's growing support in the state, as well as the numerous commercial benefits, Van Buren reversed his previous opposition, effectively clearing the bill for passage. Clinton was sworn into office on July 1, and three days later he participated in a groundbreaking event in Rome, in Oneida County. The Erie Canal proposal was scarcely mentioned in the 1812 campaign, but it was an idea that was commonly mocked by state and national politicians. Gradually, it earned political support and became the foundation for Clinton's revitalization in public life.[36]

Along the way there was also tragedy, as Clinton's wife Maria died on July 30, 1818. At age forty-two, her health declined significantly after the birth of the couple's tenth child the previous year. The family was still young, and they were brought closer together around their father. As he was still mourning the loss of Maria, Clinton injured himself in a fall, fractured a leg, and was never again able to walk normally. On a happier note, in April 1819 Clinton married thirty-six-year-old Catherine Jones. The new Mrs. Clinton was the daughter of a New York doctor and was the niece of the famous Philadelphia physician John Jones. Accustomed to the obligations of being a woman of society, she embraced the social responsibilities of being the governor's wife.[37]

Vice President Tompkins challenged Clinton's reelection in April 1820. In spite of his support for the Erie Canal project, Van Buren and his Bucktails formed the leading agent of opposition to Governor Clinton during his tenure. They recruited Tompkins to challenge the incumbent, but Clinton prevailed in a race that had less than a 2 percent spread. Van Buren's machine was beatable, but still very formidable. The Bucktail-dominated Council of Appointment purged a significant number of Clinton's appointees from state government after the election. The need to amend the New York constitution commanded widespread support, but Clintonians and Bucktails had differing motives. Clinton favored steps toward democratization but balked at the Bucktails' demand that a convention hold blank-check authority to completely overhaul everything in government. After voters overwhelmingly approved a referendum to call a generally unrestricted convention, deliberations began on August 28, 1821.[38]

The Bucktails aimed to use the convention as a means to consolidate their own strength at the expense of the Clintonians. Though Clinton technically presided over the convention, Bucktails and their sympathizers dominated the proceedings. Most notably, the Council of Appointment was abolished, for that body was now functioning as an instrument of patronage and exerting inordinate influence over local and state government. The Council of Revision, which diluted the legislature's powers, was also eliminated. In lieu of the latter council, the governor was given a veto, which could be overridden by two-thirds of both chambers of the legislature. The governor's term was shortened from three years to two, which displeased Clinton. Nor did he favor the reorganization of the judiciary, where he had allies under the existing system. Property qualifications for white male voters were also drastically reduced, which Clinton supported.[39]

By a large margin, voters approved the new constitution in January 1822, thereby implementing some sensible democratic reforms but also ending Governor Clinton's term one year earlier than originally scheduled. He declined to run for reelection and returned to private life, save for his continued service on the Erie Canal Commission. With the easy election that year of Joseph Yates to the governorship, the Bucktails now controlled the state, even as Van Buren was now in the US Senate. The Bucktails in the legislature were now commonly referred to as the "Albany Regency," a pejorative label meant to liken them to some sinister royal cabal. Not content to let Clinton's political career slowly fade away, they endeavored to humiliate him once more.[40]

The Erie Canal Commission, on which the former governor had been serving for fourteen years without pay, was Clinton's remaining institutional post, thus maintaining his status as a relevant figure in state politics as the massive project moved toward completion. In the legislature, the Albany Regency successfully assembled a coalition to remove Clinton from the commission in April 1824. Not only was this an act of political vindictiveness, but it was also an effort to damage the state's new People's Party, to which many Clintonians had migrated. While Van Buren and the Albany Regency supported the presidential nomination of William Crawford in 1824, the People's Party opposed his candidacy, as well as the outdated congressional nominating caucus that selected him. Clinton decided to support Andrew Jackson for the presidency.[41]

Public reaction to Clinton's dismissal generated a backlash in New York and created new momentum for him to run for governor that November. Clinton may have had a reputation as an ambitious intriguer, but by now his work on behalf of the Erie Canal was widely appreciated. Even Van Buren seemed to realize that his allies had overplayed their hand. The People's Party nominated Clinton for the governorship, and he prevailed by a convincing margin. The party also captured the lieutenant governorship and a working majority in the legislature. In addition to Clinton's removal from the Erie Canal Commission, another campaign issue was New York's method of selecting presidential electors. The state was one of only six that still allocated electoral votes by the legislature. Clinton and the People's Party favored giving the choice to the voters, while the Albany Regency opposed any major immediate changes to New York's existing process.[42]

Clinton took office on New Year's Day 1825, although soon after taking the oath of office he turned down an offer from the new president, John Quincy Adams, to be the American minister to Britain. During his third term, Clinton got to see the completion of the Erie Canal, which was the subject of much fanfare in New York. The waterway had already been in limited use since 1821, and on October 26, 1825, the project was formally finished. For the opening celebration, Clinton personally traveled on the canal route from Buffalo, and then down the Hudson River to New York City. The festive party lasted for several days, including cannons and fireworks, as well as speeches and musical acts at various stops along the way. At long last, the governor got the final laugh at his critics who mocked the idea as "Clinton's Big Ditch" and "Clinton's Folly."[43]

Recreational boats and tourists are the primary users of the Erie Canal today, but in the 1820s it represented a major achievement in American infrastructure. It was the longest canal in the Western Hemisphere, and the economic benefits of the 363-mile-long artery were numerous. Michigan became a state in 1837 and owes much of its growth and development to the canal. Most notably, shipping costs were reduced, and travel became more efficient. New York, and even other states, now had greater access to the Great Lakes. Materials and news could move with greater speed, whether going to or coming from New York City. In addition to Clinton's leadership in making the canal a reality, immigrant workers and slaves labored on the project. Slavery was not fully abolished in New York until July 4, 1827, as part of the state's twenty-eight-year-long gradual emancipation policy. Interestingly, the Erie Canal would someday be used as a route on the Underground Railroad to transport escaped slaves to Canada.[44]

Other Clinton initiatives did not advance much during his remaining tenure. The governor proposed education reforms, as well as further internal improvements and agricultural modernizations, but had little luck with the legislature. New York did indeed change its presidential election law to enable voters to choose electors in 1828, but there was little else. The Albany Regency had been sidelined for the time being, but they would be back, and Clinton found that his People's Party was a hot mess. The loose coalition included supporters of President Adams, Henry Clay, and Andrew Jackson. Their unity at election time revolved more around opposition to Crawford and Van Buren's operatives in Albany. Now that it was time to govern, the cracks were definitely showing, but Clinton had established a national identity beyond just that of his losing presidential candidacy. Other states were encouraged by the accomplishment of the Erie Canal, and their leaders solicited the New York governor's input about possible similar projects. In November 1826, he was narrowly reelected.[45]

Meanwhile, Clinton was making his peace with Van Buren, and the force bringing them together was the political momentum of Andrew Jackson.

The New York governor reached out to Van Buren about a possible Jacksonian alliance with the Little Magician's Albany Regency. Crawford, who suffered from a paralytic stroke in 1823, was no longer presidential material, even though his health had stabilized. Van Buren undertook to find a national figure who shared his priorities, although it would not be easy to overcome years of rivalry and distrust between his team and the Clinton people. The process was in motion to bring these two adversaries together, revealing the powerful impulse of Jacksonian democracy to realign existing political divisions.[46]

In his final year in office, Clinton was dealing with a bizarre scandal that ended up being the catalyst for a new anti-Mason movement in America. A gentleman named William Morgan, who was planning to reveal the secrets of the Freemasons in a book, vanished in Genesee County in September 1826. He was never heard from again and was assumed to have been murdered. A long line of powerful American men, going back to George Washington, were members of the fraternal organization. The Morgan case brought attention to conspiracy theorists who always hated the mere existence of the Freemasons. Clinton himself was a member of the society, but he publicly vowed to bring any possible perpetrators to justice, including a cash reward. Had Clinton continued in office, the Morgan disappearance may have derailed the governor's political future, given the anti-Mason hysteria that was spreading throughout New York.[47]

On February 11, 1828, Clinton died in his personal library after a busy day of meetings and a speech in front of the Senate. Lethargic and overweight, the governor had been steadily growing frailer for a decade, including a recent nasty bout with the flu. He was just shy of fifty-nine years old. Funeral and memorial services were ubiquitous in all of New York. Van Buren saluted his old ally, adversary, and renewed partner in politics: "The triumph of his talent and patriotism cannot fail to become monuments of high and enduring fame," he told the US Senate. "It gives me a deep-felt though melancholy satisfaction, to know, and more so, to be conscious that the deceased also felt and acknowledged, that our political differences have been wholly free from that most venomous and corroding of all poisons—personal hatred." Catherine and the children, four of whom were still underage, were left with debts and unpaid obligations. A permanent burial was initially too expensive. Many of Clinton's possessions were auctioned off, although after some debate the legislature did award a small financial aid package to the family. Many years later, a permanent interment for the body was finally established in Greenwood Cemetery in Brooklyn.[48]

AMERICA'S FIRST WARTIME ELECTION ASSESSED

All presidential elections are worthy of scrutiny. Every national plebiscite where a chief executive is chosen reveals something about the country at that given point in time. Presidential elections across history may share similarities with each other, but no two are identical. In all likelihood, each election will either provide one or more firsts for the nation, and/or exist under the context of a previously unprecedented situation for the country. Every election features new modes of communication and technology, or perhaps new party rules and procedures, as well as new laws concerning voting. In 2016 an election was held with the first female presidential nominee of a major political party. In 2008 an election was held with the first African American presidential nominee of a major political party. In 1864 citizens voted in the middle of a civil war. In 1812 a presidential race took place in the middle of a domestic American war with Britain.

The results validated the war's overall popularity and confirmed the nation's Democratic-Republican majority. The outcome also demonstrated the tricky task of running an anti-war campaign, as well as the difficulties of forging a fusion ticket in an era of institutionally weak political parties. There is evidence to suggest that the war generated increased interest in the election among voters, but not to a major degree. In his summary study of voter participation going back to the founding of the republic, Walter Dean Burnham estimated a national voter turnout rate of 34.9 percent in 1808, which then rose to 38.2 percent in 1812. Even the highly competitive 1800 presidential race produced an estimated turnout of only 32.2 percent. Michael McDonald estimated a 40.4 percent turnout of the voting eligible population in 1812, as compared to 36.8 percent in 1808. These numbers suggest that there was a small upward pressure on voter participation amid an environment of a controversial war and the perception of a competitive election. Significant variation between turnouts in states is also noteworthy. Burnham estimated a 54.9 percent turnout in Maryland, 75.5 percent in New Hampshire, 37.6 percent in Pennsylvania, and 17.8 percent in Virginia.[49] The latter state did not even present the illusion of being a tight contest, which is reflected by the dismal voter participation figure.

The 1812 also race spawned the beginning of absentee voting. Large numbers of male troops were in the field and so were not available to vote at their respective polling places for elections. Once can conjecture that an easier availability of suffrage for enlisted soldiers and sailors would have worked to Madison's benefit. Subsequently, Governor Snyder and the Pennsylvania legislature adopted a law in late March 1813 to address this issue.

The measure mandated that if the state's military personnel were stationed more than two miles from their home precinct, the men must be allowed to cast ballots in a manner established by the appropriate commanding officers. Democratic-Republicans in New Jersey, now back in control of their state, followed with their own military absentee ballot law in 1815.[50]

Abraham Lincoln was a commander in chief defending a nation against a domestic insurrection that, by 1864, permeated all aspects of life in the United States. Even when events on the battlefield looked grim, he stoutly rejected any notion that the upcoming election should be postponed or terminated.[51] Although he did not say so directly, he was acting on the precedent that Madison set fifty-two years beforehand: even a war on American soil cannot justify suspending or canceling a presidential election. There is no evidence that Madison ever contemplated trying to postpone or cancel the 1812 presidential election. It is hard to imagine a strict constitutionalist like the fourth president claiming the authority for himself or the federal government to execute such a policy. This was an era when states were almost entirely free to run their elections as they saw fit. In addition, the slow pace of communications would have made any abrupt national changes to the law confusing and maddening for voters.

The incumbent president also had the advantage of math in 1812. The 1810 census revealed population growth and migration in the decade of the 1800s, and the overall results dropped more electoral votes into the lap of Madisonian Democratic-Republicans. States that voted for DeWitt Clinton gained fifteen electoral votes from the new apportionments. The states carried by Madison earned an increase of twenty-seven electoral votes, as compared to four years earlier. Clinton's New York saw impressive growth, but Madison benefited even more from the burgeoning population in frontier states like Kentucky, Louisiana, Ohio, and Tennessee.[52]

A strong party system imposes discipline on campaigns for president and other offices. Even the calendar is rigidly structured around the actions of political parties. State and federal laws governing election campaigns are constructed around the activities of parties. Today, the presidential campaign is segmented into a pre-primary rollout and fundraising phase, followed by primaries and caucuses, then formal nomination at conventions, and finally the general election phase. Even as they have lost institutional strength in the twenty-first century, parties still play a major role within each of these steps.

In 1812 the electoral calendar was a decentralized mess. The nominating phase overlapped with the general election segment, and electors were chosen across a month-long period in state after state. Races for other offices were scattered across the calendar all over the country. Under a framework like this, weak political parties would be unable to impose much control over the process at a national level. The constraints of the early party system were all there, including a generally elite-centered model that kept out far more persons than it admitted. Voter suffrage laws across the nation were a combination of racist, sexist, and classist restrictions. Secretive private meetings and caucuses made major decisions that impacted political outcomes. Party organizations and electoral procedures were decentralized and often very poorly coordinated across state lines. The slow pace of communications in this era only exacerbated these constraints.

We can also observe the early signs of a transition into a new model of party competition that came into full maturity more than two decades later. Complaints against the congressional nominating caucus grew louder, gradually building a case for a more democratic and transparent method of choosing candidates. The first steps toward national party conventions surprisingly came from Federalists, though their assembly in New York City was not tightly organized, and the post-meeting messaging was in disarray. The Jacksonian party system centered on white male populism, and as early as 1812 very small movements in that direction were gaining momentum. Property qualifications were lifted in Maryland and South Carolina, while the trend in the western frontier states was already in favor of diminishing these rules. The existence of a controversial war in the middle of a presidential election opened the door for both parties to engage the citizenry with populist arguments about foreign policy. At the moment, however, the parties were not well-equipped to accomplish that task.

One of the lessons from the 1812 election is that for an effective fusion to occur, there must be a system in place of institutionally strong political parties. Whether the coalition is between two or more parties or, as in 1812, one aggrieved party faction joining forces with the opposition party, it is essential that there be a robust, organized, and structured framework in position to manage all relevant actors. A fusion ticket for president, or any elective office, will require coordinated action between politicians and activists who are not accustomed to working together or trusting each other. Who the leaders and followers are must be clearly established. Messaging must be consistent, simple, and easily digestible for the targeted audience. Accusations and attacks from the other side must be answered promptly.

In 1812 these objectives fell short, in part because of mutual distrust between the fusion partners, which was related to a lack of Federalist enthusiasm for Clinton. Nor would the immaturity of the existing party system permit a smooth fusion between Madison's opponents. Actual coordination between Federalist newspapers and pro-Clinton publications was irregular and ineffective. Politicians within both of these camps did little to collaborate messaging and strategy. Political parties were highly decentralized, with only a very thin layer of national leadership that otherwise might have been able to facilitate an effective alliance among Clintonians and Federalists. Subsequent American party systems were more nationalized, and bipartisan collective action was more feasible in future presidential races, especially as communications technology evolved into speedier and more efficient modes. Even so, further into the nineteenth century, as the party system became more institutionalized and entrenched into American civic life, problems with fusion presidential tickets still remained.

As this account has shown, a fusion ticket is always going to present challenges and vulnerabilities that the opposition party may or may not be able to exploit. DeWitt Clinton was a smart but conventional politician with a reputation for intrigue and ambition in an era that frowned upon those characteristics. A promising fusion ticket candidate would be a person who avoids vituperative smears upon his or her adversaries, shuns hardball political tactics, and has solid credentials as a bipartisan agent of compromise. Even if those boxes are checked, however, the nominee must be a consistent messenger, and this is where the Clinton campaign faltered.

Avoiding a fully pacifist campaign based on an ideological commitment to peace, Clinton's supporters generally maneuvered their efforts toward making a pragmatic anti-war argument, but it broke down and failed to meet numerous challenges. Pro-Madison newspapers regularly labeled him as a calculating politician who would say whatever was expedient at the moment. Fairly or not, the fact that he accepted the nomination of the opposition party only lent credence to these arguments. Newspapers and campaign committees working on Clinton's behalf around the country disseminated a mixed stew of messaging that could have formed the basis for an effective case for his candidacy. They hit upon Virginia's presidential dynasty. They promoted commerce and responsible trade policy. They celebrated Clinton's skills as a problem-solving pragmatist, and implied that he would bring the war to an honorable conclusion. They denounced the Madison administration for ineffective war preparations and for poor decisions on the battlefield, and made assertions that the war would benefit France. Specifics about how the war would be ended were not provided.

In a war that has already been commenced—however flawed—it will be easier for the incumbent commander in chief to make the crisp case for finishing the job. The president's task will be to establish clearly defined objectives and a plan for executing military operations. Just like in any presidential campaign, the incumbent has the advantage of access to the machinery of government. In a wartime election, the commander in chief has an even greater ability to master events, rather than being a servant to developments on the ground. If the challenger opposes the war, he or she must tell citizens how peace will be achieved. The candidate has the choice of proposing vague solutions, in the hope that just an anti-war stance is enough to prevail. Alternatively, the challenger could offer specific policy plans aimed at ending the war. Whatever choice the challenger makes, new questions will be raised that will open the candidate to criticism. He or she will be accused of some combination of political opportunism, lack of seriousness, and a lack of patriotism. Although such lines of attack are normal in campaigns, in the context of domestic wartime mania this can be especially difficult for an anti-war challenger to overcome.

While it is fair to say that the theme of Clinton's campaign revolved around inconsistent messaging, we also must put our assessments of his campaign in the context of 1812's political landscape. Decentralized parties inevitably meant a decentralized message coming from the candidate's supporters. In this media environment, accusations and attacks could not be promptly refuted and widely disseminated. Nor should Madison be free from criticism for being an inconsistent messenger and administrator. Shifting pre-war foreign and trade policies sometimes bewildered the president's critics, supporters, and European actors. Though Madison's Democratic-Republicans were also divided and decentralized, they also came into the 1812 campaign from a strong majority position in multiple key states, supplemented by the political rally effects of a newly declared war. Custom dictated that presidential candidates not give stump speeches or even appear to be promoting their own election. Hence, it was impossible for Clinton to regain control of the narrative by stepping up to the stage to make statements that could steer the campaign's message in the desired direction. Today, a presidential candidate who is losing control of the news cycle would have that option.

Newspapers spread vitriolic and hyperbolic rhetoric. Baltimore erupted into riots. A congressman was beaten, and other politicians were burned in effigy. Partisan state legislatures used hardball tactics to achieve an advantage for their side. The notion that presidential campaigns in the distant past were somehow more genteel and issue-oriented is simply a falsehood.

Strong parties function to either restrain the worst effects of partisanship or at least channel them into a positive direction. In 1812 parties were institutionally weak, but intense sentiment about the war fused into passionate advocacy for citizens' respective candidates. Political scientists today have observed a similar phenomenon of weaker parties at the institutional level, alongside an American public with red-hot feelings of sharply cynical and negative partisanship.[53]

Not only is this state of affairs dangerous for democracy, but it also poses major risks when the country goes to war, if that policy decision does not command universal support. Just like in 1812, the Civil War, and the war with Iraq, feelings of partisanship increased during these controversial moments. In the contemporary era, where communications move instantaneously across a wide variety of mediums, the substance of discourse has deteriorated and intensified to a place where one must ask if our political system is capable of having a debate about war and peace in the middle of a presidential election. Cable news, social media, and internet message boards do not lend themselves to polite debate and reasoned conversation based on facts and evidence. Rather, an argument can be made that these instruments serve to exacerbate and worsen ideological and cultural cleavages in American society. The presidential election of 1812 reveals that any war will be disruptive to the existing domestic equilibrium. It also provides a lesson about what happens when weak, clumsy, and disorganized parties operate in an atmosphere of passionate divisions about the war itself. A controversial war thrown into the current political landscape of the United States could produce ruinous consequences for American politics, and potentially even threaten the country's constitutional democracy.

APPENDIX A ELECTOR SELECTION DATES AND METHODS IN 1812

State	Elector Selection Date(s)	Selection Method
Pennsylvania	October 30	Voters at-large
Ohio	October 30	Voters at-large
Vermont	October 30	Legislature and Governor's Council
Connecticut	October 30	Legislature
New York	November 2–9	Legislature
New Hampshire	November 2	Voters at-large
Virginia	November 2	Voters at-large
New Jersey	November 5*	Legislature
Tennessee	November 5–6	Voters by district
Georgia	November 9	Legislature
Kentucky	November 9	Voters by district
Maryland	November 9	Voters by district
Delaware	November 10	Legislature
Massachusetts	November 12	Voters by district
Rhode Island	November 18	Voters at-large
North Carolina	November 21	Legislature
Louisiana	November 30	Legislature
South Carolina	December 1	Legislature

* Originally scheduled for November 3–4 in New Jersey.

APPENDIX B ELECTORAL COLLEGE RESULTS IN 1812
(LISTED IN THE ORDER THAT EACH STATE VOTED)

State	Winner	Electors Awarded
Pennsylvania	Madison	25
Ohio*	Madison	7
Vermont	Madison	8
Connecticut	Clinton	9
New York	Clinton	29
New Hampshire	Clinton	8
Virginia	Madison	25
New Jersey	Clinton	8
Tennessee	Madison	8
Georgia	Madison	8
Kentucky	Madison	12
Maryland	Split Decision	Madison 6/Clinton 5
Delaware	Clinton	4
Massachusetts	Clinton	22
Rhode Island	Clinton	4
North Carolina	Madison	15
Louisiana	Madison	3
South Carolina	Madison	11

* One of the eight Ohio electors failed to show up to cast his vote.

TOTAL ELECTORAL VOTES

Madison	128 electoral votes
Clinton	89 electoral votes

APPENDIX C FINAL ROLL CALL VOTE IN THE STATES WHERE THE LEGISLATURE CHOSE PRESIDENTIAL ELECTORS

	Final Results	
State	Candidate	Votes
Connecticut	NA*	NA
Delaware	Clinton	19
	Madison	6
Georgia	NA	NA
Louisiana	Clinton	16
	Madison	23
New Jersey	Clinton	29
	Madison	23
New York	Clinton	74
	Unnamed Federalist	45
	Blank	23–33
North Carolina	Clinton	60
	Madison	130
South Carolina	Clinton	0
	Madison	139–153
Vermont**	NA	NA

* Final legislative tally is unavailable for Connecticut, Georgia, and Vermont.

** The *Vermont Mirror* reported that "about 12 or 14" Democratic-Republicans voted with Federalists for the Clintonian ticket; see "Vermont Electors," *Vermont Mirror*, November 4, 1812, 3.

APPENDIX D AVAILABLE STATEWIDE TALLY WHERE VOTERS CHOSE PRESIDENTIAL ELECTORS

Final Results

State	Candidate	Votes	Percentage
Kentucky[a]	Clinton	433	4.8%
	Madison	8,501	95.2%
Maryland	Clinton	14,270	49.0%
	Madison	14,826	51.0%
Massachusetts	Clinton	50,488	65.0%
	Madison	27,169	35.0%
New Hampshire[b]	Clinton	18,858	54.2%
	Madison	15,907	45.8%
Ohio[c]	Clinton	3,301	30.8%
	Madison	7,420	69.2%
Pennsylvania	Clinton	29,639	37.4%
	Madison	49,695	62.6%
Tennessee[d]	Clinton	0	0%
	Madison	0	0%
Rhode Island	Clinton	4,032	65.9%
	Madison	2,084	34.1%
Virginia	Clinton	0	0%
	Madison	15,128	73.0%
	King	5,584	27.0%

TOTAL VOTES

Clinton	121,021	45.3%
Madison	140,730	52.6%
King	5584	2.1%

Note: Unless otherwise noted, the highest vote total is recorded for each state's pro-Clinton elector candidates. Similarly, the highest vote tally is counted for each state's pro-Madison elector candidates.

a. Popular vote tallies for two of Kentucky's three electoral districts are currently in existence. See chapter 6, note 53.

b. In the case of New Hampshire, the second-highest vote total for Clinton electors is counted. See chapter 6, note 35 for more explanation.

c. See chapter 6, note 18.

d. Popular vote totals for Tennessee are lost to history.

NOTES

PREFACE

1   John Thomson, *An exact and authentic narrative, of the events which took place in Baltimore, on the 27th and 28th of July last. Carefully collected from some of the sufferers and eyewitnesses. To which is added a narrative of Mr. John Thomson, one of the unfortunate sufferers, &c*, Printed for the Purchasers, 1812, 62.

1. THE POLITICAL TERRAIN OF THE EARLY REPUBLIC

1   Irving Brant, *James Madison: Secretary of State, 1800–1809* (vol. 4), (Indianapolis: Bobbs-Merrill, 1953), 419–421; Noble E. Cunningham Jr., *The Jeffersonian Republicans in Power: Party Operations, 1801–1809* (Chapel Hill: University of North Carolina Press, 1963), 83–86, 108–109.
2   "The Notice Calling the Caucus of 1808," S. R. Bradley (Edwin Gray Papers, Duke University), in Noble E. Cunningham Jr. ed., *The Making of the American Party System, 1789 to 1809* (Englewood Cliffs, NJ: Prentice Hall, 1965), 125–126.
3   Brant, *James Madison* (vol. 4), 424–425.
4   Signatories included Clinton and Monroe supporters. See "James Madison's Opponents Denounce the Caucus" (*National Intelligencer*, March 7, 1808), in Cunningham, *The Making of the American Party System*, 129–130; also see "Thomas Ritchie Defends the Caucus" (*Richmond Enquirer*, February 2, 1808), in Cunningham, 129; "Representative Edwin Gray Protests the Summoning of the Caucus of 1808" (Edwin Gray Papers, Duke University), in Cunningham, 126.
5   Evan Cornog, *The Birth of Empire: DeWitt Clinton and the American Experience, 1769–1828* (Oxford: Oxford University Press, 1998), 86–88; John P. Kaminski, *George Clinton: Yeoman Politician of the New Republic* (Madison, WI: Madison House, 1993), 278–289.
6   Twelve members who were absent from the caucus officially recorded their public support for Madison or Clinton (twelve votes and two votes, respectively); Brant, *James Madison* (vol. 4), 426; Cunningham, *The Jeffersonian Republicans in Power*, 114–115.
7   Harry Ammon, *James Monroe: The Quest for National Identity* (Charlottesville: University of Virginia Press, 1971), 273.
8   Brant, *James Madison* (vol. 4), 423, 430–431, 441; Cornog, *The Birth of Empire*, 86–88; Cunningham, *The Jeffersonian Republicans in Power*, 118–121; Kaminski, *George Clinton: Yeoman Politician*, 278–289.
9   David Hackett Fischer, *The Revolution of American Conservatism: The Federalist Party in the Era of Jeffersonian Democracy* (Chicago: University of Chicago Press, 1965), 84–87.

10 "A Federalist View of Eight Years under Jefferson" (*Connecticut Courant*, April 6, 1808), in Cunningham, *The Making of the American Party System*, 161–162.
11 Ralph Ketcham, *James Madison* (Charlottesville: University of Virginia Press, 1971), 468.
12 "Republicans Attempt to Transfer Jefferson's Popularity to Madison" (*Columbian Phenix*, June 18, 1808), in Cunningham, *The Making of the American Party System*, 163–164.
13 Cunningham, *The Jeffersonian Republicans in Power*, 118–119.
14 Cunningham, 119–121.
15 Ammon, *James Monroe*, 276–277. Phil Lampi shows a slightly different tally, but with the same overarching trend: Madison 15,683, Monroe 3,505, and Pinckney 761; see Philip J. Lampi, Lampi Collection of American Electoral Returns, 1788–1825, American Antiquarian Society and Tufts Archival Research Center, 2007, https://elections.lib.tufts.edu/catalog/7w62f982h (hereafter cited as Lampi Collection of American Electoral Returns).
16 Popular results from New Jersey delivered a convincing, but not overwhelming, victory for Madison. See Lampi Collection of American Electoral Returns, https://elections.lib.tufts.edu/catalog/mg74qm9in; De Alva Stanwood Alexander, *A Political History of the State of New York*, vol. 1 (New York: Holt & Co., 1906), 166–167.
17 Donald A. Zinman, *The Heir Apparent Presidency* (Lawrence: University Press of Kansas, 2016), 38–42.
18 Paul F. Boller Jr., *Presidential Campaigns: From George Washington to George W. Bush* (Oxford: Oxford University Press, 2004), 22–25.
19 On Madison the jokester, see Hilarie M. Hicks, "The Mischievous Mr. Madison," *Montpelier's Digital Doorway*, 2020, https://digitaldoorway.montpelier.org/2020/03/26/the-mischievous-mr-madison/.
20 Ketcham, *James Madison*, 1–24.
21 Ketcham, 25–50.
22 Ketcham, 41–63.
23 Ketcham, 63–64.
24 Ketcham, 77; Richard Franklin Bensel, *The American Ballot Box in the Mid-Nineteenth Century* (Cambridge: Cambridge University Press, 2004).
25 J. C. A. Stagg, "James Madison: Life before the Presidency," Miller Center of Public Affairs, University of Virginia, https://millercenter.org/president/madison/life-before-the-presidency.
26 Stagg, "James Madison: Life before the Presidency."
27 Stagg.
28 Ketcham, *James Madison*, 185, 190–195.
29 James Madison, *Federalist*, nos. 48 and 55, https://guides.loc.gov/federalist-papers/text-41-50#s-lg-box-wrapper-25493415 and https://guides.loc.gov/federalist-papers/text-51-60#s-lg-box-wrapper-25493431.
30 Ketcham, *James Madison*, 194–230.
31 Ketcham, 239–249; James Madison, *Federalist*, no. 45, https://guides.loc.gov/federalist-papers/text-41-50#s-lg-box-wrapper-25493409.

32 Ketcham, *James Madison*, 249–264.
33 Center for the Study of the American Constitution, Madison, University of Wisconsin, https://csac.history.wisc.edu/states-and-ratification/.
34 Ketcham, *James Madison*, 275–276.
35 Ketcham, 275–277; Ammon, *James Monroe*, 70–73.
36 Chris DeRose, *Founding Rivals: Madison vs. Monroe, the Bill of Rights, and the Election that Saved a Nation* (Washington, DC: Regnery Publishing, 2011); Ammon, 75–77; Ketcham, 277; Lampi Collection of American Electoral Returns, https://elections.lib.tufts.edu/catalog/bn999842j.
37 Ketcham, 226–227; Ammon, 77.
38 Ketcham, 289–292; had the apportionment amendment been ratified, the size of the House would today include over 6,000 members. Ironically, Madison himself warned against the dangers of large legislative bodies in *Federalist*, no. 55. See Dylan Matthews, "The Case for Massively Expanding the US House of Representatives, in One Chart," *Vox*, June 4, 2018, https://www.vox.com/2018/6/4/17417452/congress-representation-ratio-district-size-chart-graph.
39 Ketcham, 108–111.
40 Ketcham, 376–390, 615–616.
41 New Jersey served as an exception. This was the only state, following ratification of the US Constitution, to permit property-holding women to vote. Coverture, however, limited female suffrage to unmarried women. The state legislature revoked female suffrage in 1807. See Judith Apter Klinghoffer and Lois Elkis, "'The Petticoat Electors': Women's Suffrage in New Jersey, 1776–1807," *Journal of the Early Republic* 12, no. 2 (Summer 1992): 159–193. African American suffrage was permitted in half of the eighteen states as of 1812. See Alexander Keyssar, *The Right to Vote: The Contested History of Democracy in the United States* (New York: Basic Books, 2000), 325–401.
42 Keyssar, *The Right to Vote*, 328–336.
43 See *Marbury v. Madison* 5 US 137 (1803).
44 William Hogeland, *The Whiskey Rebellion: George Washington, Alexander Hamilton, and the Frontier Rebels Who Challenged America's Newfound Sovereignty* (New York: Scribner, 2006); James Madison to Hubbard Taylor, November 15, 1794, *Founders Online*, National Archives, https://founders.archives.gov/documents/Madison/01-15-02-0291.
45 "An Act in Addition to the Act, Entitled 'An Act for the Punishment of Certain Crimes against the United States,'" Yale Law School, Lillian Goldman Law Library, Avalon Project: Documents in Law, History and Diplomacy, http://avalon.law.yale.edu/18th_century/sedact.asp; as an example of Madison's cooperative effort with Jefferson to oppose the measures, see James Madison, Virginia Resolution, December 21, 1798, *Founders Online*, National Archives, https://founders.archives.gov/documents/Madison/01-17-02-0128.
46 George Washington: "Farewell Address," September 19, 1796, The American Presidency Project, http://www.presidency.ucsb.edu/ws/?pid=65539.
47 Alexander Hamilton, *Federalist*, no. 9, and James Madison, *Federalist*, nos. 10

and 51, https://www.congress.gov/resources/display/content/The+Federalist+Papers.

48 Jefferson to Francis Hopkinson, March 13, 1789, *Founders Online*, National Archives, https://founders.archives.gov/documents/Jefferson/01-14-02-0402.
49 John Adams to Jonathan Jackson, October 2, 1780, *Founders Online*, National Archives, https://founders.archives.gov/documents/Adams/06-10-02-0113.
50 On the formation of early political parties, see Richard Hofstadter, *The Idea of a Party System: The Rise of Legitimate Opposition in the United States, 1780–1840* (Berkeley: University of California Press, 1969).
51 Hamilton's comprehensive economic plans were articulated in three reports he submitted to Congress. See "Report Relative to a Provision for the Support of Public Credit," January 9, 1790, *Founders Online*, National Archives, https://founders.archives.gov/documents/Hamilton/01-06-02-0076-0002-0001; "Final Version of the Second Report on the Further Provision Necessary for Establishing Public Credit (Report on a National Bank)," December 13, 1790, *Founders Online*, https://founders.archives.gov/documents/Hamilton/01-07-02-0229-0003; "Alexander Hamilton's Final Version of the Report on the Subject of Manufactures," December 5, 1791, *Founders Online*, https://founders.archives.gov/documents/Hamilton/01-10-02-0001-0007. See also Gordon S. Wood, *Empire of Liberty: A History of the Early Republic, 1789–1815* (Oxford: Oxford University Press, 2009), 89–139.
52 A. James Reichley, *The Life of the Parties: A History of American Political Parties* (Lanham, MD: Rowman & Littlefield, 2000), 36–38, 55–57; Bernard A. Weisberger, *America Afire: Jefferson, Adams, and the Revolutionary Election of 1800* (New York: Harper Collins, 2000), 190–192; Leonard D. White, *The Jeffersonians: A Study in Administrative History, 1801–1829* (New York: Free Press, 1951), 29–30.
53 Ronald P. Formisano, "Federalists and Republicans: Parties, Yes—System, No," in Paul Kleppner, ed., *The Evolution of American Electoral Systems* (Westport, CT: Greenwood Press, 1981), 33–76.
54 Alan I. Abromowitz and Steven W. Webster, "Negative Partisanship: Why Americans Dislike Parties but Behave Like Rabid Partisans," *Political Psychology* 39 (February 2018): 119–135.
55 This is a core argument in Hofstadter, *The Idea of a Party System*.
56 Wood, *Empire of Liberty*, 247–250.
57 Wood, 168.
58 Fischer, *The Revolution of American Conservatism*, 224–225. Fischer notes, however, that Maryland Catholics of British heritage favored Federalists.
59 Reichley, *The Life of the Parties*, 45.
60 Reichley, 44; Fischer, *The Revolution of American Conservatism*, 225.
61 Reichley, 44, Fischer, 224–225. The Delmarva Peninsula refers to the state of Delaware, in addition to the eastern shores of Maryland and Virginia.
62 Reichley, 43, 45.
63 "Letter from Alexander Hamilton, Concerning the Public Conduct and Character of John Adams, Esq. President of the United States," October 24, 1800,

Founders Online, National Archives, https://founders.archives.gov/documents/Hamilton/01-25-02-0110-0002.

64 David McCullough, *John Adams* (New York: Simon & Schuster, 2001), 539–540.

65 Ketcham, 306–315; Joseph J. Ellis, *Founding Brothers: The Revolutionary Generation* (New York: Knopf, 2000), 48–80.

66 Nonetheless, Jefferson was uncomfortable with arbitrary acts of violence and revenge that would define France's Reign of Terror. See Thomas Jefferson, "Letter to William Short" (January 3, 1793), Thomas Jefferson Papers at the Library of Congress, Series 1, Reel 17.

67 See the Pacificus-Helvidius debates of 1793–1794. This anonymous exchange of essays between Hamilton (Pacificus) and Madison (Helvidius) centers on Washington's proclamation, the American alliance with France, and the president's constitutional authority to assert this policy in the absence of congressional action. Alexander Hamilton, *The Pacificus-Helvidius Debates of 1793–1794: Toward the Completion of the American Founding* [1793], Online Library of Liberty, Liberty Fund, http://oll.libertyfund.org/titles/hamilton-the-pacificus-helvidius-debates-of-1793-1794; Ketcham, *James Madison*, 345–348.

68 Ketcham, 306–315, 319–323.

69 Donald R. Hickey, *The War of 1812: A Forgotten Conflict*, Bicentennial ed. (Urbana: University of Illinois Press, 2012), 11–12.

70 Ketcham, *James Madison*, 356–364; George Washington, "Message to the House of Representatives Regarding Documents Relative to the Jay Treaty," March 30, 1796, The American Presidency Project, http://www.presidency.ucsb.edu/ws/?pid=65520.

71 Jeffrey L. Pasley, *The First Presidential Contest: 1796 and the Founding of American Democracy* (Lawrence: University Press of Kansas, 2013).

72 Adams broke with his party over British attacks on American ships, which he strongly denounced. He supported Jefferson's Embargo Act even though his home state of Massachusetts was economically harmed by the policy. Adams resigned from the US Senate when it became clear that his state's legislature would not reelect him. In 1808 Adams partook in the Democratic-Republican congressional nominating caucus that picked Madison for president. Charles N. Edel, *Nation Builder: John Quincy Adams and the Grand Strategy of the Republic* (Cambridge, MA: Harvard University Press, 2014), 92–94, 96.

73 Hofstadter, *The Idea of a Party System*, 194–203.

74 See the protest letter written by anti-caucus members of Congress, "To the People of the United States," *National Intelligencer*, March 7, 1808, 2–3.

75 James W. Ceaser, *Presidential Selection: Theory and Development* (Princeton, NJ: Princeton University Press, 1979), 103–104, 113–121; William G. Morgan, "The Origin and Development of the Congressional Nominating Caucus," *Proceedings of the American Philosophical Society* 113, no. 2 (April 1969): 184–196.

76 Thomas Jefferson to Spencer Roane, September 6, 1819, Library of Congress, http://www.loc.gov/exhibits/jefferson/137.html.

77 Boller, *Presidential Campaigns*, 10–18; James Roger Sharp, *The Deadlocked Elec-*

tion of 1800: Jefferson, Burr, and the Union in the Balance (Lawrence: University Press of Kansas, 2010), 104–108.

78 Cunningham, *The Jeffersonian Republicans: The Formation of Party Organization*, 239–240.
79 Hofstadter, *The Idea of a Party System*, 136–140.
80 Alexander Hamilton to Theodore Sedgwick, May 10, 1810, *Founders Online*, National Archives, https://founders.archives.gov/documents/Hamilton/01-24-02-0387.
81 Morgan, "The Origin and Development of the Congressional Nominating Caucus," 187; Wood, *Empire of Liberty*, 439–440; on the Burr affair, see Peter Charles Hoffer, *The Treason Trials of Aaron Burr* (Lawrence: University Press of Kansas, 2008).
82 Tadahisa Kuroda walks readers through the entire congressional debate over the Twelfth Amendment in *The Origins of the Twelfth Amendment: The Electoral College in the Early Republic, 1787–1804* (Westport, CT: Greenwood Press, 1994).
83 Ketcham, *James Madison*, 406–407.
84 Donald A. Zinman, "The Heir Apparent Presidency of James Madison," *Presidential Studies Quarterly* 41, no. 4 (December 2011), 724; Historical Party Divisions of the US Senate and US House, https://www.senate.gov/history/partydiv.htm and http://history.house.gov/Institution/Party-Divisions/Party-Divisions/.
85 Norman K. Risjord, *The Old Republicans: Southern Conservatism in the Age of Jefferson* (New York: Columbia University Press, 1965).
86 Noble E. Cunningham Jr., "Who Were the Quids?," *Mississippi Valley Historical Review* 50, no. 2 (1963): 252–263.
87 Cunningham, *The Jeffersonian Republicans in Power*, 78–88; Risjord, *The Old Republicans*, 40–71.
88 Cunningham, "Who Were the Quids?," 252–258.
89 John K. Lee, *George Clinton: Master Builder of the Empire State* (Syracuse, NY: Syracuse University Press, 2010), 29–30; Kaminski, *George Clinton: Yeoman Politician*, 113–139.
90 Clinton carried 67 out of 108 votes on the first ballot. Cunningham, *The Jeffersonian Republicans in Power*, 104; also see Kaminski, *George Clinton: Yeoman Politician*, 274.
91 Hofstadter, *The Idea of a Party System*, 159–161.
92 Wood, *Empire of Liberty*, 293.
93 Hofstadter, *The Idea of a Party System*, 155–158.
94 William D. Adler and Jonathan Keller, "A Federal Army, Not a Federalist One: Regime Building in the Jeffersonian Era," *Journal of Policy History* 26, no. 2 (April 2014): 167–187.
95 Forrest McDonald, *The Presidency of Thomas Jefferson* (Lawrence: University Press of Kansas, 1976), 61–63, 76–80.
96 This was to be known as the Cumberland Road, which would eventually stretch from western Maryland to Vandalia, Illinois. Ground was not broken on the new road, however, until 1811; Wood, *Empire of Liberty*, 482.

97 McDonald, *The Presidency of Thomas Jefferson*, 142.
98 J. C. A. Stagg, *Mr. Madison's War: Politics, Diplomacy, and Warfare in the Early American Republic, 1783–1830* (Princeton, NJ: Princeton University Press, 1983), 20–22.
99 Ketcham, *James Madison*, 448–449; Risjord, *The Old Republicans*, 87.
100 Gary Hart, *James Monroe* (New York: Times Books, 2005), 45–47.
101 Napoleon Bonaparte, *Berlin Decree*, November 21, 1806. History website of the Foundation Napoleon, https://www.napoleon.org/en/history-of-the-two-empires/articles/the-berlin-decree-of-november-21-1806/.
102 Hickey, *The War of 1812*, 17; Wood, *Empire of Liberty*, 646.
103 Ketcham, *James Madison*, 452–455.
104 Ketcham, 456.
105 Wood, *Empire of Liberty*, 649–650. Senator John Quincy Adams was the only Federalist to break ranks. For House and Senate roll calls see Jeffrey B. Lewis, Keith Poole, Howard Rosenthal, Adam Boche, Aaron Rudkin, and Luke Sonnet, 2019, *Voteview: Congressional Roll-Call Votes Database*, https://voteview.com/.
106 Wood, 655.
107 White, *The Jeffersonians*, 426–432.
108 Wood, *Empire of Liberty*, 652–654.
109 Brant, *James Madison* (vol. 4), 402–403; Wood, 651–652.
110 "Embargo," *National Intelligencer & Washington Advertiser*, December 23, 1807, 3.
111 Brant, *James Madison* (vol. 4), 402–403.
112 James Madison to William Pinkney, December 23, 1807, *The Writings of James Madison, Vol. 7, Online Library of Liberty*, Liberty Fund, http://oll.libertyfund.org/titles/madison-the-writings-vol-7-1803-1807.
113 Ketcham, *James Madison*, 456–461, 463–465.

2. MADISON'S DILEMMA

1 James Madison, Inaugural Address, *The American Presidency Project*, https://www.presidency.ucsb.edu/node/204053.
2 The statement continued, "Obviously indicating the necessity of continuing the succession of the powers of administering the government in those hands, that would give a fair scope to, by securing a perseverance in, those political measures, originated by the present administration, now in the full tide of successful experiment." Democratic Republican Citizens, New Castle, Delaware, *At a very numerous and respectable meeting of the Democratic Republican citizens of New-Castle County in the State of Delaware, on the 3d of September, . . . Convened pursuant to a resolution of a former meeting, dated the 19th of August last*, 1808, https://www.loc.gov/item/rbpe.01304000.
3 A major theme of David Hackett Fischer's *The Revolution of American Conservatism: The Federalist Party in the Era of Jeffersonian Democracy* (New York: Harper & Row, 1965), is the Federalist Party's messaging, organizing, and tactics after being displaced from power in the 1800 election.

4   Leonard W. Levy, *Jefferson and Civil Liberties: The Darker Side* (New York: Quadrangle, 1963), 121–141.
5   Levy, *Jefferson and Civil Liberties*, 105–107, 114–120.
6   James Madison to William Pinkney, January 3, 1809, *Online Library of Liberty*, Liberty Fund, https://oll.libertyfund.org/titles/1939#lf1356-08_mnt010.
7   Marque and reprisal is a constitutionally authorized procedure whereby Congress can commission private actors to seize the property of foreign governments or citizens, usually as compensation for some harm that nation, or its citizens, have allegedly done to the United States. See *Constitution of the United States*, Article I, Section 8, Clause 11.
8   Brant, *James Madison* (vol. 4), 477–480; McDonald, *The Presidency of Thomas Jefferson*, 156–158.
9   James Madison to William Pinkney, February 11, 1809, *Letters and Other Writings of James Madison, Fourth President of the United States* (Philadelphia: J. B. Lippincott, 1865), 429–431; Irving Brant, *James Madison: The President, 1809–1812*, vol. 5 (Indianapolis: Bobbs-Merrill, 1956), 16, 37.
10 Hickey, *The War of 1812*, 20–21.
11 James Madison, Proclamation—Suspension of Prohibition of Trade between the United States and Great Britain, *The American Presidency Project*, https://www.presidency.ucsb.edu/node/205581.
12 Robert Allen Rutland, *The Presidency of James Madison* (Lawrence: University Press of Kansas, 1990), 39–41.
13 "French Minister," *Northern Whig*, May 2, 1809, 3; See Fischer, *The Revolution of American Conservatism*, 424–429, for a full bibliography of newspapers that supported the Federalist Party between 1800 and 1820.
14 "Boston, May 8," *American*, May 12, 1809, 2–3.
15 Rutland, *The Presidency of James Madison*, 41–43; James Madison, Proclamation—Renewal of Prohibition of Trade between the United States and Great Britain, *The American Presidency Project*, https://www.presidency.ucsb.edu/node/204365.
16 Wood, *Empire of Liberty*, 665.
17 Wood, 665; Irving Brant, *James Madison* (vol. 5), 126–129; Stagg, "James Madison: Life before the Presidency," 27–28.
18 Brant (vol. 5), 137–140; Ketcham, *James Madison*, 499; Rutland, *The Presidency of James Madison*, 62–63; Stagg, 28–29.
19 A review of presidential veto messages from George Washington through Andrew Jackson, and to some extent beyond, reveals a strong emphasis on the government's proper constitutional authority and the president's role in halting legislation he deemed to be unconstitutional. For a repository of presidential veto messages, see *The American Presidency Project*, https://www.presidency.ucsb.edu/documents/app-categories/presidential/vetoes. See also Robert J. Spitzer, *The Presidential Veto: Touchstone of the American Presidency* (Albany: State University of New York Press, 1988).
20 John Armstrong and Duc De Cadore, *Duc de Cadore to John Armstrong, August 5*, August 5, 1810, https://www.loc.gov/item/mjm022051/.

21 James Madison, Proclamation—Suspension of Prohibition of Trade with France, *The American Presidency Project*, https://www.presidency.ucsb.edu/node/204918.
22 Rutland, *The Presidency of James Madison*, 66, 80–81; Wood, *Empire of Liberty*, 666.
23 Hickey, *The War of 1812*, 21; Ketcham, *James Madison*, 502–506; Stagg, "James Madison: Life before the Presidency," 55–58.
24 Hickey, 21.
25 Eric Lomazoff, *Reconstructing the National Bank: Politics and Law in the Early American Republic* (Chicago: University of Chicago Press, 2018), 78.
26 Lomazoff, *Reconstructing the National Bank*, 69–70; Brant, *James Madison* (vol. 5), 265–270; Rutland, *The Presidency of James Madison*, 68–70; Garry Wills, *James Madison* (New York: Times Books, 2002), 75–77; Henry Adams, *The Life of Albert Gallatin* (New York: J. B. Lippincott, 1943), 426–430. The House roll call was technically a procedural defeat rather than a vote on the actual substance of renewal. The House voted 65–64 to table the recharter measure indefinitely.
27 *Annals of Congress*, 11th Cong., 3rd sess., 346–347. Similarly, the Senate vote was a roll call to table the measure.
28 *Annals of Congress*, 11th Cong., 3rd sess., 651–659. Desha was an opponent of the National Bank on constitutional grounds, but he also objected to the foreign—especially British—influence that infused the institution. Desha was also aligned with the War Hawk faction; Risjord, *The Old Republicans*, 111, 116, 129.
29 Brant, *James Madison* (vol. 5), 265–270; Risjord, 111; Rutland, *The Presidency of James Madison*, 69.
30 Lomazoff, *Reconstructing the National Bank*, 94–95.
31 James Madison, Veto Message, *The American Presidency Project*, https://www.presidency.ucsb.edu/node/205221.
32 James Madison, Veto Message, *The American Presidency Project*, https://www.presidency.ucsb.edu/node/205267.
33 Rutland, *The Presidency of James Madison*, 77–78.
34 Rutland, 203.
35 James Madison, Veto Message, *The American Presidency Project*, https://www.presidency.ucsb.edu/node/205162.
36 On the first presidential Cabinet, see Lindsay M. Chervinksy, *The Cabinet: George Washington and the Creation of an American Institution* (Cambridge, MA: Harvard University Press, 2020). As party cleavages and internal factions began to take shape in subsequent administrations, presidents had to be more closely attuned to the task of political balance.
37 Andrew Jackson serves as the first and best example of a president who utilized a Kitchen Cabinet that held at least equal political influence as the official Cabinet. See Jon Meacham, *American Lion: Andrew Jackson in the White House* (New York: Random House, 2008), for several examples.
38 Rutland, *The Presidency of James Madison*, 32–36; Wills, *James Madison*, 63–64.

39 Hickey, *The War of 1812*, 41; Rutland, 32–36, 41–42, 120; White, *The Jeffersonians*, 80–81, 217–218, 271; Wills, 116–117.
40 Rutland, 74; Stagg, "James Madison: Life before the Presidency," 55–57.
41 Wills, *James Madison*, 89–90.
42 James Madison, "Memorandum on Robert Smith" [ca. 11 April] 1811, *Founders Online*, National Archives, https://founders.archives.gov/documents/Madison/03-03-02-0317; Rutland, *The Presidency of James Madison*, 74.
43 Brant, *James Madison* (vol. 5), 302–307; Robert Smith, *An Address to the People of the United States* (London: Hatchard, 1811), 42–43. The manuscript, totaling about forty pages, was published in major American newspapers.
44 Ammon, *James Monroe*, 287–288.
45 Mark O. Hatfield, with the Senate Historical Office, *Vice Presidents of the United States, 1789–1993* (Washington, DC: Government Printing Office, 1997), 49–58.

3. DEMOCRATIC-REPUBLICANS GO TO WAR WITH BRITAIN AND THEMSELVES

1 "The Closing Point," *Columbian*, June 22, 1812, 2.
2 James Sterling Young, *The Washington Community: 1800–1828* (New York: Columbia University Press, 1966), 173–174.
3 Risjord, *The Old Republicans*, 112–117.
4 Risjord, 74, 116–119; Ammon, *James Monroe*, 270–273, 283–286.
5 "The Spirit of 'Seventy-Six," Library of Congress, https://www.loc.gov/item/sn82014068/.
6 Risjord, *The Old Republicans*, 126–127, 141–147; see also Reginald Horsman, "Who Were the War Hawks?," *Indiana Magazine of History* 60, no. 2 (June 1964): 121–136.
7 Risjord, 116–117.
8 Risjord, 116–117; Leland R. Johnson, "The Suspense Was Hell: The Senate Vote for War in 1812," *Indiana Magazine of History* 65, no. 4 (1969): 247–267; John S. Pancake, "The 'Invisibles': A Chapter in the Opposition to President Madison," *Journal of Southern History* 21, no. 1 (February 1955): 17–37; Stagg, "James Madison: Life before the Presidency," 50.
9 Brant, *James Madison* (vol. 5), 293–294; Stagg, 50–51.
10 Pancake, "The 'Invisibles,'" 33.
11 Cornog, *The Birth of Empire*, 62; Johnson, "The Suspense Was Hell," 264–267; Horsman, "Who Were the War Hawks?," 133–136.
12 Historian Donald Hickey has found that use of the "War Hawk" label actually goes back to the 1790s. See Hickey, *The War of 1812*, 336–337.
13 Hickey, 29; Johnson, "The Suspense Was Hell," 247–267.
14 James Madison, Third Annual Message, *The American Presidency Project*, https://www.presidency.ucsb.edu/node/204473.
15 Hickey, *The War of 1812*, 28–34; James Madison, Proclamation—Granting Pardon to All Deserters Who Return to Duty, *The American Presidency Project*, https://www.presidency.ucsb.edu/node/205217.

16 Jeffrey L. Pasley, *The Tyranny of Printers: Newspaper Politics in the Early American Republic* (Charlottesville: University Press of Virginia, 2001), 132–152; Charles Holt to Jefferson, October 25, 1810, *Founders Online*, National Archives, https://founders.archives.gov/documents/Jefferson/03-03-02-0124, see footnote 1; "Original Prospectus," *Columbian*, November 1, 1809, 1.
17 Stefan Bielinski, "Solomon Southwick," New York State Museum, https://exhibitions.nysm.nysed.gov/albany/bios/s/sosouthwick.html.
18 Johnson, "The Suspense Was Hell," 247–267; Hickey, *The War of 1812*, 28–29; Stagg, "James Madison: Life before the Presidency," 52–53; Wills, *James Madison*, 69.
19 Cornog, *The Birth of Empire*, 14; Dorothie Bobbé, *DeWitt Clinton* (New York: Minton, Balch & Co., 1933), 20, 25.
20 Cornog, 15–17; Bobbé, 25–35.
21 Cornog, 18–21; "Letter IV," *New-York Journal*, January 10, 1788, 2. Also see "Miscellany," *New-York Journal*, December 6, 1787; and "Letter II," *New-York Journal*, December 13, 1787.
22 Cornog, 22–30.
23 Cornog, 45, 54–68, 104–117; Harry B. Yoshpe, "Record of Slave Manumissions in New York during the Colonial and Early National Periods," *Journal of Negro History* 26, no. 1 (January 1941): 78–107.
24 Cornog, 30–34; Lampi Collection of American Electoral Returns, https://elections.lib.tufts.edu/catalog/3f462543d.
25 Cornog, 34–38; Grotius, *A Vindication of Thomas Jefferson* (New York: David Denniston, 1800).
26 Cornog, 34, 39–43; "DeWitt Clinton's Duel with John Swartwout," *Troy Weekly Times*, September 21, 1872, 4.
27 Cornog, 43–44.
28 Cornog, 44–49; see the Naturalization Act of 1802; on the politics and process of creating the Twelfth Amendment, see Tadahisa Kuroda, *The Origins of the Twelfth Amendment*.
29 Cornog, 54–61.
30 Cornog, 73–78.
31 Cornog, 75–78.
32 Lampi Collection of American Electoral Returns, https://elections.lib.tufts.edu/catalog/s1784m933; Cornog, 84–86, 89; De Alva Stanwood Alexander, *A Political History of the State of New York*, vol. 1 (New York: Holt, 1906), 168.
33 Cornog, 89–90. In Governor Tompkins's 1810 reelection, the Federalist candidate, Jonas Platt, carried New York City; see Lampi Collection of American Electoral Returns, https://elections.lib.tufts.edu/catalog/3n204020s.
34 Cornog, 91–92; Lampi Collection of American Electoral Returns, https://elections.lib.tufts.edu/catalog/8k71nj015.
35 Stagg, "James Madison: Life before the Presidency," 52–53, 111, 114; Johnson, "The Suspense Was Hell," 264–267; Roger H. Brown, *The Republic in Peril: 1812* (New York: Columbia University Press, 1964), 143–147.
36 Cornog, *The Birth of Empire*, 109, 112.

37 Madison to Congress, December 23, 1811, *Founders Online*, National Archives, https://founders.archives.gov/documents/Madison/03-04-02-0096, and see footnote 4.
38 Madison to Congress, December 23, 1811, footnote 2, Bayard to Caesar A. Rodney, December 22, 1811; Cornog, *The Birth of Empire*, 90–94.
39 Hickey, *The War of 1812*, 22–23.
40 On the battle, see "The Little Belt Affair," US Navy, https://www.history.navy.mil/content/history/nhhc/our-collections/art/exhibits/conflicts-and-operations/the-war-of-1812/the-little-belt-affair.html
41 "Washington City," *National Intelligencer*, May 30, 1811, 2; "Independence," *Boston Patriot*, July 13, 1811, 2; Paul Hamilton to Madison, September 17, 1811, *Founders Online*, National Archives, https://founders.archives.gov/documents/Madison/03-03-02-0552.
42 Hickey, *The War of 1812*, 22–25.
43 Hickey, 22–25; Brant, *James Madison* (vol. 5), 190–193.
44 Brant (vol. 5), 384–389.
45 Hickey, *The War of 1812*, 22–25; casualty reports estimate that the Native fighters totaled 38 dead (wounded figures were unknown), and Harrison's losses were 62 dead and 126 wounded. See Walter R. Borneman, *1812: The War that Forged a Nation* (New York: Harper Collins, 2004), 32–37.
46 James Madison, Special Message, *The American Presidency Project*, https://www.presidency.ucsb.edu/node/205428.
47 "For Congress and the Administration," *Reporter*, November 23, 1811, 2; Hickey, *The War of 1812*, 25.
48 "Indian War!!," *Republican*, Savannah, Georgia, December 12, 1811, 3; "More of the Indian War," *Republican Star*, Easton, Maryland, November 26, 1811, 6; "War! War! War!," *Supporter*, Chillicothe, Ohio, November, 30, 1811, 3.
49 Morgan Friedman, The Inflation Calculator, https://westegg.com/inflation/; Hickey, *The War of 1812*, 34–36; Monroe to Joel Barlow, February 22, 1812, *Papers of James Monroe*, University of Mary Washington, Fredericksburg, Virginia, http://monroepapers.com/items/show/2255; Stagg, "James Madison: Life before the Presidency," 93–94.
50 James Madison, Special Message, *The American Presidency Project*, https://www.presidency.ucsb.edu/node/206024.
51 *National Intelligencer*, March 10, 14, 17, 21, and 24, 1812, cited in Brant, *James Madison* (vol. 5), 414–415.
52 All quotations are taken from the *Concord Gazette*, April 7, 1812, 1–2, which was a compilation of stories and editorials about the Henry affair from various publications.
53 Hickey, *The War of 1812*, 34–36.
54 "A fearful prostitution of the first office in our country!," bellowed Delaware's Federalist senator James A. Bayard. John Randolph denounced the payoff and the documents' publication as a "dirty electioneering trick." Vice President Clinton privately disapproved of releasing the papers. Madison's Democratic-Republican skeptics like the Invisibles and Clintonians focused upon the

deception of the president and the secretary of state, rather than any British wrongdoing. See Brant, *James Madison* (vol. 5), 414–420, Stagg, "James Madison: Life before the Presidency," 95, 97–99.

55 Brant (vol. 5), 175–189; Ketcham, *James Madison*, 500–502; Rutland, *The Presidency of James Madison*, 60–62; Wills, *James Madison*, 77–79.

56 Brant (vol. 5), 175–189; Ketcham, 500–502; Rutland, 60–62; Wills, 77–79.

57 James Madison, Proclamation 16—Taking Possession of Part of Louisiana (Annexation of West Florida), *The American Presidency Project*, https://www.presidency.ucsb.edu/node/204872.

58 Brant, *James Madison* (vol. 5), 175–189; Ketcham, *James Madison*, 500–502; Rutland, *The Presidency of James Madison*, 60–62; Wills, *James Madison*, 77–79.

59 Hubert Bruce Fuller, *The Purchase of Florida: Its History and Diplomacy* (Cleveland, Ohio: Burrows Brothers, 1906), 187–188; Madison to Congress, January 3, 1811, *Founders Online*, National Archives, https://founders.archives.gov/documents/Madison/03-03-02-0112.

60 Madison to Jefferson, April 24, 1812, *Founders Online*, National Archives, https://founders.archives.gov/documents/Jefferson/03-04-02-0546. In a letter terminating Mathews's service, Secretary Monroe told the rebellious general that "the measures which you appear to have adopted for obtaining possession of Amelia Island and other parts of East Florida, are not authorized by the law of the United States or the instructions founded on it, under which you have acted." Monroe to Mathews, April 4, 1812, *Papers of James Monroe*, http://monroepapers.com/items/show/2273; for a comprehensive account, see James G. Cusick, *The Other War of 1812: The Patriot War and the American Invasion of Spanish East Florida* (Athens: University of Georgia Press, 2003); Wills, *James Madison*, 79.

61 Brant, *James Madison* (vol. 5), 227–228.

62 The letter was written from the vicinity of St. Augustine, Florida, on the date of June 22, 1812, which was four days after the congressional declaration of war in Washington, DC. While this news would not have traveled that fast in 1812, a political environment of imminent Anglo-American war certainly existed at the time. See also Paul Kruse, "A Secret Agent in East Florida: General George Mathews and the Patriot War," *Journal of Southern History* 18, no. 2 (May 1952): 193–217; Mathews to Monroe, June 22, 1812; Cusick, *The Other War of 1812*, 189–190.

63 "East Florida," *Charleston Courier*, April 1, 1812, 2.

64 William H. Crawford to Monroe, August 6, 1812, *Papers of James Monroe*, http://monroepapers.com/items/show/2341; Frank Lawrence Owsley Jr. and Gene A. Smith, *Filibusters and Expansionists: Jeffersonian Manifest Destiny, 1800–1821* (Tuscaloosa: University of Alabama Press, 1997), 72–74.

65 Owsley and Smith, *Filibusters and Expansionists*, 74–76.

66 *Annals of Congress*, 12th Cong., 1st sess., 326; Cusick, *The Other War of 1812*, 190–192.

67 See Stagg, "James Madison: Life before the Presidency"; Jasper M. Trautsch,

"'Mr. Madison's War' or the Dynamic of Early American Nationalism?," *Early American Studies* 10, no. 3 (Fall 2012): 630–670.
68 James Madison, Special Message, *The American Presidency Project*, https://www.presidency.ucsb.edu/node/206055.
69 Hickey, *The War of 1812*, 36–37; Stagg, "James Madison: Life before the Presidency," 96–97, 101–102.
70 Zinman, "The Heir Apparent Presidency of James Madison," 721, tables 2 and 3. As House elections and senatorial selections by state legislatures took place over a period of several months, some contests were held into 1811.
71 Trautsch, "'Mr. Madison's War,'" 650–651; "New Patriotic Song," *Carthage Gazette*, March 8, 1811, 2.
72 Reginald Horsman, *The Causes of the War of 1812* (Philadelphia: University of Pennsylvania Press, 1962), 186–187; Harlow Giles Unger, *Henry Clay: America's Greatest Statesman* (Boston: Da Capo Press, 2015), 47, 49, 70–73, 265.
73 Kentucky used a district-based electoral vote allocation at the time, and though Democratic-Republicans were dominant in the state, there were some pockets of Federalist support. See David S. Heidler and Jeanne T. Heidler, *Henry Clay: The Essential American* (New York: Random House, 2010), 47–48.
74 Unger, *Henry Clay*, 51–57.
75 "Washington City," *National Intelligencer*, May 30, 1812, 3; Brant, *James Madison* (vol. 5), 469–470, speculates that Monroe could have written the editorial; Ketcham, *James Madison*, 525–526.
76 Brant (vol. 5), 478; Hickey, *The War of 1812*, 38–40.
77 James Madison, Special Message, *The American Presidency Project*, https://www.presidency.ucsb.edu/node/204937.
78 Ketcham, *James Madison*, 528–529.
79 James Madison, Proclamation—Announcement of a State of War between the United States and the United Kingdom, *The American Presidency Project*, https://www.presidency.ucsb.edu/node/205331; Brant, *James Madison* (vol. 5), 477.
80 Samuel Harrison to Madison, May 11, 1812, *Founders Online*, National Archives, https://founders.archives.gov/documents/Madison/03-04-02-0400.
81 Morgan, "The Origin and Development of the Congressional Nominating Caucus," 190–191; Brant, *James Madison* (vol. 5), 452–453.
82 Brant (vol. 5), 452–459.
83 "Nomination of Electors," *Richmond Enquirer*, February 18, 1812, 2.
84 Simon Snyder to James Madison, April 6, 1809, *Founders Online*, National Archives, https://founders.archives.gov/documents/Madison/03-01-02-0118.
85 James Madison to Simon Snyder, April 13, 1809, *Founders Online*, National Archives, https://founders.archives.gov/documents/Madison/03-01-02-0132.
86 For a narrative on this episode, see Mary E. Cunningham, "The Case of the Active," *Pennsylvania History: A Journal of Mid-Atlantic Studies* 13, no. 4 (1946): 229–247; see also Saul Cornell, *A Well-Regulated Militia: The Founding Fathers and the Origins of Gun Control in America* (Oxford: Oxford University Press,

2008), 117–123; Brant, *James Madison* (vol. 5), 28–30; Rutland, *The Presidency of James Madison*, 53–55.
87 "The Voice of Pennsylvania," *Democratic Press*, March 18, 1812, 2; Brant (vol. 5), 455.
88 Brant (vol. 5), 456–457, 459.
89 "Prorogation," *Albany Register*, March 31, 1812, 4; Cornog, *The Birth of Empire*, 94–96, notes that on the National Bank issue, Clinton was "in a tight spot," lest he offend pro-Bank Federalists, whose support he would require in the upcoming presidential campaign.
90 Solomon Southwick, "Republican Tickets," *Albany Register*, April 14, 1812, 2; Solomon Southwick, "Presidential Election," *Albany Register*, April 3, 1812, 2.
91 Brant, *James Madison* (vol. 5), 456.
92 *Weekly Register*, March–September 1812, vol. II, 192–193; Brant (vol. 5), 458.
93 *Weekly Register*, March–September 1812, vol. II, 196.
94 *Weekly Register*, March–September 1812, vol. II, 276.
95 *Weekly Register*, March–September 1812, vol. II, 276.
96 George Billias, *Elbridge Gerry: Founding Father and Republican Statesman* (New York: McGraw-Hill, 1976), 264–289.
97 Gerry embarked on various efforts, with varying levels of success, to reduce Federalist influence at state-chartered banks, hospitals, the Massachusetts Medical Society, and Harvard University. The judicial branch of state government was reorganized to give the governor new powers to appoint more judges and sheriffs. Voter suffrage laws were liberalized, strengthening Democratic-Republicans at local levels. A law was passed to reduce state support for the officially established Congregationalist Church, which was a Federalist constituency. Billias, *Elbridge Gerry*, 185–205, 314–323.
98 Billias, 185–205, 314–323; "The Gerry-mander," *Boston Gazette*, March 26, 1812, 2.
99 Elbridge Gerry to James Madison, April 16, 1812, *Founders Online*, National Archives, https://founders.archives.gov/documents/Madison/03-04-02-0339.
100 On the role of collectors in the early republic, see White, *The Jeffersonians*, 148–161.
101 Albert Gallatin to Joseph H. Nicholson, May 21, 1812, in *The Writings of Albert Gallatin*, vol. 1, ed. Henry Adams (Philadelphia: J. B. Lippincott, 1879), https://oll.libertyfund.org/titles/1953#lf1358-01_head_329.
102 "Vice Presidency," *National Intelligencer*, June 27, 1812, 2.
103 "Presidential Election," *National Intelligencer*, October 10, 1812, 1–2.
104 "Presidential Nomination," *Essex Register*, June 13, 1812, 3.
105 *Weekly Register*, March–September 1812, vol. II, 276.
106 Benjamin Ludlow et al., "Republican Convention," *Centinel of Freedom*, July 28, 1812, 1; Ludlow et al., "Address. To the President of the U. States," *Centinel of Freedom*, July 28, 1812, 1.
107 James Madison to Benjamin Ludlow, July 25, 1812, *Founders Online*, National Archives, https://founders.archives.gov/documents/Madison/03-05-02-0063.
108 "Presidential Nomination," *Columbian Phenix*, July 11, 1812, 2.
109 "Presidential Nomination," *New Hampshire Patriot*, October 20, 1812, 2.

4. FEDERALISTS AND CLINTONIANS: A WARTIME ALLIANCE

1. "Grand Caucus," *Public Advertiser*, September 19, 1812, 2.
2. Fisher Ames to Thomas Dwight, April 16, 1802, *Works of Fisher Ames* (Boston: Little, Brown, 1854), 297–298. In this letter, Ames was celebrating the party's recent victory in the Massachusetts gubernatorial election.
3. In *Federalist*, no. 1, Hamilton made his views very clear on leaders who rely on populist appeals to the citizenry: "Of those men who have overturned the liberties of republics, the greatest number have begun their career by paying an obsequious court to the people; commencing demagogues, and ending tyrants." Alexander Hamilton, *Federalist*, no. 1, https://guides.loc.gov/federalist-papers/text-1-10#s-lg-box-wrapper-25493264.
4. *Connecticut Courant*, cited in Manning Dauer, "Federalist Platform," in Arthur M. Schlesinger Jr., Fred L. Israel, and William P. Hansen, eds., *History of American Presidential Elections, 1789–1968*, vol. 1 (New York: Chelsea House Publishers, 1971), 178.
5. Humphrey Marshall, *The History of Kentucky*, vol. 2 (Frankfort, KY: G. S. Robinson, 1824), 319; Fischer, *The Revolution of American Conservatism*, 156, 410.
6. Fischer, xviii–xix, 70.
7. Fischer, 60–90, 97–100, 110–128.
8. Pasley, *The Tyranny of Printers*, 202–208; Morgan, "The Origin and Development of the Congressional Nominating Caucus," 185–186; Sharp, *The Deadlocked Election of 1800*, 90–91, 112–113.
9. Fischer, 83–84.
10. Fischer, 85–87; Samuel E. Morison, "The First National Nominating Convention, 1808," *American Historical Review* 17, no. 4 (July 1912): 744–763; Samuel Eliot Morison, *The Life and Letters of Harrison Gray Otis, Federalist, 1765–1848*, vol. 1 (Boston: Houghton Mifflin, 1913), 304–306.
11. Dinah Mayo-Bobee, "Understanding the Essex Junto: Fear, Dissent, and Propaganda in the Early Republic," *New England Quarterly* 88, no. 4 (2015): 623–656; David H. Fischer, "The Myth of the Essex Junto," *William and Mary Quarterly* 21, no. 2 (1964): 191–235.
12. Fischer, *The Revolution of American Conservatism*, 85–87; Morison, "The First National Nominating Convention, 1808," 750–753.
13. Morison, "The First National Nominating Convention, 1808," 750–754; Morison, *The Life and Letters of Harrison Gray Otis*, 304–306; Fischer surmises that New York Federalists sent Egbert Benson, an accomplished lawyer, jurist, and politician, as well as Abraham Van Vechten, a lawyer and state legislator. Fischer also lists Connecticut's David Daggett as a probable attendee. In addition to being active in Federalist politics, with previous stints in the Connecticut General Assembly and State Council, Daggett was a supporter of proactive party-building, Fischer, *The Revolution of American Conservatism*, 62–63, 86, 296, 300–301, 318–319.
14. See "Official Notification of the Result of the Federalist National Convention of 1808," a document published by the party's New York Committee of Corre-

spondence (September 1808), in Morison, *The Life and Letters of Harrison Gray Otis*, 306–307, 314–315.
15 Morison, "The First National Nominating Convention, 1808," 751–753.
16 "Presidential Election," *National Intelligencer*, March 26, 1812, 3.
17 Cornog, *The Birth of Empire*, 76.
18 Brant, *James Madison* (vol. 5), 456; Ketcham, *James Madison*, 509.
19 Lansing was lobbying for his son's appointment as a surgeon in the army, and he subsequently reminded Madison of his election-year support of the president. Abraham G. Lansing to James Madison, May 8, 1813, *Founders Online*, National Archives, https://founders.archives.gov/documents/Madison/03-06-02-0278; see also Brant (vol. 5), 456.
20 Cornog, *The Birth of Empire*, 96; Ketcham, *James Madison*, 521, 569; White, *The Jeffersonians*, 301; Steven E. Siry, *DeWitt Clinton and the American Political Economy: Sectionalism, Politics, and Republican Ideology, 1787–1828* (New York: Peter Lang, 1990), 160–161. Madison ultimately fired Granger in March 1814, as the latter was allotting ever more local postmasterships to allies of the Invisibles. The final straw may have been when Granger appointed Senator Michael Leib to the prestigious Philadelphia postmaster job in February 1814. See Stagg, "James Madison: Life before the Presidency," 365.
21 Cornog, 96–97; John Jay Knox, *A History of Banking in the United States* (New York: Bradford Rhodes, 1900), 397. The *National Intelligencer* reported the attendance as ninety-one members whereas the *Albany Register* reported ninety. "Presidential Nomination," *National Intelligencer*, June 4, 1812, 2; "The Presidential Nomination," *Albany Register*, June 5, 1812, 2.
22 "Republican Presidential Nomination," *Orange County Patriot*, June 9, 1812, 3.
23 "Presidential Nomination," *Albany Register*, June 2, 1812, 2.
24 "Presidential Nomination," *National Intelligencer*, June 4, 1812, 2.
25 "For the Columbian," *Columbian*, June 9, 1812, 3.
26 "Washington City," *National Intelligencer*, June 18, 1812, 2.
27 "The Presidential Nomination," *Albany Register*, June 5, 1812, 2.
28 "Presidential Election," *New York Evening Post*, June 6, 1812, 3. The newspaper later became known as the *New York Post*, which promotes a sensationalist brand of journalism and today functions as a leading organ for American conservatives.
29 For a full original printing of the proclamation of Clinton's nomination by his supporters in the state legislature see "Address," *Albany Register*, August 28, 1812, 2–3. Quotes from the next six paragraphs are from this source.
30 William Plumer Jr., ed., and A. P. Peabody, *Life of William Plumer* (Boston: Phillips, Sampson, 1857), 401 (September 11, 1812).
31 According to Rufus King, Pinckney had told the Federalist Corresponding Committee of Philadelphia that he would decline another presidential nomination. Reportedly, the general recommended John Jay or King as candidates. See footnote from King's notes from the Federalist meeting in New York City (September 15–17, 1812), Charles R. King, ed., *The Life and Correspondence of*

    Rufus King, vol. 5, 1807–1816 (New York: G. P. Putnam's Sons, Knickerbocker Press, 1898), 280–281.
32 Jay stepped away from contributing to *The Federalist Papers* due to illness. Fischer, *The Revolution of American Conservatism*, 6–10; Morison, *The Life and Letters of Harrison Gray Otis*, 309, 319–320.
33 This obscure case concerned the American seizure of a Danish ship that was allegedly violating a trade embargo with France. Adams's orders pursuant to this law ran contrary to the statute enacted by Congress. Furthermore, if the ship's commander obeyed an illegal directive, he could be held liable for damages. *Little v. Barreme*, 6 US 170 (1804).
34 Rufus King, diary entry, July 27, 1812, *The Life and Correspondence of Rufus King*, 266. See also the entry for August 29, 1812, 271–272; Fischer, *The Revolution of American Conservatism*, 89.
35 King, diary entry, August 29, 1812, 271–272, and his notes from the Federalist meeting in New York City (September 15–17, 1812), 280–281; Fischer, 89.
36 Fischer, 87–88; William Sullivan, *The Public Men of the Revolution: Including Events from the Peace of 1783 to the Peace of 1815* (Philadelphia: Carey & Hart, 1847), see editor's footnote, John Turner Sargent Sullivan, 349–351.
37 "Grand Caucus," *Commonwealth*, October 6, 1812, 2; John S. Murdock, "The First National Nominating Convention," *American Historical Review* 1, no. 4 (July 1896): 680–683. Secondary accounts of the meeting assert that there were upward of 60 men at the event. William Sullivan counted 70 delegates in his notes and identified the size of each state's delegation as 18 from New York, 12 from New Jersey, 10 from Pennsylvania, 8 from Massachusetts, 6 from Connecticut, 4 from South Carolina, 3 each from Maryland and Rhode Island, and 2 each from Delaware, New Hampshire, and Vermont. See William Sullivan, *Familiar Letters on Public Characters, and Public Events: From the Peace of 1783, to the Peace of 1815*, 2nd ed. (Boston: Russell, Odiorne & Metcalfe, 1834), 327. King cited "more than sixty Gentlemen" at the gathering; King, *The Life and Correspondence of Rufus King*, 277.
38 Fischer, *The Revolution of American Conservatism*, 321–322; Peter A. Jay to John Jay, September 17, 1812, *The Papers of John Jay*, Columbia University.
39 Risjord, *The Old Republicans*, 148–149.
40 Gaillard Hund and James Brown Scott, eds., *The Debates in the Federal Convention of 1787, Which Framed the Constitution of the United States of America, Reported by James Madison* (Oxford: Oxford University Press, 1920), August 8, 1787, https://avalon.law.yale.edu/18th_century/debates_808.asp.
41 Rufus King, diary entry, August 5, 1812, *The Life and Correspondence of Rufus King*, 268–271.
42 "Meeting of the Friends of Liberty, Peace and Commerce," *New York Evening Post*, August 18, 1812, 2; Richard P. McCormick, *The Presidential Game: The Origins of American Presidential Politics* (New York: Oxford University Press, 1982), 98.
43 "Convention of New Jersey," *Trenton Federalist*, July 20, 1812, 1.

44 "Public Meetings," *Trenton Federalist*, June 15, 1812, 2; "Public Meeting," *Federal Republican*, May 22, 1812, 1.
45 For references to local peace meetings, see "Appeal for Peace, of the Town of Boston," *Rhode Island American*, June 23, 1812, 2–3; "Salem," *Connecticut Courant*, July 7, 1812, 3; "Freemen of All Parties," *Lancaster Journal*, June 12, 1812, 2.
46 The document was principally written by Rep. Josiah Quincy of Massachusetts, along with some input from Sen. James A. Bayard of Delaware. The letter was signed by thirty-four Federalists in the House of Representatives. Donald R. Hickey, ed., "What Are the United States to Gain by this War?," in *The War of 1812: Writings from America's Second War of Independence* (New York: Library of America, 2013), 46–53.
47 Hickey, "What Are the United States to Gain by this War?," 46–53.
48 Rufus King, diary entries, August 3–5, 1812, in King, *The Life and Correspondence of Rufus King*, 267–271; see also King to Christopher Gore, September 19, 1812, in the same, 276–280.
49 King, 267–271, 276–280.
50 Sullivan, *The Public Men of the Revolution*, 351; Morison, *The Life and Letters of Harrison Gray Otis*, 309–310.
51 King, *The Life and Correspondence of Rufus King*, 276–280.
52 Fischer, *The Revolution of American Conservatism*, 87–90; King, 276–281; Morison, *The Life and Letters of Harrison Gray Otis*, 306–312; Sullivan, *The Public Men of the Revolution*, 349–351.
53 Peter A. Jay to John Jay, September 17, 1812, *The Papers of John Jay*, Columbia University.
54 "Federal Nomination," *Boston Patriot*, September 23, 1812, 2.
55 "The New York Coalition," *National Intelligencer*, October 15, 1812, 3; "The New York Coalition," *National Intelligencer*, November 10, 1812, 2.
56 "To the Editor of the Evening Post," *New York Evening Post*, October 20, 1812, 2.
57 "The New York Coalition," *National Intelligencer*, October 24, 1812, 3. The pro-Clinton New York legislature appointed the Committee of Correspondence, which held a convention in New York City on October 19 asserting the nominee's Democratic-Republican credentials and attacking critics in the media.
58 May 3, 1812, entry, *The Diaries of Gouverneur Morris*, digital edition, Melanie Randolph Miller, ed. (Charlottesville: University of Virginia Press, Rotunda, 2015).
59 "To the Public," *New York Evening Post*, October 23, 1812, 2; "To the Editors of the Fed. Republican," *Federal Republican*, November 16, 1812, 2–3.
60 "The Convention of the Delegates . . . ," *Virginia Patriot*, October 6, 1812, 2; Fischer, *The Revolution of American Conservatism*, 79.
61 "Extract of a Letter from a Member of the Late Convention at Staunton, to His Friend in this City," *Virginia Patriot*, October 6, 1812, 3.
62 "The Convention of the Delegates . . . ," *Virginia Patriot*, October 6, 1812, 2.
63 Fischer, *The Revolution of American Conservatism*, 387–388.

64 "Extract of a Letter from a Member of the Late Convention at Staunton, to His Friend in this City," *Virginia Patriot*, October 6, 1812, 3.
65 John Steele to Joseph Pearson, August 31, 1812, John Steele and Henry McGilbert Wagstaff (ed.), *The Papers of John Steele*, vol. 2 (Raleigh, NC: Edwards & Broughton, 1924), 679–682; Fischer, *The Revolution of American Conservatism*, 390–391.
66 Steele to Pearson, August 31, 1812, *The Papers of John Steele*, 679–682; Risjord, *The Old Republicans*, 126–127, 148–149.
67 Hawkins's message to the North Carolina General Assembly on November 18, 1812, leaves no doubt about his belligerence toward Britain and commitment to a military solution. See Samuel A'Court Ashe, ed., *Biographical History of North Carolina from Colonial Times to the Present*, vol. 5 (Greensboro, NC: C. L. Van Noppen, 1906), 154–159.
68 Irving Brant, *James Madison: Commander in Chief, 1809–1812*, vol. 6 (Indianapolis: Bobbs-Merrill, 1961), 106; William Boylan to John Steele, September 5, 1812, *The Papers of John Steele*, 689, see note 1; Madison to Jefferson, October 14, 1812, *Founders Online*, National Archives, https://founders.archives.gov/documents/Madison/03-05-02-0301, see footnote 8.
69 Brant, *James Madison* (vol. 6), 105–106.
70 Lampi Collection of American Electoral Returns, 1788–1825, American Antiquarian Society, 2007, https://elections.lib.tufts.edu/catalog/8k71nh141; Fischer, *The Revolution of American Conservatism*, 332–353, 428.
71 "Extract of a Letter from Lancaster," *Carlisle Gazette*, September 11, 1812, 3. The author of the August 28 letter, first published in the *York Exposition*, is unidentified.
72 "Democrats Opening Their Eyes," *Lancaster Journal*, September 4, 1812, 3; "Presidential Nomination in Pennsylvania," *Poulson's American Daily Advertiser*, September 1, 1812, 2; Sanford W. Higginbotham, *The Keystone in the Democratic Arch: Pennsylvania Politics, 1800–1816* (Harrisburg: Pennsylvania Historical and Museum Commission, 1952), 259–260.
73 "Voice of Pennsylvanians," *Virginia Patriot*, September 18, 1812, 4.
74 Higginbotham, *The Keystone in the Democratic Arch*, 259–260; Victor A. Sapio, *Pennsylvania and the War of 1812* (Lexington: University of Kentucky Press, 1970), 172–174; "Voice of the People," *Lancaster Journal*, September 18, 1812, 3; "Voice of Pennsylvanians," *Lancaster Journal*, September 29, 1812, 3; "The Democratic Republicans," *Commonwealth*, September 29, 1812, 2.
75 Fischer, *The Revolution of American Conservatism*, 339–340; on the life of Jared Ingersoll Sr., see Lawrence Henry Gipson, *American Loyalist: Jared Ingersoll* (New Haven, CT: Yale University Press, 1971).
76 Hund and Scott, *The Debates in the Federal Convention of 1787*, September 17, 1787, https://avalon.law.yale.edu/18th_century/debates_917.asp.
77 "Senate Holds Editor in Contempt," United States Senate, https://www.senate.gov/about/origins-foundations/parties-leadership/duane-republican-editor-contempt.htm; Matthew Schafer, "That Time the Senate Issued an Arrest Warrant for a Reporter," Medium.com, June 27, 2021, https://medium.com/les

sons-from-history/that-time-the-senate-issued-an-arrest-warrant-for-a-reporter-a58faa4408d; see also William Duane to Jefferson, June 10, 1801, *Founders Online*, National Archives, https://founders.archives.gov/documents/Jefferson/01-34-02-0241; William Duane to Jefferson, March 24, 1800, *Founders Online*, National Archives, https://founders.archives.gov/documents/Jefferson/01-31-02-0396.

78 Kathryn Turner, "The Appointment of Chief Justice Marshall," *William and Mary Quarterly* 17, no. 2 (April 1960): 143–163.

79 *Chisholm v. Georgia*, 2 US 419 (1793) and *Hylton v. United States*, 3 US 171 (1796).

80 "Grand Caucus," *Public Advertiser*, September 19, 1812, 2.

81 "Mr. Ingersoll; York," *Lancaster Journal*, September 25, 1812, 7; Sapio, *Pennsylvania and the War of 1812*, 173–174.

5. THE CAMPAIGN FOR A WARTIME PRESIDENCY

1 For a comprehensive narrative of the war, see Hickey, *The War of 1812: A Forgotten Conflict*; Stagg, "James Madison: Life before the Presidency," 204–205.

2 "EVACUATION OF CANADA!! AND SURRENDER OF DETROIT!!!!," *Trenton Federalist*, September 14, 1812, 2; story was carried from the *Buffalo Gazette*, a newspaper also affiliated with the Federalist Party.

3 "Monday, September 7," *New York Evening Post*, September 7, 1812, 2.

4 "The War," *Federal Republican and Commercial Gazette*, September 9, 1812, 3.

5 "News from Detroit," *National Intelligencer*, September 8, 1812, 2.

6 "General Hull," *Boston Patriot*, September 12, 1812, 2.

7 "Gen. Hull's Army," *New Hampshire Patriot*, September 15, 1812, 3.

8 "Treason Stalks Abroad," *The Reporter*, September 5, 1812, 1.

9 Jonathan Dayton to Madison, September 17, 1812, *Founders Online*, National Archives, https://founders.archives.gov/documents/Madison/03-05-02-0239; Dayton sent the letter without a signature, but his identity was known to the president.

10 "Heroism," *National Intelligencer*, September 10, 1812, 3.

11 "INDIAN MURDERS," *Richmond Enquirer*, September 29, 1812, 1.

12 "SAVAGE ALLIES—CONFIRMED," *Independent Chronicle*, September 28, 1812, 2.

13 "From the United States Gazette," *New York Evening Post*, October 28, 1812, 2. This *United States Gazette* article was carried by the *Post*.

14 "Queries!," *Trenton Federalist*, November 2, 1812, 3.

15 "Count the Cost," *Connecticut Courant*, September 15, 1812, 3.

16 Rutland, *The Presidency of James Madison*, 120; Stagg, "James Madison: Life before the Presidency," 275–277, 289–290.

17 "A Pitiful Shift," *New York Evening Post*, June 29, 1812, 2; "War Taxes," *Lancaster Journal*, October 2, 1812, 3, carrying a story from the *Frederick-Town Herald*.

18 "Washington City," *National Intelligencer*, October 31, 1812, 2; Hickey, *The War of 1812: A Forgotten Conflict*, 83–84.

19 James Madison to the Delegations of Several Indian Nations, [ca. August 22,] 1812, *Founders Online*, National Archives, https://founders.archives.gov/documents/Madison/03-05-02-0137.

20 Annual Message to Congress, November 4, 1812, *Founders Online*, National Archives, https://founders.archives.gov/documents/Madison/03-05-02-0334.

21 Annual Message to Congress, November 4, 1812, *Founders Online*, National Archives, https://founders.archives.gov/documents/Madison/03-05-02-0334, see footnotes; Madison to Congress, November 12, 1812, *Founders Online*, National Archives, https://founders.archives.gov/documents/Madison/03-05-02-0354, see footnotes.

22 "Documents," *American and Commercial Daily Advertiser*, November 7, 1812, 5; Brant, *James Madison* (vol. 6), 111.

23 Madison, Annual Message, *Founders Online*, National Archives, https://founders.archives.gov/documents/Madison/03-05-02-0334.

24 "ANGLO SAVAGE HOSTILITY," *National Intelligencer*, August 6, 1812, 1; "Citizens of West Tennessee," *Carthage Gazette*, July 11, 1812, 2; "Our Frontier," *New Hampshire Patriot*, September 1, 1812, 3; "The Spirit of the People," *Savannah Republican*, September 17, 1812, 5. The *Savannah Republican* carried this story from the *Pittsburgh Mercury*.

25 Brant, *James Madison* (vol. 6), 105; "New York, October 7, 1812," *New York Evening Post*, October 21, 1812, 2.

26 Milo (pseudonym), *Letters Addressed to a Friend at Pittsburg on the Character and Conduct of DeWitt Clinton, Esq.* (New York: n.p., 1812).

27 "Who Shall Be Our Next President," *National Intelligencer*, October 17, 1812, 2; article is reprinted from the *Fredonian*. In Greek mythology, Proteus was a god of the sea who could change his appearance at will and foresee the future.

28 "Picture of Federalism!," *True American*, October 26, 1812, 2.

29 "Presidential Election," *New Hampshire Gazette*, October 13, 1812, 3.

30 "DeWitt Clinton," *Rhode Island Republican*, October 8, 1812, 3.

31 "To the Democratic Republicans of Pennsylvania," *National Intelligencer*, October 24, 1812, 2.

32 "To the People of New Hampshire," *New Hampshire Patriot*, October 13, 1812, 5.

33 "The Next President," *Concord Gazette*, September 22, 1812, 3; "Miscellany," *New England Palladium*, September 18, 1812, 1; "Grand Madisonian Warfare!," *Albany Register*, October 9, 1812, 2; "The Voice of Clinton!," *Trenton Federalist*, October 5, 1812, 1.

34 "People of Pennsylvania," *Lancaster Journal*, October 26, 1812, 3; "Hints to the Well Meaning," *Vermont Mirror*, October 14, 1812, 1; letter from Saratoga is reprinted in the *Mirror* from the *Baltimore Whig*; "Presidential Election," *The Star*, September 25, 1812, 4; letter from Americanus is reprinted in *The Star* from *The Yankee* in Boston; "For the Columbian," *Columbian*, October 10, 1812, 2–3.

35 "Communication," *Columbian*, September 17, 1812, 3; article is reprinted from the *Baltimore Whig* into the New York *Columbian*.

36 "No. VI," *Charleston Courier*, September 1, 1812, 1.

37 "Friday, September 11," *New York Evening Post*, September 11, 1812, 2.

38 "Hartford, September 29," *Connecticut Courant*, September 29, 1812, 3.

6. IN THE HANDS OF THE LEGISLATORS AND SOME VOTERS

1. "List of the Polls," *Columbian*, April 29, 1812, 3; on the influence of free booze in elections, see W. J. Rorabaugh, *The Alcoholic Republic: An American Tradition* (New York: Oxford University Press, 1979), 152–155.
2. Madison to Jefferson, October 14, 1812, *Founders Online*, National Archives, https://founders.archives.gov/documents/Madison/03-05-02-0301.
3. Higginbotham, *The Keystone in the Democratic Arch*, 253, 258–259, 265–266; Sapio, *Pennsylvania and the War of 1812*, 46–47, 131, 154–157, 176. For a full accounting of the 1812 Pennsylvania congressional elections, see Wilkes University Election Statistics Project, https://staffweb.wilkes.edu/harold.cox/rep/Congress%201812.pdf.
4. "The New York Coalition," *National Intelligencer*, October 27, 1812, 3; Duane's statement is reprinted from the *Aurora*; Higginbotham, 267.
5. "Presidential Election," *Lancaster Journal*, October 23, 1812, 2; Higginbotham, 267.
6. Various articles, *Whig Chronicle*, October 14, 1812, 1–3; "The War," *Whig Chronicle*, October 19, 1812, 2; Si Sheppard, *The Partisan Press: A History of Media Bias in the United States* (Jefferson, NC: McFarland, 2008), 69.
7. "A Burlesque," *Whig Chronicle*, October 23, 1812, 2.
8. "Presidential Election," *Public Advertiser*, October 31, 1812, 2; statement is reprinted from the *Aurora*.
9. Jefferson to Madison, June 29, 1812, *Founders Online*, National Archives, https://founders.archives.gov/documents/Madison/03-04-02-0555.
10. Jefferson to Madison, August 5, 1812, *Founders Online*, National Archives, https://founders.archives.gov/documents/Madison/03-05-02-0095; Augustus John Foster and Richard Beale Davis, eds., *Jeffersonian America: Notes on the United States of America* (San Marino, CA: Huntington Library, 1954), 101–102; Brant, *James Madison* (vol. 6), 104.
11. "Cecil County Election," *Lancaster Journal*, October 9, 1812, 3.
12. Sapio, *Pennsylvania and the War of 1812*, 192–193.
13. Lampi Collection of American Electoral Returns, 1788–1825, American Antiquarian Society, 2007, https://elections.lib.tufts.edu/catalog/8k71nh141, and https://elections.lib.tufts.edu/catalog/gq67js486.
14. "Wednesday, November 11, 1812," November 11, 1812, *Commonwealth*, 2; "The Presidential Election," November 10, 1812, *National Intelligencer*, 2; "What More Could Be Done?," November 11, 1812, *Whig Chronicle*, 2.
15. Fred J. Milligan, *Ohio's Founding Fathers* (Lincoln, NE: iUniverse, 2003), 185; Donald J. Ratcliffe, "The Experience of Revolution and the Beginnings of Party Politics in Ohio, 1776–1816," *Ohio History* 85 (Summer 1976): 207–210.
16. "Oration," *Scioto Gazette*, July 15, 1812, 1.
17. "Return Jonathan Meigs, Jr.," *The Supreme Court of Ohio & The Ohio Judicial System*, https://www.supremecourt.ohio.gov/SCO/formerjustices/bios/meigs.asp; Lampi Collection of American Electoral Returns, Ohio, US House, 1812, https://elections.lib.tufts.edu/; Richard P. McCormick, *The Second American*

Party System: Party Formation in the Jacksonian Era (New York: W. W. Norton, 1966), 260; Milligan, *Ohio's Founding Fathers*, 185.

18 "Electoral Election," *National Intelligencer*, November 14, 1812, 2; Lampi Collection of American Electoral Returns, https://elections.lib.tufts.edu/catalog/r207tq33w; full results survive from the counties of Licking and Trumbull. See Lampi's footnotes for more explanations of a few other counties, where some incomplete unofficial returns are revealed.

19 Lampi Collection of American Electoral Returns, https://elections.lib.tufts.edu/catalog/cf95jc369, https://elections.lib.tufts.edu/catalog/n583xw521, and https://elections.lib.tufts.edu/catalog/p5547s59r; Pliny Holton White, *Jonas Galusha, the Fifth Governor of Vermont: A Memoir Read before the Vermont Historical Society*, YA Pamphlet Collection (Montpelier, VT: E. P. Walton, printer, 1866), 10. Federalists did retain the treasurer position, as the long-tenured Benjamin Swan had no major opponent and held bipartisan support; see Lampi, https://elections.lib.tufts.edu/catalog/tt44pn102; "Election Results," *Green Mountain Farmer*, September 9, 1812, 3.

20 "Vermont Election," *Washingtonian*, September 7, 1812, 3; "Vermont Electors," *Vermont Mirror*, November 4, 1812, 3.

21 Lampi Collection of American Electoral Returns, https://elections.lib.tufts.edu/catalog/6m311p94g; "Republicans of Vermont," *Green Mountain Farmer*, December 2, 1812, 3. For extensive footnotes on the saga of the 1813 gubernatorial election in Vermont, see Lampi, https://elections.lib.tufts.edu/catalog/jq085m35s, and https://elections.lib.tufts.edu/catalog/mw22v689v.

22 Fischer, *The Revolution of American Conservatism*, 224.

23 "For the Courant," *Connecticut Courant*, September 29, 1812, 1.

24 National Governors Association, Washington, DC, https://www.nga.org/governor/roger-griswold/; "New Haven, Nov. 5," *Connecticut Journal*, November 5, 1812, 3; "For the Courant," *Connecticut Courant*, September 15, 1812, 1; Lampi Collection of American Electoral Returns, https://elections.lib.tufts.edu/catalog/qb98mg27v. Griswold died on October 25.

25 "Election," *New York Evening Post*, April 28, 1812, 2; Jabez D. Hammond, *The History of Political Parties in the State of New York*, vol. 1 (Cooperstown, NY: H & E Phinney, 1846), 320–321; Rufus King to William King, October 23, 1812, *The Life and Correspondence of Rufus King* (vol. 5), 288.

26 Lampi Collection of American Electoral Returns, see New York, electoral college, 1812, https://elections.lib.tufts.edu/; Hammond, 320–321.

27 "From Our Correspondent," *New York Evening Post*, November 12, 1812, 2; Lampi, https://elections.lib.tufts.edu/catalog/ht24wj97t; Martin Van Buren and John C. Fitzpatrick (ed.), *The Autobiography of Martin Van Buren* (Washington, DC: Government Printing Office, 1920), 40–41.

28 Van Buren, *The Autobiography*, 40–41; Lampi Collection of American Electoral Returns, https://elections.lib.tufts.edu/catalog/ht24wj97t; "Extract-Dated Albany, Nov. 9, 1812," *Public Advertiser*, November 13, 1812, 2.

29 Van Buren, *The Autobiography*, 37.

30 Cornog, *The Birth of Empire*, 131–132.

31 Lampi Collection of American Electoral Returns, https://elections.lib.tufts.edu/catalog/cz30pt443, and https://elections.lib.tufts.edu/catalog/zw12z6405.

32 "New Hampshire Rising!," *New England Palladium*, August 11, 1812, 1; *Speech of the Hon. George Sullivan, at the Late Rockingham Convention: With the Memorial and Resolutions, and Report of the Committee of Elections*, 2nd ed. (Exeter, NH: Constitutionalist Press, E. C. Beals, 1812); "War; Armies; Alas," *Portsmouth Oracle*, October 31, 1812, 5.

33 Lampi Collection of American Electoral Returns, https://elections.lib.tufts.edu/catalog/rj430513s, and https://elections.lib.tufts.edu/catalog/cv43nx37f.

34 "Presidential Election," *Constitutionalist*, November 10, 1812, 3; "Clinton's Election Sure," *Concord Gazette*, November 10, 1812, 2. In another article reporting the results on that same date, the *Gazette* asserted that Clinton was "more than probable" to carry Pennsylvania. "Presidential Election," *Concord Gazette*, November 10, 1812, 3.

35 Lampi Collection of American Electoral Returns, https://elections.lib.tufts.edu/catalog/rx913r35v. Some minor discrepancies exist between the popular vote count of individual men running for presidential elector, given that they often ran on at-large tickets. In the case of New Hampshire, the second-highest vote total for Clinton electors is counted. Lampi identifies one somewhat significant aberration in 1812: a New Hampshire elector named John Goddard, who was thought to be pledged to Madison but switched his allegiance to Clinton prior to the citizen balloting. Word of his defection did not reach all voters in time, and Goddard received several hundred more votes than he was likely intended to receive. See Lampi, note 9, https://elections.lib.tufts.edu/catalog/1831cm17t.

36 "For the Enquirer," *Richmond Enquirer*, September 11, 1812, 1.

37 "For the Repository" and "Patriotic Meeting," *Farmers' Repository*, October 16, 1812, 1.

38 "Friday, October 30," *Alexandria Gazette*, October 30, 1812, 3.

39 Lampi Collection of American Electoral Returns, https://elections.lib.tufts.edu/catalog/7w62f982h, and https://elections.lib.tufts.edu/catalog/5425kc16f.

40 See Lampi Collection of American Electoral Returns, https://elections.lib.tufts.edu/, and see Virginia, US House results, 1813; Risjord, *The Old Republicans*, 150–151; "The 36th Anniversary," *Richmond Enquirer*, July 28, 1812, 4.

41 Fischer, *The Revolution of American Conservatism*, 116; Rudolph J. Pasler and Margaret C. Pasler, *The New Jersey Federalists* (Rutherford, NJ: Fairleigh Dickinson University Press, 1975), 142–148.

42 "The Election," *Trenton Federalist*, October 5, 1812, 3; "New-Jersey Election," *Trenton Federalist*, October 26, 1812, 3; "New-Jersey Election!," *True American*, October 19, 1812, 3.

43 Pasler and Pasler, *The New Jersey Federalists*, 146; Lampi Collection of American Electoral Returns, https://elections.lib.tufts.edu/catalog/3t945r80k, and https://elections.lib.tufts.edu/, New Jersey, 1813 elections, US House of Representatives.

44 Lampi Collection of American Electoral Returns, https://elections.lib.tufts

.edu/catalog/np193b858, and https://elections.lib.tufts.edu/catalog/5425kc112; "Joint Meeting," *Trenton Federalist*, November 9, 1812, 3; "The Election," *True American*, November 16, 1812, 3.

45 "Citizens of New-Jersey!," *Centinel of Freedom*, November 10, 1812, 2; "The Legislature," *True American*, November 16, 1812, 2; "Joint-Meeting," *Trenton Federalist*, November 2, 1812, 3.

46 Pasler and Pasler, *The New Jersey Federalists*, 148–149.

47 Steven Levitsky and Daniel Ziblatt, *How Democracies Die* (New York: Penguin Random House, 2018), 109–112.

48 Willie Blount to Madison, November 23, 1811, *Founders Online*, National Archives, https://founders.archives.gov/documents/Madison/03-04-02-0035; Madison to Willie Blount, December 10, 1811, *Founders Online*, National Archives, https://founders.archives.gov/documents/Madison/03-04-02-0066.

49 Sampson Williams, campaign document, 1812, https://www.google.com/books/edition/To_the_Electors_of_the_Counties_of_Rhea/d3jSmgEACAAJ?hl=en; "Elections: Historical Notes," University of Tennessee: County Technical Assistance Service, 2022, 3, https://www.ctas.tennessee.edu/node/97050/printable/pdf; Lampi Collection of American Electoral Returns, https://elections.lib.tufts.edu/catalog/h128nf260; for more Tennessee results use the search engine at https://elections.lib.tufts.edu/.

50 "Georgia Legislature, November 9," *Alexandria Herald*, November 23, 1812, 3; "Glorious News from Savannah," *Investigator*, October 9, 1812, 3.

51 "Election Returns," *The Reporter*, August 15, 1812, 5; "Election Returns," *Frankfort Argus*, August 19, 1812, 3; see also the letter from Sidney, "Isaac Shelby," *The Reporter*, July 11, 1812, 3.

52 It was common in the era of state legislative selection of US senators for the legislature to send instructions on how to vote on key issues. Although these demands were nonbinding, a senator likely understood that displeasing legislators in the state capital could result in being sent home from Washington, DC, when his term ended. George T. Blakey, "Rendezvous with Republicanism: John Pope vs. Henry Clay in 1816," *Indiana Magazine of History* 62, no. 3 (September 1966): 246; Leland R. Johnson, "The Suspense Was Hell: The Senate Vote for War in 1812," *Indiana Magazine of History* 65, no. 4 (1969): 250–251, 264–265; "News of the Declaration of War," *The Reporter*, July 1, 1812, 5; "Senator Pope," *Trenton Federalist*, July 27, 1812, 3.

53 Lampi only finds full county-level returns from Fayette and Franklin counties. He cites a letter from a soldier who reported that Clinton's vote was negligible in two counties (Nicholas and Mason) and zero in another (Fleming); Lampi Collection of American Electoral Returns, https://elections.lib.tufts.edu/catalog/sn009z195; "To the People of Kentucky," *The Reporter*, October 31, 1812, 3; "Presidential Election," *The Reporter*, November 14, 1812, 3; "Presidential Election," *The Reporter*, November 25, 1812, 5.

54 "Taxes! Taxes! Up to the Eyes," *Federal Republican*, February 18, 1812, 2; "Poor Madison," *Federal Republican*, June 5, 1812, 2.

55 "Baltimore, Saturday, June 20," *Federal Republican*, June 20, 1812, 2.

56 Hickey, *The War of 1812*, 54.
57 "A Mobocracy," *Federal Republican*, July 27, 1812, 3.
58 Hickey, *The War of 1812*, 58–59; The *Baltimore Whig* was a hawkish Democratic-Republican paper with ties to the Smiths, and accordingly, a hostile attitude toward Madison. Ultimately, the *Whig* endorsed Clinton, and the *Baltimore Patriot* subsequently surfaced in the city on September 28, 1812, as a fully pro-administration publication. See J. Thomas Scharf, *The Chronicles of Baltimore: Being a Complete History of "Baltimore Town" and Baltimore City from the Earliest Period to the Present Time* (Baltimore: Turnbull Brothers, 1874), 89–90.
59 Hickey, 58–61; for a bio, see *Military Hall of Honor*, James McCubbin Lingan, https://militaryhallofhonor.com/honoree-record.php?id=2769.
60 "The Massacre at Baltimore," *Federal Republican*, August 3, 1812, 2; Hickey, 60–62; Bobbé, *DeWitt Clinton*, 191.
61 Madison to John Montgomery, August 13, 1812, *Founders Online*, National Archives, https://founders.archives.gov/documents/Madison/03-05-02-0119; on the Baltimore riot, see Josh S. Cutler, *Mobtown Massacre: Alexander Hanson and the Baltimore Newspaper War of 1812* (Charleston, SC: History Press, 2019).
62 Monroe to Madison, August 4, 1812, *Founders Online*, National Archives, https://founders.archives.gov/documents/Madison/03-05-02-0094.
63 "Mobs and Riots," *National Intelligencer*, August 13, 1812, 3; "whataboutism," *Merriam-Webster*, https://www.merriam-webster.com/dictionary/whataboutism.
64 "Toasts," *Boston Gazette*, July 13, 1812, 1; "Monday, August 17, 1812," *Trenton Federalist*, August 17, 1812, 3; "Martyr for the Liberty of the Press," *Poulson's American Daily Advertiser*, August 6, 1812, 3; "Alexandria, Sept. 5," *New-York Gazette*, September 8, 1812, 2.
65 Lampi Collection of American Electoral Returns, https://elections.lib.tufts.edu/catalog/pk02cb09k; Election Returns, Maryland State Archives, http://guide.msa.maryland.gov/pages/series.aspx?id=S106; Philip J. Lampi, "The Federalist Party Resurgence, 1808–1816: Evidence from the New Nation Votes Database" *Journal of the Early Republic* 33, no. 2 (Summer 2013): 265.
66 Lampi Collection of American Electoral Returns, https://elections.lib.tufts.edu/catalog/6682x4715 and https://elections.lib.tufts.edu/catalog/xg94hq10j; Linda H. Lamone, *A History of Maryland's Electoral College Meetings, 1789–2016* (Annapolis: Maryland State Board of Elections, 2016), 33–34.
67 Lampi Collection of American Electoral Returns, https://elections.lib.tufts.edu/, see Maryland Electoral College results, 1812.
68 "An Account Current," *Richmond Enquirer*, November 20, 1812, 3.
69 Fischer, *The Revolution of American Conservatism*, 53, 63, 75, 106–107; Carol E. Hoffecker, *Democracy in Delaware* (Wilmington, DE: Cedar Tree Books, 2004), 70; Lampi Collection of American Electoral Returns, https://elections.lib.tufts.edu/catalog/k069880rr.
70 "Delaware Election," *Poulson's American Daily Advertiser*, October 10, 1812, 3; John Thomas Scharf, *History of Delaware: 1609–1888*, vol. 1 (Philadelphia: L. J. Richards, 1888), 403; Lampi Collection of American Electoral Returns, https://elections.lib.tufts.edu/catalog/9880vs00r, and https://elections.lib.tufts.edu

/catalog/v692t686f; "Delaware Election," *American Watchman and Delaware Republican*, October 17, 1812, 3; see Lampi's database for full Delaware legislative election returns from 1812; "Pennsylvania," *New Hampshire Patriot*, November 10, 1812, 3.
71 John Adams to William Stephens Smith, October 15, 1812, *Founders Online*, National Archives, https://founders.archives.gov/documents/Adams/99-03-02-2202.
72 "After the Election," *Repertory*, October 20, 1812, 2.
73 Lampi Collection of American Electoral Returns, https://elections.lib.tufts.edu/catalog/0c483j55p; Lampi, "The Federalist Party Resurgence, 262; "Representatives Elected," *Columbian Centinel*, May 9, 1812, 2.
74 *Resolves of the General Court of the Commonwealth of Massachusetts* (Boston: Russell & Cutler, 1813), 94–96; "Massachusetts Erect," *Repertory*, October 23, 1812, 2.
75 Massachusetts electors were apportioned as follows: Eastern District One (3), Eastern District Two (3), Eastern District Three (1), Middle District (5), Southern District (4), and Western District (6), Lampi Collection of American Electoral Returns, https://elections.lib.tufts.edu/, see Massachusetts Electoral College results, 1812.
76 Brant, *James Madison* (vol. 6), 103.
77 Lampi Collection of American Electoral Returns, https://elections.lib.tufts.edu/catalog/b2773x122.
78 "Rhode Island Election," *Newport Mercury*, April 18, 1812, 2; "A Proclamation," *Newport Mercury*, July 18, 1812, 3; Hickey, 262–272; Lampi Collection of American Electoral Returns, https://elections.lib.tufts.edu/catalog/qz20sv07x, and https://elections.lib.tufts.edu/catalog/wh246s9on.
79 Lampi Collection of American Electoral Returns, https://elections.lib.tufts.edu/catalog/zw12z6694.
80 "Laws of North Carolina," *The Star*, January 24, 1812, 4.
81 "State of North Carolina, Lincoln County," *The Star*, February 28, 1812, 3; "State of North Carolina, Johnston County," *The Star*, April 3, 1812, 3; "State of North Carolina," *The Star*, April 17, 1812, 3.
82 James H. Broussard, *The Southern Federalists, 1800–1816* (Baton Rouge: Louisiana State University Press, 1978), 150–151; Arthur M. Schlesinger Jr. and Fred L. Israel (eds.), *History of American Presidential Elections, 1789–1844*, vol. 1 (New York: Chelsea House, 1971), 271 (article by Norman K. Risjord, "Election of 1812"); New Bern, in Craven County, used to be referred to as "Newbern."
83 "Legislature of N. Carolina," *Carolina Federal Republican*, November 28, 1812, 2; Broussard, 151; Steele and Wagstaff, *The Papers of John Steele*, vol. 2, 680, note 3.
84 Brant, *James Madison* (vol. 6), 111–112; "The Electoral Election," *National Intelligencer*, November 19, 1812, 2; "The Electoral Election," *National Intelligencer*, November 24, 1812, 3.
85 "Saturday, May 8, 1813," *Carolina Federal Republican*, May 8, 1813, 3; Lampi

Collection of American Electoral Returns, https://elections.lib.tufts.edu/, see North Carolina US House results, 1813.

86 Archie Vernon Huff Jr., *Langdon Cheves of South Carolina* (Columbia: University of South Carolina Press, 1977), 53, 56, 63–64; Risjord, *The Old Republicans*, 121, 124–125.

87 South Carolina Legislature to Madison, August 29, 1812, *Founders Online*, National Archives, https://founders.archives.gov/documents/Madison/03-05-02-0168.

88 Madison to the South Carolina Legislature, October 10, 1812, *Founders Online*, National Archives, https://founders.archives.gov/documents/Madison/03-05-02-0288.

89 Lampi Collection of American Electoral Returns, https://elections.lib.tufts.edu/, see South Carolina US House results, 1812; "Republicans!," *Investigator*, October 12, 1812, 3; "Charleston, May 23," *Eastern Argus*, June 18, 1812, 1; article reprinted from the *Charleston Courier*.

90 "Charleston," *Investigator*, December 5, 1812, 3; Broussard, *The Southern Federalists*, 152–153; Lampi Collection of American Electoral Returns, https://elections.lib.tufts.edu/catalog/mc87pq92p.

91 "An Account Current," *Richmond Enquirer*, November 20, 1812, 3; "Bad News," *Columbian Centinel*, November 28, 1812, 2; "Presidential Election," *Vermont Mirror*, December 2, 1812, 3; "Electoral Returns," *The Yankee*, November 27, 1812, 1; "Boston, November 20," *Albany Gazette*, November 26, 1812, 3.

92 "State of Louisiana," *National Intelligencer*, December 29, 1812, 1; "New Orleans, Dec. 1, 1812," *Investigator*, January 6, 1813, 3; W.C.C. Claiborne to Albert Gallatin, December 29, 1812, in Dunbar Rowland, ed., *Official Letter Books of W.C.C. Claiborne, 1801–1816*, vol. 6 (Jackson: Mississippi Department of Archives and History), 1917, 205–206.

93 "Presidential Election," *National Intelligencer*, December 3, 1812, 3; "Chillicothe, Dec. 2," *Columbian*, December 18, 1812, 3; Dave Leip, *Atlas of U.S. Presidential Elections*, https://uselectionatlas.org/USPRESIDENT/GENERAL/pe1812.html.

94 See Appendix D. Calculations performed by the author from the database in Lampi Collection of American Electoral Returns, https://elections.lib.tufts.edu/. The popular votes are counted from the highest tally of each candidate's elector slate. The one exception to this methodology is from the Clinton total from New Hampshire. As noted in note 35, the last-minute flip of Madison elector John Goddard distorted the returns, given that many voters were unaware that he was now a Clinton man. His tally was 20,286, while all other Clinton electors polled between 18,739 and 18,858. For this popular vote analysis, the second-highest Clinton elector tally (18,858) was used from New Hampshire. See also Walter Dean Burnham, *Voting in American Elections: The Shaping of the American Political Universe since 1788* (Bethesda, MD: Academica Press, 2010), 60; Michael J. Dubin, *United States Presidential Elections, 1788–1860: The Official Results by County and State* (Jefferson, NC: McFarland, 2002), 19–22.

95 Gerry to Madison, December 12, 1812, *Founders Online*, National Archives,

https://founders.archives.gov/documents/Madison/03-05-02-0408; "Pennsylvania Election," *Public Advertiser*, November 19, 1812, 2; "Accurate Votes for President and V. President," *Columbian Centinel*, December 26, 1812, 2.
96 "From Harrisburgh," *Commonwealth*, December 9, 1812, 2; "Constitutional Question," *Statesman*, December 17, 1812, 2; "Accurate Votes for President and V. President," *Columbian Centinel*, December 26, 1812, 2.
97 *Annals of Congress*, 12th Cong., 2nd Sess., 1020–1021.
98 "Party Divisions of the House of Representatives, 1789 to Present," United States House of Representatives, https://history.house.gov/Institution/Party-Divisions/Party-Divisions/, and "Party Division," United States Senate, https://www.senate.gov/history/partydiv.htm.

7. MADISON AND CLINTON: THE WAR OF 1812 AND THE BALLOT BOX

1 Ketcham, *James Madison*, 556–557; "From the National Intelligencer," *American and Commercial Daily Advertiser*, March 8, 1813, 2.
2 James Madison, Inaugural Address, *The American Presidency Project*, https://www.presidency.ucsb.edu/documents/inaugural-address-22.
3 James Madison, Inaugural Address.
4 Hickey, *The War of 1812*, 104–106; Ketcham, *James Madison*, 573–575, 582–583.
5 Brant, *James Madison* (vol. 5), 132; Hickey, 141–145. In an effort to improve his legacy, Wilkinson published *Memoirs of My Own Times* in 1816 (Philadelphia: Abraham Small).
6 Hickey, 285–298.
7 Hickey, 299–300.
8 "Peace!!!," *Rhode Island Republican*, February 22, 1815, 3; article is reprinted from the *National Intelligencer*; "Celebration of Returning Peace," *Connecticut Courant*, February 21, 1815, 3; "Friday, February 17, 1815," *Albany Register*, 2; reprint of an editorial by Charles Holt from the *Columbian*.
9 Hickey, *The War of 1812*, 220–223. Scattered fighting, mostly at sea and in the West, continued as word of the peace agreement had not yet arrived. The books on Jackson's political ascendance, as well as the era that bears his name, are voluminous. Among others, see Meacham, *American Lion*; Arthur M. Schlesinger Jr., *The Age of Jackson* (Boston: Little, Brown, 1945); and Charles Sellers, *The Market Revolution: Jacksonian America, 1815–1846* (New York: Oxford University Press, 1991).
10 Madison, Seventh Annual Message, *The American Presidency Project*, https://www.presidency.ucsb.edu/node/204622; Ketcham, *James Madison*, 602–603, 606.
11 Madison, Veto Message, *The American Presidency Project*, https://www.presidency.ucsb.edu/node/205266; Ketcham, 606.
12 Stagg, "James Madison: Life before the Presidency," 365; *Biographical Directory of the United States Congress*, Washington, DC, https://bioguide.congress.gov/search/bio/S000609, https://bioguide.congress.gov/search/bio/G000183, https://bioguide.congress.gov/search/bio/L000229; Madison to Jefferson,

February 13, 1814, *Founders Online*, National Archives, https://founders.archives.gov/documents/Madison/03-07-02-0254.
13 Lampi Collection of American Electoral Returns, https://elections.lib.tufts.edu/catalog/n583xv14d; *Biographical Directory of the United States Congress*, https://bioguide.congress.gov/search/bio/R000047; Risjord, *The Old Republicans*, 262–263, 277–278.
14 Morgan, "The Origin and Development of the Congressional Nominating Caucus," 193–195; the first New Yorker to win the presidency would be Martin Van Buren in 1836.
15 For a narrative of the 1824 election, see Donald Ratcliffe, *The One-Party Presidential Contest: Adams, Jackson, and 1824's Five-Horse Race* (Lawrence: University Press of Kansas, 2015).
16 Wills, *James Madison*, 161.
17 Ketcham, *James Madison*, 646–658.
18 Ketcham, 659; Keyssar, *The Right to Vote*, appendix, table A.2.
19 Richard Brookhiser, *James Madison* (New York: Basic Books, 2011), 234–235.
20 For Calhoun's views on the matter of nullification, see the *South Carolina Exposition and Protest*, December 1828. The documents were written anonymously. See also Ross M. Lence, ed., *Union and Liberty: The Political Philosophy of John C. Calhoun* (Indianapolis: Liberty Fund, 1992).
21 Madison to Edward Everett, August 28, 1830, *Founders Online*, National Archives, https://founders.archives.gov/documents/Madison/99-02-02-2138. The Virginia Resolution was a 1798 document written in opposition to the federal Alien and Sedition Acts. See Virginia Resolutions, December 21, 1798, *Founders Online*, National Archives, https://founders.archives.gov/documents/Madison/01-17-02-0128.
22 Morgan Robinson, "The American Colonization Society," White House Historical Association, 2020, https://www.whitehousehistory.org/the-american-colonization-society; Jim Humphrey and Rich Wallace, "Randolph Slaves," Shelby County, Ohio, Historical Society, 1997, https://www.shelbycountyhistory.org/schs/archives/blackhistoryarchives/randolphbhisA.htm.
23 Catherine Allgor, *Dolley Madison: The Problem of National Unity* (Boulder, CO: Westview Press, 2013), 145–148.
24 Gerry to Madison, December 19, 1812, *Founders Online*, National Archives, https://founders.archives.gov/documents/Madison/03-05-02-0423; Billias, *Elbridge Gerry*, 324, 327–329.
25 Michael J. Dubin, *United States Congressional Elections, 1788–1997: The Official Results* (Jefferson, NC: McFarland, 1998), 53–56.
26 Theodore Dwight, *History of the Hartford Convention: With a Review of the Policy of the United States Government Which Led to the War of 1812* (New York: N. & J. White, 1833), 352–379.
27 "The Internal Enemy," *Boston Patriot*, March 25, 1815, 2.
28 "Toasts," *Centinel of Freedom*, July 18, 1815, 3.
29 Lampi Collection of American Electoral Returns, https://elections.lib.tufts.edu/catalog/mw22v7026. For nearly one year, there was an interruption in King's

Senate service because the legislature struggled to fill the seat after his term expired in early 1819. In January 1820 a diverse legislative coalition chose King for another term. See Lampi, https://elections.lib.tufts.edu/catalog/m9o0nw0ow, and https://elections.lib.tufts.edu/catalog/js956h02f; *Biographical Directory of the United States Congress*, Washington, DC, https://bioguide.congress.gov/search/bio/K000212.

30 In his description, historian Paul F. Boller Jr. calls the 1816 race "dull as dishwater" in his volume of presidential elections. See Boller, *Presidential Campaigns: From George Washington to George W. Bush* (Oxford: Oxford University Press, 2004), 29–30.

31 William Howard Adams, *Gouverneur Morris: An Independent Life* (New Haven, CT: Yale University Press, 2003), 292–293.

32 Cornog, *The Birth of Empire*, 102; Bobbé, *DeWitt Clinton*, 190–191.

33 Bobbé, 189–190.

34 Bobbé, 201; Cornog, *The Birth of Empire*, 34–38, 103.

35 Bobbé, 216–217; "Communication," *Albany Argus*, March 28, 1817, 3; Lampi Collection of American Electoral Returns, https://elections.lib.tufts.edu/catalog/rx913p98q.

36 Bobbé, 209–210, 214; Cornog, *The Birth of Empire*, 117.

37 Bobbé, 224–227.

38 Bobbé, 231–240; Cornog, *The Birth of Empire*, 142–144; Lampi Collection of American Electoral Returns, https://elections.lib.tufts.edu/catalog/d791sg234, and https://elections.lib.tufts.edu/catalog/3b591978g.

39 Bobbé, 231–242; Cornog, 142–144.

40 Lampi Collection of American Electoral Returns, https://elections.lib.tufts.edu/catalog/wp988m05s; Cornog, 144–149.

41 Cornog, 148–151.

42 Cornog, 150–153; Lampi Collection of American Electoral Returns, https://elections.lib.tufts.edu/catalog/r207tp382, and https://elections.lib.tufts.edu/catalog/zw12z5905.

43 Cornog, 154–156.

44 Cornog, 155–157; Willis F. Dunbar and George S. May, *Michigan: A History of the Wolverine State*, 3rd ed. (Grand Rapids, MI: Eerdmans, 1995), 159–160; Sam Roberts, "200 Years Ago, Erie Canal Got Its Start as Just a 'Ditch,'" *New York Times*, June 26, 2017, https://www.nytimes.com/2017/06/26/nyregion/history-of-the-erie-canal.html.

45 Cornog, 173–179.

46 Cornog, 173–179.

47 Cornog, 179–180.

48 Bobbé, *DeWitt Clinton*, 291–297; Martin Van Buren address on the death of DeWitt Clinton, February 19, 1828, *Papers of Martin Van Buren*, Cumberland University, Lebanon, TN, https://vanburenpapers.org/document-mvb00667.

49 Burnham, *Voting in American Elections*, 57–60. See also Burnham's introductory essay, in which he walks readers through the challenges of estimating

50 Josiah H. Benton, *Voting in the Field: A Forgotten Chapter of the Civil War* (Norwood, MA: Plimpton Press, 1915), 189–190, 269–270.

51 Boller, *Presidential Campaigns*, 115–122; Roy P. Basler, ed., "Abraham Lincoln, Memorandum Concerning His Probable Failure of Re-election," August 23, 1864, in *Collected Works of Abraham Lincoln*, vol. 7 (Springfield, IL: Abraham Lincoln Association, 1953), 514, and "Lincoln, Response to a Serenade," November 10, 1864, vol. 8 of the same, 101–102.

52 Maryland, which produced a split verdict between the candidates, is irrelevant to this analysis given that the state neither gained nor lost electoral votes from the 1810 census.

53 Julia Azari, "Weak Parties and Strong Partisanship Are a Bad Combination," *Vox*, November 3, 2016, https://www.vox.com/mischiefs-of-faction/2016/11/3/13512362/weak-parties-strong-partisanship-bad-combination; on partisanship during the American Civil War, see Nathan P. Kalmoe, *With Ballots and Bullets: Partisanship and Violence in the American Civil War* (Cambridge: Cambridge University Press, 2020).

(continued: voter turnout in the nineteenth century, 15–51; Michael P. McDonald, *United States Elections Project*, http://www.electproject.org/national-1789-present.)

BIBLIOGRAPHIC ESSAY

This book was made possible by a diverse collection of primary and secondary sources, including databases, newspaper archives, memoirs, and biographies, as well as academic articles and books. Writing a book on an American presidential election opens up avenues of additional research concerning people, institutions, and episodes in the political universe. In contrast to the past, the internet now makes many of these rich resources easily available for scholars and students.

Presidential campaigns have evolved over 230 years. Today they are longer and more professionalized civic affairs. The selection process has undergone several rounds of changes, both at the general election level and at the party nomination phase. For a collection of colorful short narratives on every presidential campaign from 1789 to 2000, see Paul F. Boller Jr., *Presidential Campaigns: From George Washington to George W. Bush* (Oxford: Oxford University Press, 2004). Also see Richard P. McCormick, *The Presidential Game: The Origins of American Presidential Politics* (New York: Oxford University Press, 1982), as well as James W. Ceaser, *Presidential Selection: Theory and Development* (Princeton, NJ: Princeton University Press, 1979).

Assuming office after Thomas Jefferson, James Madison fits into a rare category of heir-apparent presidents, analogous to Martin Van Buren, Harry Truman, and George H. W. Bush. Arguably there are a few other chief executives who fall under this label. As I discuss at various points in my previous book, presidents in the heir-apparent role face unique challenges in their efforts to win a second term, although these challenges are not insurmountable. On the leadership dilemma of these particular presidents, see Donald A. Zinman, *The Heir Apparent Presidency* (Lawrence: University Press of Kansas, 2016).

Biographies of Madison are numerous and have attracted renewed attention in recent years. Irving Brant produced a meticulous multi-volume biography of Madison, *James Madison* (Indianapolis: Bobbs-Merrill, 1941–1961), although a reasonable assessment can be made that sometimes the author could have been more critical of his subject. Brant also covers the 1812 election more than most Madison biographers. Ralph Ketcham's comprehensive biography, *James Madison* (Charlottesville: University of Virginia Press, 1971), remains a highly respected narrative of the fourth president. More recently, there is Richard Brookhiser, *James Madison* (New York: Basic Books, 2011), and Lynne Cheney, *James Madison: A Life Reconsidered* (New York: Viking Press, 2014). For readers who want a briefer account of Madison's life, see Garry Wills, *James Madison* (New York: Times Books, 2002).

For an account of Madison's presidency, see Robert Rutland's *The Presidency of James Madison* (Lawrence: University Press of Kansas, 1990). The book is part of UPK's long-running series on the tenure of American presidents. Brant's fifth (1956) and sixth (1961) volumes also cover the presidential years. All of Madison's public proclamations and messages as president can be found in Gerhard Peters and John T. Woolley, eds., *The American Presidency Project*, https://www.presidency.ucsb.edu/ (Santa Barbara: University of California). On the famous 1789 congressional election between Madison and James Monroe, see Chris DeRose, *Founding Rivals: Madison vs. Monroe, The Bill of Rights, and The Election that Saved a Nation* (Washington, DC: Regnery, 2011). For a full sample of Madison's early constitutional philosophy, see his essays in *The Federalist Papers*, particularly nos. 10, 39, 43, 45, 46, 48, 51, and 55. To find this historic defense of the Constitution online see full text of *The Federalist Papers*, https://guides.loc.gov/federalist-papers/full-text (Washington, DC: Library of Congress). For a full collection of a lifetime of Madison's correspondence, public proclamations, and speeches, see *Founders Online*, https://founders.archives.gov/ (Washington, DC: National Archives). This online repository also includes similar documents for other leading figures of the American Founding and the early republic.

As a young anti-federalist, DeWitt Clinton wrote essays as "Countryman" that articulated his opposition to the new Constitution in a slightly amusing prose. See *New-York Journal*, December 6 and December 13, 1787, and January 10, 1788. Clinton's late-blooming political career is also the subject of biographical accounts, although his presidential campaign tends to be treated as an insignificant chapter in his life. Dorothie Bobbé completed an early biography of Clinton: *DeWitt Clinton* (New York: Minton, Balch, 1933). Evan Cornog's *The Birth of Empire: DeWitt Clinton and the American Experience, 1769–1828* (Oxford: Oxford University Press, 1998) covers his political and governmental life very thoroughly, but with more emphasis on New York. Steven Siry has also written about Clinton's role within the Democratic-Republican Party, most notably as a leading advocate of commerce, manufacturing, and developing American infrastructure. See Siry, *DeWitt Clinton and the American Political Economy: Sectionalism, Politics, and Republican Ideology, 1787–1828* (New York: Peter Lang, 1990).

The supporting actors in this book deserve their dues as well. The vice presidency was not a highly prestigious office in 1812, but both nominees had distinguished careers. On Elbridge Gerry, see George Billias, *Elbridge Gerry, Founding Father and Republican Statesman* (New York: McGraw-Hill, 1976). Jared Ingersoll Jr.'s papers are spread throughout the Library of Congress, the American Philosophical Society Library, the Historical Society of Pennsylvania, the New York State Library, Pennsylvania State University, and Princeton University. Future presidents, such as Martin Van Buren, sometimes played an important role in the 1812 campaign. Van Buren's autobiography was published long after the eighth president had died: see Martin Van Buren and John C. Fitzpatrick (ed.), *The Autobiography of Martin Van Buren* (Washington, DC: Government Printing Office, 1920).

A detailed record of Rufus King's correspondence was very valuable in the process of preparing this manuscript, including the national Federalist meeting in New York City in September 1812. See Charles R. King, ed., *The Life and Correspondence of Rufus King (vol. 5), 1807–1816* (New York: G. P. Putnam's Sons, Knickerbocker Press, 1898). William Sullivan was also in attendance at the Federalist conclave, and his notes provide helpful details. See Sullivan, *Familiar Letters on Public Characters, and Public Events: From the Peace of 1783, to the Peace of 1815*, 2nd ed. (Boston: Russell,

Odiorne & Metcalfe, 1834). A subsequent edition was published in 1847 entitled *The Public Men of the Revolution: Including Events from the Peace of 1783 to the Peace of 1815* (Philadelphia: Carey & Hart, 1847). Samuel Eliot Morison documented the correspondence and political life of Harrison Gray Otis in *The Life and Letters of Harrison Gray Otis, Federalist, 1765–1848 (vol. 1)* (Boston: Houghton Mifflin, 1913). On the life and impact of Gouverneur Morris, see William Howard Adams, *Gouverneur Morris: An Independent Life* (New Haven, CT: Yale University Press, 2003). His observations about politics can be seen in Melanie Randolph Miller, ed., *The Diaries of Gouverneur Morris*, digital ed. (Charlottesville: University of Virginia Press, Rotunda, 2015). Some comments from the New York meeting can also be found in *The Papers of John Jay* (Columbia University) in correspondence from Peter Jay to his father.

On the Democratic-Republican side, Albert Gallatin's story is told in Henry Adams, *The Life of Albert Gallatin* (New York: J. B. Lippincott, 1943). Harry Ammon produced a classic biography of Madison's presidential successor in *James Monroe: The Quest for National Identity* (Charlottesville: University of Virginia Press, 1971). A shorter account of his life can be found in Gary Hart, *James Monroe* (New York: Times Books, 2005). For primary source documents, see Papers of James Monroe, http://monroepapers.com/ (Fredericksburg, VA: University of Mary Washington). On Henry Clay, see David S. Heidler and Jeanne T. Heidler, *Henry Clay: The Essential American* (New York: Random House, 2010), and Harlow Giles Unger, *Henry Clay: America's Greatest Statesman* (Boston: Da Capo Press, 2015).

For those who prefer an emphasis on Thomas Jefferson's tenure as president, readers may consult another volume from the UPK series mentioned previously: see Forrest McDonald, *The Presidency of Thomas Jefferson* (Lawrence: University Press of Kansas, 1976). For Jefferson's post-presidency correspondence with Madison, the *Founders Online* archive was used. On the heavy-handed tactics of the Jefferson administration to enforce the Embargo Act, see Leonard W. Levy, *Jefferson and Civil Liberties: The Darker Side* (New York: Quadrangle, 1963). Jefferson was a leading actor in the first two competitive presidential elections in America. On his 1796 race with John Adams, see Jeffrey L. Pasley, *The First Presidential Contest: 1796 and the Founding of American Democracy* (Lawrence: University Press of Kansas, 2013). On his rematch with the incumbent President Adams, see James Roger Sharp, *The Deadlocked Election of 1800: Jefferson, Burr, and the Union in the Balance* (Lawrence: University Press of Kansas, 2010). Both books are part of the UPK series on presidential elections, which now includes this volume. The 1800 contest has spawned numerous other narratives, given the special status of that race and its consequences for democracy. See Bernard A. Weisberger, *America Afire: Jefferson, Adams, and the Revolutionary Election of 1800* (New York: Harper Collins, 2000). Also see John Ferling, *Adams vs. Jefferson: The Tumultuous Election of 1800* (Oxford: Oxford University Press, 2004).

The 1812 presidential election was an opportunity for Federalists to revitalize their organization at a national level, although this challenge is covered in varying degrees by other scholarly accounts of the party. David Hackett Fischer's *The Revolution of American Conservatism: The Federalist Party in the Era of Jeffersonian Democracy* (Chicago: University of Chicago Press, 1965) centers on the party's messaging, organizing, and tactics after being displaced from power in the 1800 election. Among Federalists, generational differences existed in attitudes about party organizing, as the older men in their ranks held to more traditional and antipopulist views about parties' relationships with the American people. Younger Federalists, in contrast, were more ready to accept the reality and necessity of grassroots party organizing in a political environment that was becoming more populist by the day. Fischer's book is rich with examples, charts, anecdotes, and an entire section dedicated to biographical information about Federalist elites.

Among the additional useful books about more specific aspects of the Federalist Party is James H. Broussard, *The Southern Federalists, 1800–1816* (Baton Rouge: Louisiana State University Press, 1978); this book is especially illuminating given that much other literature emphasizes the Northern roots of the party. In one of those states, Federalists maximized their advantages in 1812, even though they proved to be temporary. See Rudolph J. Pasler and Margaret C. Pasler, *The New Jersey Federalists* (Rutherford, NJ: Fairleigh Dickinson University Press, 1975). Philip J. Lampi covers the temporary comeback of the Federalist Party in "The Federalist Party Resurgence, 1808–1816: Evidence from the New Nation Votes Database," *Journal of the Early Republic* 33, no. 2 (Summer 2013): 255–281.

Lampi's article comes from his large database of elections covering the early American republic. Users can examine results in races ranging from the presidential contest all the way down to local offices. Where possible, electoral data breaks down into the county, city, and town levels. Results from major cities like Philadelphia and Baltimore are sometimes broken down into individual wards. The database is free of charge and available for any user to browse at Lampi Collection of American Electoral Returns, 1788–1825, https://elections.lib.tufts.edu/ (American Antiquarian Society and Tufts Archival Research Center, 2007). Lampi's footnotes are especially illustrative, providing readers with additional avenues for research.

Beyond politics, for a sweeping historical account of the early republic, see Gordon S. Wood, *Empire of Liberty: A History of the Early Republic, 1789–1815* (Oxford: Oxford University Press, 2009). Voter suffrage varied from state to state and was openly discriminatory against Americans of color, women, and poorer citizens. See Alexander Keyssar, *The Right to Vote: The Contested History of Democracy in the United States* (New York: Basic Books, 2000). On the unique situation concerning women's voting rights in New Jersey, see Judith Apter Klinghoffer and Lois Elkis, "'The Petticoat Electors': Women's Suffrage in New Jersey, 1776–1807," *Journal of the Early Republic* 12, no. 2 (Summer 1992):159–193.

Noble E. Cunningham Jr. has contributed significantly to our knowledge of the Democratic-Republican Party. See Cunningham, *The Jeffersonian Republicans: The Formation of Party Organization, 1789–1801* (Chapel Hill: University of North Carolina Press, 1957), and *The Jeffersonian Republicans in Power: Party Operations, 1801–1809* (Chapel Hill: University of North Carolina Press, 1963). Cunningham also edited *The Making of the American Party System, 1789 to 1809* (Englewood Cliffs, NJ: Prentice Hall, 1965). Norman K. Risjord gives vital attention to Democratic-Republicans from the Randolph wing, as well as other internal party critics who espoused principles of limited government and states' rights. See Risjord, *The Old Republi-*

cans: Southern Conservatism in the Age of Jefferson (New York: Columbia University Press, 1965).

As the governing party for a generation, Democratic-Republicans adjusted and transformed the Federalist model envisioned by Alexander Hamilton. See Leonard D. White, *The Jeffersonians: A Study in Administrative History, 1801–1829* (New York: Free Press, 1951). The institutional development of the Bank of the United States, including under Democratic-Republican administrations, is covered in Eric Lomazoff, *Reconstructing the National Bank: Politics and Law in the Early American Republic* (Chicago: University of Chicago Press, 2018). The Bank's expiration in 1811 was part of a broader failure to prepare the nation for war with Britain, thereby teaching many Democratic-Republicans a painful lesson.

The story of the War of 1812 has been thoroughly told by historians. For this book, the account by Donald R. Hickey was most useful. See Hickey, *The War of 1812: A Forgotten Conflict* (Urbana: University of Illinois Press, 2012). Also see Reginald Horsman, *The Causes of the War of 1812* (Philadelphia: University of Pennsylvania Press, 1962). For a more sweeping account that goes well beyond the war and into the politics of the early republic, see J. C. A Stagg, *Mr. Madison's War: Politics, Diplomacy, and Warfare in the Early American Republic, 1783–1830* (Princeton, NJ: Princeton University Press, 1983). For a breakdown of the congressional roll call votes in Congress, see Leland R. Johnson, "The Suspense Was Hell: The Senate Vote for War in 1812," *Indiana Magazine of History* 65, no. 4 (1969): 247–267. On the House side of the vote, see Reginald Horsman, "Who Were the War Hawks?," *Indiana Magazine of History* 60, no. 2 (June 1964), 121–136.

As the brass ring of the campaign, Pennsylvania received significant attention in this book. On the politics of the state in the early republic, see Sanford W. Higginbotham, *The Keystone in the Democratic Arch: Pennsylvania Politics, 1800–1816* (Harrisburg: Pennsylvania Historical and Museum Commission, 1952). Also see Victor A. Sapio, *Pennsylvania and the War of 1812* (Lexington: University of Kentucky Press, 1970), for a closer look at the period under scrutiny in this book. On the Pennsylvania fiasco involving the British sloop the *Active*, see Mary E. Cunningham, "The Case of the *Active*," *Pennsylvania History: A Journal of Mid-Atlantic Studies* 13, no. 4 (1946): 229–247.

The pro-war and anti-British rioting that plagued Baltimore was recently documented in Josh S. Cutler, *Mobtown Massacre: Alexander Hanson and the Baltimore Newspaper War of 1812* (Charleston, SC: History Press, 2019). Primary accounts of the state's political violence were drawn from newspapers, including Baltimore's *Federal Republican and Commercial Gazette*, the *Baltimore Whig*, and the *Baltimore Patriot*, and the *National Intelligencer*. Other newspapers around the country also commented on the city's riots, as reactions usually depended on each publication's specific partisan orientation.

Newspapers reflected the country's partisan divisions and often revealed the internal tensions within the large Democratic-Republican tent, as well as the clumsy fusion between Federalists and Clintonians. *America's Historical Newspapers* provides a rich archive of newspapers going back to the seventeenth century. Some publications in the repository have long since faded into obscurity, while others contributed significantly to the development of journalism in the United States. The online collection can be found at http://tinyurl.com/ycxz3zm8 (Readex/Newsbank, Naples, FL).

Among the newspapers used extensively in this book was the *National Intelligencer*, a pro-Madison organ based in Washington, DC, and arguably the closest resemblance to a national publication in the early nineteenth century. Many other mainline Democratic-Republican papers were used in the research as well, including the *Richmond Enquirer*, based in the Virginia state capital, and the *True American* out of Trenton, New Jersey. From Newark there was the *Centinel of Freedom*, and from South Carolina, the *Investigator*. In North Carolina *The Star* propounded the party message from Raleigh. In Massachusetts the *Boston Patriot* defended the Madison administration, despite being hopelessly outnumbered within the state's political environment. The *New Hampshire Patriot* promoted the administration in one of 1812's most fiercely competitive battleground states. Pennsylvania's pro-Madison organs included John Binns's *Democratic Press* in Philadelphia and the *Commonwealth* in Pittsburgh. William Duane's *Aurora* was based out of Philadelphia, although the paper was a late and lukewarm supporter of Madison's reelection. In Clinton's New York, Madison had papers speaking on his behalf, including the *Public Advertiser* in the city. In heavily Federalist Delaware, Wilmington's *American Watchman and Delaware Republican* spread the Democratic-Republican message. In the sometimes violently contested state of Maryland, pro-Madison presses included the *American and Commercial Daily Advertiser* out of Baltimore and the *Baltimore Patriot*, which emerged as an ally of the Madison administration late in the campaign. In Vermont, the *Green Mountain Farmer* in Bennington advocated for the president; in Kentucky the Lexington *Reporter* strongly promoted his reelection. Newspapers for some states were more easily obtainable than for others. In the period covering the 1812 election, the states of Georgia, Louisiana, Ohio, and Tennessee were less represented in the repository.

Clintonian Democratic-Republican organs were centered in New York. Charles Holt published the *Columbian* in New York City, and Solomon Southwick published the *Albany Register* in the state capital. The *Whig Chronicle* in Philadelphia was quickly thrown together to promote Clinton in Pennsylvania but disappeared soon after his defeat. Newspapers that opposed Madison were not always easy to categorize as pro-Federalist or pro-Clinton. In Boston, there was the *Yankee* and the *Boston Pilot* to speak for Democratic-Republicans that were against Madison, although the *Yankee* had still been supportive of the president and the war as recently as August 1812. The *Baltimore Whig* had ties to the Smith political family in Maryland. The paper supported Clinton, although it was very much in favor of the war.

Federalist publications were numerous throughout the country, even in some states where their party was decisively in the minority. The *New York Evening Post* was founded by Alexander Hamilton and remains to this day a major organ of American conservatism. New Jersey had the *Trenton Federalist*, while Virginia had the *Alexandria Gazette*. Most notable in Baltimore was Alexander Contee Hanson's *Federal Republican and Commercial Gazette*, which was the target of pro-war rioters. The *Lancaster Journal* was an important voice for Pennsylvania Federalists, as was

Poulson's American Daily Advertiser in Philadelphia. Although its influence was declining, the *United States' Gazette* (formerly the *Gazette of the United States*) was also a Federalist newspaper in Philadelphia.

In New England, Federalists maintained some influential publications. The *Connecticut Courant* is now known as the *Hartford Courant* and is today the oldest active newspaper in America. Rhode Island had the *Newport Mercury* among others, while New Hampshire had the *Portsmouth Oracle*, Exeter's *Constitutionalist*, and the *Concord Gazette*. In Vermont, Federalists were represented by the *Brattleboro Reporter*, the *Vermont Mirror* in Middlebury, and the *Washingtonian* in Windsor. In Massachusetts the party was well-represented in the presses: in Boston there was the *New England Palladium*, the *Repertory*, the *Columbian Centinel*, and the *Boston Gazette*.

In the West and the South, Federalist newspapers included the *Supporter* in Chillicothe, Ohio, and the Charleston *Courier* and the *Carolina Federal Republican*, based in New Bern, North Carolina. Federalist presses, just like their Democratic-Republican counterparts, were in the habit of sharing their news content and opinion pieces with their respective allies across the country. News moved slowly, especially in the frontier pockets of America, but political momentum was still a real phenomenon that could be discerned by looking at the headlines across the country. Similar to today's media, journalists in 1812 were prone to prognostications that sometimes proved to be inaccurate, as well as using hyperbole and stating falsehoods.

Access to many of these primary documents and very old secondary sources was made possible by the Internet Archive; see https://archive.org/, as well as the HathiTrust Digital Library; see https://www.hathitrust.org/. Scholarly journal articles were obtained through JSTOR, an online repository of academic publications. See https://www.jstor.org/.

INDEX

Abbot, David, 175
absentee voting, 198–199
Active (prison ship), 81–82
Adams, John
  defeat of, 26
  on Democratic-Republican caucus, 213n72
  Democratic-Republican Party and, 18
  freedom of speech and, 16
  Madison, viewpoint of, 167
  nomination of, 92
  as peacemaker, 22
  People's Party and, 196
  political party, viewpoint of, 18
Adams, John Quincy, 25, 181, 185, 195
  Embargo Act, viewpoint of, 213n72
  resignation of, 213n72
African Americans, 162, 198
Albany Regency, 195, 196
Albany Register (newspaper), 57, 58, 83, 98, 132–133, 182
alcohol, at elections, 9, 140
Alexandria Gazette (newspaper), 155
Alien and Sedition Acts, 16–17
Amelia Island, 72, 221n60
amendments, ratification of, 14–15
American Academy of the Arts, 60
American and Commercial Daily Advertiser (newspaper), 127–128
American Colonization Society, 188
American System of robust internal improvements, 185
Ames, Fisher, 90
Anderson, Joseph, 55
Anglo-American party, 20
Anglo-American war proclamation, 73
anti-Indian propaganda, 128–129
apportionment, 186–187, 199
arbitration, with Britain, 24

Armstrong, John, Jr., 180
Articles of Confederation, 10, 11, 12
Association of Democratic Young Men, 144–145
Aurora (newspaper), 5, 49, 55, 75, 82, 117, 143

Baker, Anthony St. John, 182
Baltimore Patriot (newspaper), 235n58
Baltimore Whig (newspaper), 75, 133, 163, 235n58
Bank of America, 83, 97
Bank of the United States, 32, 44–45
Baptists, 21, 46
Barry, William T., 44
Battle of Monguagon, 123
Battle of Tippecanoe, 67–68, 78
Bayard, James A., 66, 95, 181, 220n54, 227n46
Bee (newspaper), 57–58
Benson, Egbert, 224n13
Berlin Decree, 33–34
Bill of Rights, 14
Blackledge, William, 115, 172
Blount, Willie, 159, 160
Bonaparte, Napoleon, 33–34, 42–43, 145, 167–168, 181
Boston Gazette (newspaper), 70, 85
Boston Patriot (newspaper), 67, 110, 121, 190
Boston Pilot (newspaper), 169
Boudinot, Elias, 104
Boyd, Adam, 157
Bradley, Stephen R., 2
Brant, Irving, 80
bribery, 9, 83, 85
Britain
  arbitration with, 24
  border disputes with, 24

Britain, *continued*
   Canada, control of, 66–67
   concessions with, 24, 77
   impressment issues regarding, 24
   negotiations of, 181
   pre-war episodes of, 66–74
   secret agent of, 69–70
   trade with, 34, 126
   treaty with, 24
   war, viewpoint of, 182
British Royal Navy, 24
Brock, Isaac, 120
Brownsville, Michigan, 121–122
Bucktails, 193, 194, 195
Burnham, Walter Dean, 198
Burr, Aaron, 15, 27–28, 61–62, 63

Cabinet, 47–48, 50, 180
Calhoun, John C., 56, 172, 185, 187
Canada, 122, 123
Canard River, 123
Carthage Gazette (newspaper), 128
Castlereagh, Lord, 127
Catholics, 21
caucus, 2, 3, 4, 26, 84. *See also specific states*
Centinel of Freedom (newspaper), 158
Charleston Courier (newspaper), 73, 134, 174
Cheves, Langdon, 56, 172, 173
Chisholm, Alexander, 118
Chisholm v. Georgia, 118
citizenship, Alien and Sedition Acts and, 16–17
Claiborne, William C. C., 175
Clay, Henry, 56, 75–76, 80, 181, 185, 188, 196
Clay, Matthew, 54, 156
Clinton, Alexander, 59
Clinton, Bill, 58
Clinton, DeWitt
   campaigning by, 6, 202
   candidacy challenges of, 129–134
   Clintonians and, 57–66
   on Council of Appointment, 61

   criticism of, 96, 131, 132, 143, 144–145, 201
   death of, 197
   dueling by, 62
   education of, 59
   election results for, 150–151, 154
   endorsements for, 142–144
   Erie Canal project of, 65–66, 193, 195–196
   as faction leader, 50
   following War of 1812, 192–197
   Gouverneur Morris and, 110–111
   as mayor, 63, 64–65
   military service of, 60
   nomination of, 97–98, 112
   personal challenges of, 194
   photo of, 136
   political service of, 61, 62, 63–65
   political standing of, 96
   potential of, 132
   proposal regarding, 3–4
   renomination of, 82–83
   reputation of, 130
   scandal of, 197
   as slaveholder, 60
   support for, 96–102, 132–133, 134, 141–142, 150, 151–152
   Twelfth Amendment, support of, 28
   vice presidential running mate of, 114–119
   writings of, 59
Clinton, George
   caucus results of, 4
   Clintonian faction and, 50
   death of, 50, 58, 65, 98
   Electoral College results of, 206
   electoral votes for, 6
   as governor, 31, 61
   influence of, 4, 30–31
   military service of, 31, 59
   Monroe alliance proposal and, 3
   National Bank, viewpoint of, 45, 50
   paper releasing, viewpoint of, 220n54
   photo of, 137

political careers of, 31
political party faction of, 30–31
support for, 2
total votes for, 208
as vice president, 4, 31, 63, 83
Clinton, George, Jr., 63
Clinton, George W., 60
Clinton, Hillary, 58
Clinton, James, 59
Clintonians
  anti-war stance of, 65
  candidacy challenges of, 129–134
  challenges regarding, 39, 89
  Columbian (newspaper) and, 51
  in Congress, 84
  decline of, 63–64
  DeWitt Clinton and, 57–66
  Federalist alliance with, 95, 104–106, 109–110, 129–134, 179–180
  Florida Territory acquisition and, 73
  following War of 1812, 192–197
  leadership of, 50
  Madison, viewpoint of, 100–101
  manifesto of, 100–101
  in New York, 150
  offensive of 1812 and, 96–102
  overview of, 57–66
  platforms of, 31, 58, 99, 100, 112–113
  support for, 98–99
  trade, viewpoint of, 112–113
  war vote of, 79
Columbian (newspaper), 51, 57, 98, 133, 182
Columbian Centinel (newspaper), 168, 174
Columbian Phenix (newspaper), 5
Commercial Gazette (newspaper), 121, 161–164
Committee of Correspondence, 227n57
Committee of Safety, Orange County, 8
Commonwealth (newspaper), 147
Concord Gazette (newspaper), 70, 132, 154
Congregationalist Church, 149, 223n97
Congress, 6–7, 14–15, 56, 75, 76, 124, 177. *See also* House of Representatives; Senate

Connecticut, 94, 141, 149, 190, 191, 205, 206, 207
Connecticut Courant (newspaper), 5, 90–91, 124, 134, 149, 182
Constitution, 9, 10–12, 13, 15–16, 76
constitutional hardball, 159
Constitutionalist (newspaper), 154
Constitutional Republicans, 30
corn, 145–146
Council of Appointment, 61, 64, 193, 194
Council of Revision, 10, 11, 194
Council of State, 9
Countryman letters (Clinton), 59–60
Crawford, William H., 53, 56, 73, 185, 195, 197
Cumberland Road, 214n96
customs duties, 124

Dambargo, 7, 39–43
Davie, William R., 113
Dayton, Jonathan, 62, 122
Delaware, 94, 103, 141, 166–167, 191, 205, 206, 207
Democratic-Republican Party
  anti-Indian sentiments of, 122
  caucus of, 26
  challenges of, 1–2, 25
  Clintonians, viewpoint of, 101–102
  in Congress, 183
  Congressional gains of, 29
  decentralization of, 30
  as disparate coalition, 24–25
  domination of, 26
  election of 1810 and, 74–75
  election result response of, 146–147
  election results of, 147
  Embargo Act, viewpoint of, 34–35, 39–40
  factions of, 30, 39, 50, 52–57, 61
  Federalist Party and, 19–20, 90–91
  governorships domination of, 6
  Hamiltonian economic system and, 32
  hostility in, 38

INDEX 253

Democratic-Republican Party, *continued*
  in House of Representatives, 74–75,
    143, 147, 149, 153, 177
  influence of, 31–32
  Jefferson's role in, 22
  justification for, 19
  nationalism and, 179–186
  nominating instrument of, 1–2,
    87–88
  nomination by, 81
  origin of, 18
  in Pennsylvania, 144
  platforms of, 18–19, 20
  political dominance of, 1
  religion and, 21
  in state legislature, 85
  strengthening of, 184
  support for, 20–21
  support for Madison from, 5–6
  War of 1812 and, 179–186
  war vote of, 79
  See also specific states
Desha, Joseph, 45, 217n28
Detroit, Michigan, 120, 121, 128
DeWitt, Mary, 59
Dolley Payne Todd, 15, 188–189
Duane, William, 5, 49, 55, 82, 117, 139,
    143, 180
dueling, 28, 62
Dunham, Josiah, 94–95

East Florida. *See* Florida Territory
economics, Hamilton's plan regarding,
    18, 22–23, 32, 44
election of 1812
  assessment of, 198–203
  campaigning for, 142–175
  disorganization of, 140–141
  electoral calendar of, 199–200
  finalizing outcome of, 175–177
  polarization during, 19
  state support breakdown of, 141–142
  voter turnout for, 198
  See also specific states
Electoral College, 27, 28, 62, 206

embargo, 36, 39–43, 74, 145, 156–157.
    See also trade
Embargo Act, 1, 2, 34–35, 39–40
Episcopalians, 21, 46
Eppes, John W., 156, 185
Erie Canal Commission, 65–66, 195
Erie Canal project, 65–66, 193,
    195–196
Erskine, David, 41
Essex Junto, 93
establishment clause, religion and, 46
Eustis, William, 48, 68, 124–125, 180
Everett, Edward, 187–188
executive branch, 11, 29, 35–36, 76, 202

Farmers' Repository (newspaper), 155
Federalist Papers, The, 12, 14, 23, 52, 188,
    224n3
Federalist Party
  accusations against, 110
  campaign of, 93
  candidacy challenges of, 129–134
  caucus of, 26, 92–93
  characteristics of, 90
  Clintonians alliance with, 95, 104–
    106, 109–110, 129–134, 179–180
  comeback of, 39
  as compared to Invisibles, 54
  Congregationalist Church and, 149
  in Congress, 6–7, 177, 189–190
  Congressional influence of, 29
  criticism of Madison from, 5
  crossovers of, 152
  decline of, 20, 61
  Democratic-Republican Party
    divisions with, 19–20, 90–91
    differences of attitudes in, 91–92
  elites, meeting of, 4–5
  Embargo Act, viewpoint of, 34–35
  endorsement of, 143–144
  Essex Junto and, 93
  factions of, 29
  Florida Territory acquisition and, 73
  following War of 1812, 189–192
  Grand Caucus of, 89

growth of, 29
Hamilton as leader of, 21–22
hierarchical party arrangement in, 92
High Federalists, 21–22
in House of Representatives, 6, 149, 153, 177
immigration and, 20
Jacobins and, 90–91
justification for, 19, 90
manifesto of, 113
newspapers of, 92
nomination process of, 93, 96, 102–114
opposition against Madison by, 22
party committee of, 93–94
party conventions of, 200
peace conventions of, 106–107
presidential campaign of 1808 and, 1
public declarations of, 106
public meetings of, 92
purpose of, 89–90
rebranding of, 179–180
religion and, 21
resolutions of, 107
secret meeting of, 89
in the Senate, 190
soul-searching by, 91
support for, 20
trade, viewpoint of, 146
War of 1812 and, 69–70
war position of, 106, 107
war vote of, 79
weakening of, 25
See also specific states
Federal Republican (newspaper), 70, 111, 121, 161–164
Fenner, James, 170
Fernandina, Florida, 72
First Amendment, 46
Fischer, David Hackett, 91, 92
Fish, Nicholas, 64
Florida Patriots, 72
Florida Territory, 30, 70–73, 159–160
flour, 145–146, 155

Floyd, Catherine "Kitty," 15
Floyd, William, 15
foreign policy, trade and, 33
Fort Dearborn, 122
Fort Harrison, 125
Fort Mackinac, 122
Fort Wayne, 125
Foster, Augustus, 80, 145
France, 22, 23, 32, 33–34, 42–43, 85, 90
Franklin, Maria, 60
Franklin, Walter, 60
Fredonian (newspaper), 131
freedom of speech, 16
fusion ticket, 114–119, 129–134, 200–201

Gallatin, Albert
  attacks on, 125
  Aurora (newspaper) and, 55
  on Cabinet, 47
  on Elbridge Gerry, 86
  on embargo, 36
  Jeffersonians and, 53
  on National Bank, 44–45
  photo of, 139
  policy work of, 41–42
  resignation of, 49, 181
  war financing plan of, 124
Galusha, Jonas, 148
Gananoque, Canada, 123
Garnett, James, 80
George III (king), 26
Georgia, 29–30, 94, 141, 160, 205, 206, 207
German, Obadiah, 55, 65
Gerry, Elbridge
  bill of rights, support of, 14
  death of, 189
  defeat of, 168
  election results of, 84, 175
  following vice presidency, 189
  gerrymandering and, 13
  influence of, 11
  John Henry and, 69
  overview of, 84–86

INDEX 255

Gerry, Elbridge, *continued*
  photo of, 136
  vice president nomination considerations of, 84–86, 116
  work of, 223n97
gerrymandering, 13, 85, 168
Giles, William Branch, 55, 184
Gilman, Nicholas, 65
Goddard, John, 233n35, 237n94
Gore, Christopher, 95
governorships, Democratic-Republican Party domination of, 6
Grand Caucus, 89
Granger, Gideon, 97, 184, 225n20
Gray, Edwin, 3, 54, 156
Green Mountain Farmer (newspaper), 148
Gregg, Andrew, 55
Griswold, Roger, 149, 170
Grundy, Felix, 56, 159, 160
Gulf of Mexico, 182

Hamilton, Alexander
  Burr and, 28
  death of, 28, 62
  economic program of, 18, 22–23, 32, 44
  Federalist Party and, 21–22
  influence of, 11–12, 27
  New York Evening Post (newspaper) and, 98
  political party, viewpoint of, 17–18
  as secretary of the treasury, 18
  See also *Federalist Papers, The*
Hamilton, Paul, 48, 67, 124–125
Hanson, Alexander Contee, 161–163
Hare, Charles Willing, 93
Harper, Robert Goodloe, 94, 108, 111
Harrison, Samuel, 79
Harrison, William Henry, 68, 125
Hartford Convention, 191, 192
Haslet, Joseph, 166–167
Hawkins, William, 115, 171–172
Heald, Nathan, 122
Henry, John, 69–70, 74

Henry, Patrick, 13
Henry-mandering, 14
High Federalists, 21–22. *See also* Federalist Party
HMS *Caledonia*, 123
HMS *Detroit*, 123
HMS *Frolic*, 123
HMS *Guerrire*, 123
HMS *Leopard*, 34
HMS *Little Belt*, 67
HMS *Macedonian*, 123
Holt, Charles, 57–58, 182
House of Representatives
  Democratic-Republican Party seats in, 74–75, 143, 147, 149, 153, 177
  districting of, 13, 15, 211n38
  Federalist Party seats in, 6, 149, 153, 177
  presidential election resolution by, 27
  Rules Committee in, 76
  war vote of, 79
Hubbard, Rubbles, 97–98
Huffy, Jacob, 157
Hull, William, 120, 121, 122, 128, 138
Hylton v. United States, 118

immigration, 20
impressment, 24, 181
Independent Chronicle (newspaper), 122
Indian-bashing, 124–129
Indian delegations, 125–126
Ingersoll, Charles Jared, 143
Ingersoll, Jared, Jr., 11, 116–118, 143, 175, 191–192
Investigator (newspaper), 173
Invisibles, 39, 48, 54–55, 73, 84, 184, 220–221n54

Jackson, Andrew, 151, 152, 182, 183, 185–186, 195, 196, 217n37
Jackson, Richard, 170
Jacksonian party, 200
Jacobins, 90–91
Jay, John, 12, 24, 61, 91, 102, 105

256 INDEX

Jay, Peter Augustus, 109–110, 150
Jay Treaty, 23–24
Jefferson, Thomas
   accusations against, 26
   Constitution of 1787, viewpoint of, 9
   Democratic-Republican Party and, 22
   Electoral College results of, 27
   embargo, viewpoint of, 145
   French Revolution, viewpoint of, 23
   Louisiana Purchase and, 71
   Madison's alliance with, 9, 22
   platform of, 32
   reelection of, 29
   resignation of, 23
   support for, 61
   support for Madison from, 5
   trade challenges of, 33
Jeffersonian faction, 26–33, 52–57, 147
Jews, political party support of, 21
Johnson, Edward, 162, 163
Johnson, Richard, 56
Jones, Catherine, 194, 197
Jones, John, 194
Jones, Samuel, 59
Jones, William, 170
JPMorgan Chase & Co., 62
judicial branch, 11, 223n97

Kentucky, 87, 94, 141, 160–161, 175, 199, 205, 206, 208
Key, Francis Scott, 181
King, Rufus
   central government, viewpoint of, 107–108
   Clintonians and, 105
   defeat of, 191
   election results of, 176
   influence of, 11
   on Madison, 150
   nomination of, 4–5
   photo of, 138
   in the senate, 191
   support for, 93, 103, 154–155
   total votes for, 208

King, William, 129, 150
Kitchen Cabinet, 47, 217n37

Lambert, John, 65, 157
Lancaster Journal (newspaper), 133, 146
Langdon, John, 84
Lansing, Abraham, 96
Lee, Henry, III, 162, 163
Lee, Robert E., 162
Lefever, Joseph, 115–16, 142–143
legislative branch, 11, 186–187.
   See also Congress; House of Representatives; Senate
Leib, Michael, 55, 84, 142, 184, 225n20
Lewis, Morgan, 30, 63
Lincoln, Abraham, 199
Lingan, James, 163, 165
Literary and Philosophical Society, 60
Little v. Barreme, 102
Lloyd, James, 95
Louisiana, 141, 174–175, 199, 205, 206, 207
Louisiana Purchase, 30, 71
Louisiana Territory, 32
Lowndes, Joseph, 172
Lowndes, William, 56

Macon, Nathaniel, 42, 54, 114–115
Macon's Bill #1, 42
Macon's Bill #2, 42
Madison, James
   Annual Message of, 126, 127, 173, 183
   Articles of Confederation and, 10, 11, 12
   background of, 7–8
   balloting win of, 3
   Bill of Rights, support of, 14
   Cabinet of, 47–48, 50, 180
   campaign of, 141, 142–175
   caucus results of, 4, 6
   as chief administrator, 54
   Congressional run of, 13–14
   as Congressman, 14–15
   Constitution, viewpoint of, 9, 10–11, 76

INDEX   257

Madison, James, *continued*
  criticism of, 4, 5, 43, 44, 45, 49, 51,
    54, 73, 121, 123, 124, 132–134, 150,
    155, 161–162
  death of, 188
  description of, 7, 8
  dispatches of, 5
  education of, 8
  election results for, 14, 115, 146, 147,
    148–149, 150–151, 154, 156, 161
    (*see also specific states*)
  Electoral College results of, 206
  electoral votes for, 6
  embargo policy, viewpoint of, 36
  faction challenges of, 52–57
  as Father of the Constitution, 11
  Federalist Party opposition to, 22
  following presidency, 186, 188
  as Founding Father, 1
  government background of, 8–9
  illness of, 8–9
  inauguration speech of, 37–38,
    178–179
  Indians, viewpoint of, 126
  influence of, 1, 186–187
  Jefferson's alliance with, 9, 22
  message to Congress by, 56
  military service of, 8–9
  mob, viewpoint of, 164
  Non-Importation Act, viewpoint of,
    33
  photo of, 135
  political defeats of, 9
  political party, viewpoint of, 17–18,
    19
  politics of the early republic and,
    7–26
  presidency, viewpoint of, 10
  presidential campaign of, 125
  presidential role of, 38
  as reluctant warrior, 80
  renomination of, 79–88
  romantic relationships of, 15
  in Second Continental Congress, 9
  as slave owner, 15–16
  support for, 2, 5–6, 38–39, 41, 84–85,
    96, 121, 132, 133, 141, 143, 146
  total votes for, 208
  at University of Virginia, 186
  vetoes of, 9–10, 46–47
  in Virginia House of Delegates, 9–10
  on Virginia's ratifying convention, 12
  war declaration by, 77–79
  as wartime president, 125–126
  See also *Federalist Papers, The*
Madison, James, Sr., 7
Madison, Nelly, 7
Maine, 168–169
Manhattan Company, 61–62, 63
Marshall, John, 32–33, 102–103,
  113–114
Marshall, Humphrey, 91
Martling Men, 96
Maryland
  agriculture in, 146
  as battleground state, 142
  campaign and election in, 161–166
  congressional contests in, 165
  Democratic-Republican Party in, 161,
    162
  election results in, 161, 165–166
  Electoral College results in, 206
  elector selection dates and methods
    in, 205
  Federalist Party committee in, 94
  Madison nomination in, 87
  property qualifications in, 200
  statewide tally in, 208
  violence in, 162–164
  voter turnout in, 198
Mason, George, 10
Massachusetts
  campaign and election in, 167–168,
    169
  election results in, 168
  Electoral College results in, 206
  elector selection dates and methods
    in, 205
  Essex Junto of, 93
  Federalist/Clintonian fusion in, 169

Federalist Party in, 158, 191
Madison nomination in, 87
modalities in, 168
state legislature in, 85
statewide tally in, 208
support for Clinton in, 141–142
Mathews, George, 71–72
McDonald, Michael, 198
McHenry, James, 22
McKean, Thomas, 30
McKee, John, 71
media, as tool, 203. *See also specific newspapers*
Meigs, Return J., Jr., 147, 184
Methodists, 21
Miami militia, 125
Michigan, 196
Milan Decree, 34
military court of inquiry, 180
Miller, James, 123
Milnor, James, 143
Milo, writings of, 131
Mitchell, David, 73
Mitchill, Samuel, 55
Monroe, James
　balloting for, 3
　campaign of, in Virginia, 4
　caucus results of, 4, 6
　Clinton alliance proposal with, 3
　Congressional run of, 13–14
　election results for, 14, 156
　mob, viewpoint of, 164
　Old Republicans and, 53–54
　political party, viewpoint of, 25
　as secretary of state, 49, 185
　support for, 2, 49, 53
　treaty ratification and, 182
　in War Department, 180
Monroe-Pinkney treaty, 5
Montgomery, John, 164
Montpelier, 188–189
Morgan, William, 197
Morison, Samuel, 94
Morris, Gouverneur, 11, 66, 105, 110–111, 192

Napoleonic Wars, 24, 33–34, 181
National Bank, 44–45, 50, 53
national defense, 19, 22, 35, 183–184
National Intelligencer (newspaper)
　anti-Indian propaganda of, 128
　on approbation, 98
　on the British, 69, 76–77, 122
　on Clinton, 110
　election result, response to, 147, 148
　on Hull, 121
　Madison's writings in, 36
　as national newspaper, 53
　opposition to Madison in, 3
　on Rodgers, 67
　violence, response to, 164
　war resolution, response to, 182
nationalism, 179–186
Native Americans, 66–68, 128–129
negative partisanship, 19
Newbold, Thomas, 157
New England Congregationalists, 21
New Hampshire, 12, 87, 142, 153–154, 198, 205, 206, 208, 233n35
New Hampshire Gazette (newspaper), 132
New Hampshire Patriot (newspaper), 121, 128, 167
New Jersey
　campaign and election in, 156–159
　Democratic-Republicans in, 158
　election results in, 158, 159
　Electoral College results in, 206
　elector selection dates and methods in, 205
　embargo, viewpoint of, 156–157
　Federalist Party in, 94, 95, 157–158, 159
　Federalist Party nomination, participation in, 103
　Madison nomination in, 87
　peace convention in, 106, 107
　roll call vote in, 207
　state legislative elections in, 157
　support for Clinton in, 142
　voting qualifications in, 211n41

INDEX 259

New Jersey, *continued*
   War of 1812, viewpoint of, 156–157
   Washington Benevolent Societies in, 157
New Orleans, Louisiana, 182, 190
New York
   bribery scandal in, 83
   campaign and election in, 149–153
   caucus in, 97
   Constitutional opponents in, 12
   constitution of, 194–195
   Council of Revision in, 10
   criticism of, 155
   Democratic-Republicans in, 150, 151, 153
   election results in, 175, 193
   Electoral College results in, 206
   elector selection dates and methods in, 205
   Federalist Party in, 94, 150–151, 153
   growth of, 199
   nomination by, 82–83, 99–100
   as political battleground state, 61
   redistricting in, 152–153
   roll call vote in, 207
   support for Clinton in, 142
New York, New York
   DeWitt Clinton as mayor of, 63
   election in, 140
New York Committee of Correspondence, 129–130
New York Evening Post (newspaper), 98, 110, 121, 134, 150
New York Historical Society, 60
New York Post (newspaper), 225n28
New York Quids, 30
Nicholson, Joseph, 86
nominations, 1–2, 25–26. *See also specific persons; specific states*
Nompère de Champagny, Jean-Baptiste de, 42–43
Non-Importation Act, 30, 33
Non-Intercourse Act, 40–41
North Carolina
   campaign and election in, 170–172
   Democratic-Republican Party in, 170, 171, 172
   district elector law in, 170–171
   election results in, 115, 175
   Electoral College results in, 206
   elector selection dates and methods in, 205
   Federalist/Clintonian fusion in, 172
   Federalist Party committee in, 94
   Federalist Party in, 170, 171
   Federalist Party nomination, participation in, 103
   legislative elections in, 171
   pre-war conflict in, 67
   roll call vote in, 207
   running mate conversations in, 114–115
Northern Whig (newspaper), 41
Northwest Territory, 122
nullification, 187–188

Ogden, Aaron, 106, 158
Ogden, David B., 106
Ohio, 87, 94, 141, 147–148, 175, 199, 205, 206, 208
Old Republicans
   accusations by, 80
   attacks from, 29–30
   challenges regarding, 39
   criticism of Madison by, 54
   decline of, 156
   influence of, 185
   overview of, 53
   platforms of, 30, 54
   in the Senate, 84
   support from, 2
   War of 1812 and, 54
   war vote of, 79
Olmsted, Gideon, 81
Orders in Council, 34, 42, 43, 77, 127
Otis, Harrison Gray, 93, 109, 111, 190

partisanship, 203
Passamaquoddy Islands, 181
Peace Party, 105

Pelopidas, writings of, 155
Peninsular War, 145
Pennsylvania
   Active (prison ship) and, 81–82
   agriculture in, 146
   as battleground state, 142
   campaign and election in, 142–146
   civil war rumors regarding, 81–82
   conflict in, 81–82
   Democratic-Republicans in, 144, 146–147
   election results in, 146, 176–177
   Electoral College results in, 206
   elector selection dates and methods in, 205
   embargo effects on, 145
   Federalist Party in, 94, 108–109, 143–144, 146
   renomination in, 81
   running mate conversations in, 115–116
   statewide tally in, 208
   voter turnout in, 198
Pennsylvania Quids, 30
People's Party, 195, 196
Perceval, Spencer, 77
Philadelphia Convention, 14
Philadelphia Federalists, 143–144
Pickering, Timothy, 22, 131
Pinckney, Charles Cotesworth, 4–5, 6, 21–22, 92–93, 102, 146, 154, 168
Pinkney, William, 40, 48
Plumer, William, 101–102, 153
political parties
   competition of, 200
   decentralization of, 202
   factions of, 29
   fusion policy of, 200
   Madison's viewpoint regarding, 17–18, 19
   as nebulous, 39
   opposition to, 18
   See also specific parties
Pope, John, 65, 160–161
Porter, Peter, 96, 193

Portsmouth Oracle (newspaper), 153
Potawatomi tribe, 122, 125
Potter, Elisha, 170
Poulson's American Daily Advertiser (newspaper), 165
Presbyterians, 21
Presidential Succession Act, 176
Prophetstown, 67–68
Public Advertiser (newspaper), 6, 89, 118, 152, 176
Publius, 12

Quakers, 21
Queenston, Upper Canada, 123
Quincy, Josiah, 227n46

Randolph, Edmund, 10
Randolph, John
   alliance agreement of, 3
   criticism from, 43
   defeat of, 156
   election of, 185
   faction of, 104
   hanging of, 174
   Old Republicans and, 29, 53, 54
   payoff denouncement by, 220n54
   photo of, 137
   reining in of, 76
   slavery and, 188
   support from, 2
   War Hawks and, 55–56
Reign of Terror, 90
religion, 21, 46
Repertory (newspaper), 167–168
Reporter (newspaper), 68, 121, 161
representative democracy, elite-based, 16
Republican (newspaper), 68
Rhode Island, 87, 95, 103, 141, 169–170, 205, 206, 208
Rhode Island Republican (newspaper), 132
Richmond Enquirer (newspaper), 3, 45, 80–81, 122, 155, 166, 174
Riker, Richard, 129

Ritchie, Thomas, 3, 45
Rittenhouse, David, 81
Rodgers, John, 67
Rodman, William, 143
Rodney, Caesar, 48
Rules Committee, 76
Russell, Jonathan, 127
Russia, 181
Rutledge, John, Jr., 94, 173

Sacket's Harbor, New York, 123
Sammons, Thomas, 84, 96
Saratoga, writings of, 133
Savannah Republican (newspaper), 128
Second Continental Congress, 9
Sedgwick, Theodore, 27
Sedition Act, 16–17, 117, 143
Senate, 6–7, 74–75, 79
Sevier, John, 159, 160
Shawnee tribe, 121–122
Shelby, Isaac, 160
slavery, 187, 188, 196
Smith, Robert, 43, 48, 49, 55
Smith, Samuel, 47–48, 55, 184
Smith, William, 167
Snyder, Simon, 81–82
social media, 131
Soubrian, Paul Emile, 69
South Carolina
    campaign and election in, 172–174
    Democratic-Republican Party in, 173, 174
    election results in, 174
    Electoral College results in, 206
    elector selection dates and methods in, 205
    Federalist Party in, 94, 174
    friends of peace in, 173–174
    nullification in, 187–188
    property qualifications in, 200
    roll call vote in, 207
    support for Madison in, 141
    tariffs in, 187
    War of 1812 support in, 172–173
Southwick, Solomon, 57, 58, 83

Spain, 30, 71–72
Speaker of the House of Representatives, 75
Spencer, Ambrose, 129
Spirit of '76, 53–54, 104
Stanford, Richard, 54, 172
Star-Spangled Banner (Key), 181
Statesman (newspaper), 176
St. Augustine, Florida, 72
Steele, John, 114
St. Lawrence River, 122
Stockton, Richard, Jr., 106
Stone, David, 115
Strong, Caleb, 85, 170
Sullivan, William, 103, 109, 226n37
Supporter (newspaper), 68
Supreme Court, 47
Swartwout, John, 62

Tait, Charles, 56
Tammany Society, 60, 61, 64, 147
tariffs, 33, 58, 187
taxation, 16, 32
Tayler, John, 129
Taylor, John, 53
Taylor, Zachary, 125
Tecumseh, 67–68, 121–122
Tennessee
    campaign and election in, 159–160
    Democratic-Republican Party in, 159
    districting in, 160
    Electoral College results in, 206
    elector selection dates and methods in, 205
    Federalist Party committee in, 94
    growth of, 199
    missing vote counts in, 175
    statewide tally in, 208
    support for Madison in, 141
Tenskwatawa, 67–68
Tertium Quids, 30
Todd, John, 15
Todd, John Payne, 15, 188–189
Tompkins, Daniel, 6, 64, 82–83, 96, 97, 152–153, 185, 194

262 INDEX

trade, 33, 34–35, 146. *See also* embargo
Treaty of Ghent, 182–183
Trenton Federalist (newspaper), 121, 123, 133, 157, 158–159, 161
Troup, George, 56, 73
True American (newspaper), 131, 157
True American, writings of, 149
Turner, Charles, Jr., 164–165, 168
Twelfth Amendment, 28, 62

Underground Railroad, 196
United States Gazette (newspaper), 123
University of Virginia, 186
USS *Chesapeake*, 34
USS *Constitution*, 123
USS *Hornet*, 74, 76
USS *President*, 67
USS *United States*, 123
USS *Wasp*, 123

Van Buren, Martin, 151–152, 192–193, 195, 196–197
Van Cortlandt, Pierre, Jr., 96–97
Van Vechten, Abraham, 224n13
Vermont, 87, 141, 148–149, 205, 206, 207
vetoes, 9–10, 46–47, 216n19
vice president, 84, 114–119. *See also specific persons*
Virginia
  agriculture in, 146
  Annapolis meeting in, 10
  campaign and election in, 154–156
  caucus balloting in, 3
  constitutional writings by, 186
  Democratic-Republicans in, 154, 155–156
  election results in, 156, 175, 176
  Electoral College results in, 206
  elector selection dates and methods in, 205
  Federalist Party in, 94, 154–155
  Federalist Party nomination, participation in, 103

Madison's role in, 9–10
Monroe campaign in, 4
ratifying convention, 12
renomination in, 80–81
statewide tally in, 208
support for Madison in, 141
voter turnout in, 198
War of 1812 popularity in, 155–156
Virginia Dynasty, 9
Virginia House of Delegates, 9–10
Virginia Patriot (newspaper), 112
Virginia Resolution, 187
voting, 16, 140, 174, 198–199, 200. *See also* election of 1812

War Hawks
  challenges regarding, 39
  in Congress, 75, 172
  criticism of, 163
  declaration of war and, 79–80
  embargo demands of, 74
  Florida Territory and, 73
  John Henry incident and, 69, 70
  overview of, 29
  platform of, 52–53, 55–56
  strengthening of, 75, 184
  support for Madison by, 159–160
  War of 1812 and, 69
  war position of, 107
War of 1812
  Battle of Monguagon, 123
  Battle of Tippecanoe, 67–68, 78
  British strategic position in, 122
  British victories in, 122–123
  defeats in, 181
  Detroit surrender in, 120, 121
  Federalist Party and, 20
  Madison's challenges regarding, 124–129
  nationalism and, 179–186
  pre-war episodes of, 66–74
  start of, 33–36, 74–79
  treaty regarding, 181–182
  United States victories in, 123
Washington, Bushrod, 103

Washington, DC, 107
Washington, George, 13, 17, 18, 23, 150, 158
Washington Benevolent Societies, 92, 157
Washingtonian (newspaper), 148
Webster, Daniel, 153
Weekly Register (newspaper), 84
Wellesley, Arthur, 145
West Florida. *See* Florida Territory
whataboutism, 164
wheat, 145–146
Whig Chronicle (newspaper), 144, 147

Whig Party, 185
Whiskey Rebellion, 16
Wilkinson, James, 180
Witherspoon, John, 8
Wolcott, Oliver, Jr., 22
Worthington, Thomas, 147
Wright, Robert, 55
Wycoff, William, 71

XYZ Affair, 85

Yankee (newspaper), 169
Yates, Joseph, 195